the mexican revolution, 1910–1940

A series of course-adoption books on Latin America

Series advisory editor:
Lyman L. Johnson, University of North Carolina at Charlotte

THE MEXICAN REVOLUTION,

1910–1940

Michael J. Gonzales

University of New Mexico Press, Albuquerque

© 2002 by the University of New Mexico Press
All rights reserved.
First edition

Library of Congress Cataloging-in-Publication Data:
Gonzales, Michael J., 1946–
The Mexican Revolution, 1910–1940 /
Michael J. Gonzales.— 1st ed.
p. cm. — (Diálogos)
ISBN 0-8263-2779-6 (cloth : alk. paper) —
ISBN 0-8263-2780-X (pbk. : alk. paper)
1. Mexico—History—Revolution, 1910–1920.
2. Mexico—Politics and government—1910–1940.
I. Title. II. Diálogos (Albuquerque, N.M.)
F1234 .G6248 2002
972.08'2—dc21
2001005644

11 10 09 08 07   4   5   6   7   8

ISBN-13: 978-0-8263-2780-2

For Michael and Ben

CONTENTS

ACKNOWLEDGMENTS

Lyman Johnson and David Holtby encouraged me to write this book, and Lyman's editorial comments improved the final product. I appreciate the support of the History Department, the Center for Latino and Latin American Studies, and the College of Liberal Arts and Sciences at Northern Illinois University. Terry Sheahan worked as my research assistant and helped me gather information about the Mexican Revolution. She also drew the maps for the book.

I am grateful to my mother, Betty A. Owen, for working hard to provide for her children and for placing their interests before her own. My wife, Gail, has accompanied me on research trips to Latin America, sometimes with young children in tow, and has always encouraged my research and writing. Her support is greatly appreciated. Our children, Michael and Ben, have been a constant source of pride and joy.

I would also like to remember my younger brother, Dave. I think that he would have liked the book.

LIST OF
ILLUSTRATIONS

IN the 1880s the Noriega brothers, two Spaniards living in Michoacán, Mexico, purchased a marsh from the town leaders of the village of Naranja. For centuries, the marsh had nourished villagers with fish, waterfowl, mussels, and crustaceans and had provided them with reeds to weave into straw mats and braids to sell in local markets. The Noriegas drained the marsh, developed a highly productive maize hacienda, and exported the corn to eastern markets via newly constructed railroads. They became wealthy and politically influential members of the regional elite. Naranjeros, meanwhile, lost their economic self-sufficiency. They suffered malnutrition. They could not buy shoes or clothing for their children. They struggled to find the money to hold religious festivals central to their cultural identity and spiritual consciousness. To survive, they worked on the Noriega's estates or migrated to labor on unhealthy sugarcane plantations.[1]

The plight of Naranja's peasants was replicated elsewhere in Mexico in areas where geographic and ecological conditions favored cultivation of cash crops in demand at home and abroad. Widespread loss of land created an economic crisis for peasants, whose desperation led them to take up arms against the seemingly impregnable regime of General Porfirio Díaz, dictator of Mexico since 1876. Regional agrarian movements spearheaded the overthrow of the dictatorship in 1911, an improbable historical event known as the Mexican Revolution.

Unregulated capitalist development and political centralization contributed to Díaz's downfall. The government facilitated hacendados' acquisition of village land and ignored peasants' plight. Moreover, the dictator, judging domestic sources of capital inadequate to generate development, offered foreign investors attractive incentives to start businesses in Mexico. Capital flowed into the country, particularly from the United States, without institutional safeguards to protect national sovereignty. The preeminence of foreign ownership over key industries became controversial and created discontent, especially among provincial elites and workers.

The Díaz government's centralization of authority also ruptured traditional patronage networks and systems of social control. Loss of political autonomy outraged notables and villagers alike. British historian Alan Knight has called local-level revolutionary movements of primarily political origin, prominent in northern Mexico and isolated regions, "serrano revolts."[2]

In 1910, Mexico's ruling elite bungled the politics of presidential succession and created an opportunity for organized political opposition to form. Could the revolution have been avoided if elites had remained united against the masses? Given the breadth and depth of the agrarian crisis, this seems doubtful. Even after the fall of Díaz, *agrarista* movements persisted until the land had been redistributed or agrarians had been defeated.

The popular and agrarian character of the revolution makes it a social revolution. The conflict pitted landless peasants, elements of the working classes, and discontented provincial gentry against the dictator Díaz, his elite supporters, and the federal army. The revolution threw out the old guard, reinvented the state, and made possible historic social and economic reforms. The revolutionary state gave landless peasants hundreds of thousands of hectares of land, nationalized foreign-owned petroleum companies, and significantly expanded public education. If the final outcome failed to eradicate poverty, create democracy, or achieve economic independence, the event still remains revolutionary.

This study begins with a discussion of the dictatorship of General Porfirio Díaz (1876–1911), whose policies provoked the revolution, and ends with an analysis of the presidency of General Lázaro Cárdenas

(1934–1940), who implemented the most far-reaching reforms. The importance of these leaders and the changes that occurred during their presidencies led me to write somewhat lengthy bookend chapters. Wedged in between is a historical narrative that discusses Mexico's most important revolutionary (and counterrevolutionary) leaders, their programs, their successes and failures. I attempt to be sensitive to regional variations that distinguish revolutionaries and their programs without losing sight of the national and international perspectives. Space limitations prevented me from delving into social and economic issues as much as I would have preferred, and discussion of cultural change is limited to the most important changes. Chapters are organized chronologically and divided by major political benchmarks.

Map 1: *The Mexican States*

Gulf of Mexico

Mexico
0   400 miles

Sonora

Baja California

Chihuahua

Sinaloa

Coahuila

Durango

Nuevo León

Zacatecas

Tamaulipas

Nayarit

San Luis Potosí

Jalisco

Guanajuato

Hidalgo

Tlaxcala

México D.F.

Michoacán

Colima

Morelos

Puebla

Veracruz

Guerrero

Oaxaca

Tabasco

Campeche

Chiapas

Yucatán

Quintana Roo

CHAPTER ONE

GENERAL PORFIRIO DÍAZ AND
THE LIBERAL LEGACY

MEXICO CITY, SEPTEMBER 1, 1910. General Porfirio Díaz, dictator of Mexico since 1876, stood on the reviewing stand and watched as the parade commemorating the centennial of Mexico's independence from Spain unfolded before him. Accompanied by foreign dignitaries and his closest advisors, the general listened as Theodore Roosevelt declared him the world's greatest living statesman and Andrew Carnegie praised him for his wisdom and character.[1] Beyond the parade grounds stretched further evidence of Díaz's achievement: broad avenues lined with majestic trees and interspersed with lovely parks, palatial homes, modern buildings, and a bustling business district. Díaz could also see in the distance a forest of factory smokestacks, evidence of industrialization and future pollution problems, and a network of railroad tracks radiating from the capital and linking it with distant provinces and the United States.

Díaz's presidency had reversed decades of political and economic chaos that had made Mexico vulnerable to foreign invasion and territorial loss. Skillful use of violence, centralization of authority at the expense of local autonomy, and electoral fraud allowed Díaz to achieve political supremacy and stability. Moreover, economic development resulted from

5

FIGURE I: General Porfirio Díaz, President of Mexico,
1876–1880, 1884–1911.

Source: Anita Brenner, *The Wind that Swept Mexico: The History of the
Mexican Revolution of 1910–1942*, with 184 historical photographs assembled by
George R. Leighton (Austin: University of Texas Press, 1971), photograph 1.

FIGURE 2: Chapultepec Castle, residence of President Díaz.

Source: Anita Brenner, *The Wind that Swept Mexico: The History of the Mexican Revolution of 1910–1942,* with 184 historical photographs assembled by George R. Leighton (Austin: University of Texas Press, 1971), photograph 30.

government programs that facilitated massive infusions of foreign capital, improvements in internal transportation networks, and exploitation of extensive natural resources.

General Díaz had also earned political capital through his role in the heroic struggle against the French imperialists from 1862 to 1867. Díaz had served in the army of the legendary liberal leader Benito Juárez, who drove the French from the motherland and executed their lackey, the Emperor Maximilian. The liberals' victory assured them control over Mexican politics and vanquished the conservatives who had openly sided with the invaders.

Nineteenth-century liberalism, rooted in the principles of emergent capitalism and utilitarianism, advocated free trade, decentralized

7

FIGURE 3: By 1910, Mexico City had broad avenues and impressive buildings,
evidence of the country's rapid economic growth.

Source: Anita Brenner, *The Wind that Swept Mexico: The History of the Mexican
Revolution of 1910–1942*, with 184 historical photographs assembled by
George R. Leighton (Austin: University of Texas Press, 1971), photograph 31.

government, individual rights, and separation of church and state. These
ideas linked Mexico with the United States and Western Europe—indus-
trializing democracies with surplus capital—and undermined Mexico's
philosophical ties with Spanish conservative traditions. Liberalism did
not, however, serve as a uniform blueprint for political and economic
policies. In fact, Díaz's methods of achieving political stability violated
every imaginable principle of liberal democracy, and he subverted free-
market concepts by offering government support to foreign-owned enterprises with extensive capital reserves and technical expertise.

As U.S. capital, technology, and personnel poured into Mexico, key
sectors of the national economy came under American control. The most
aggressive American investors recognized that Díaz's policies granted
them unprecedented opportunities in Mexico. As William Randolph
Hearst wrote to his mother, "I really don't see what is to prevent us from
owning all of Mexico and running it to suit ourselves."[2]

FIGURE 4: William Randolph Hearst, American newspaper tycoon, owned vast haciendas in northern Mexico and wrote to his mother that "I really don't see what is to prevent us from owning all of Mexico and running it to suit ourselves." Hearst is the tall man in the center of this photograph.

Source: Anita Brenner, *The Wind that Swept Mexico: The History of the Mexican Revolution of 1910–1942*, with 184 historical photographs assembled by George R. Leighton (Austin: University of Texas Press, 1971), photograph 25.

Díaz believed that this could be avoided, however, by counterbalancing U.S. interests with concessions to major European investors. Britain's Lord Cowdray, for example, helped develop Mexico's oil fields; German and French interests owned important Mexico City banks; and the French ran the biggest textile mills. Díaz also recognized that promoting French and British investment in Mexico helped mend diplomatic relations with these recent adversaries, and improved Mexico's chances of receiving future loans from European banks.[3]

Díaz also helped to trigger the expansion of commercial agriculture through authorizing confiscatory land survey schemes that facilitated the acquisition of village land by large landowners and by adopting high tariffs and restrictive labor policies that favored the interests of hacendados.[4] Although prominent foreigners such as Hearst owned large estates in Mexico, most latifundists were Mexican elites, including prominent liberals who had acquired land at the expense of the church after midcentury.

Mexico's rich natural resources and pro-business legislation would have meant little, however, without the political stability provided by the iron rule of Don Porfirio. From the 1820s to the late 1870s, domestic unrest consumed Mexico. Rival military leaders vied for power in the aftermath of liberation from Spain; liberals clashed with conservatives over separation of church and state; the United States annexed mineral-rich northern provinces following the Mexican-American War (1846–1848); and the French conquest created additional turmoil. Under these circumstances, businessmen and ordinary citizens alike feared for their lives as well as their money. Beginning in the late 1870s, General Díaz gradually restored political stability to Mexico through patronage, force, and skillful political manipulation, which included replacing unruly warlords with personal cronies who did not have ties with powerful local interests. But by 1910, generals, provincial political bosses (caudillos), and businessmen now stood beside the aging dictator and worried what would happen when he retired or died.

Sharing their concern were Mexico's Roman Catholic bishops, who had developed a comfortable political relationship with Díaz. This alliance represented a significant political comeback for the Mexican church, which had been severely discredited during the 1850s and 1860s. The church had challenged the liberal assault (called La Reforma) on its rural property and privileged judicial status by bankrolling conservative revolts in the 1850s and then by embracing the Emperor Maximilian in 1862. As a result, the patriotism of the Mexican church and its conservative allies came under scrutiny, and their political legitimacy was tainted for decades to come.

Following Maximilian's defeat and execution in 1867, Mexico's liberal leaders exiled a few bishops and kept the anticlerical legislation on the books. However, widespread political retribution did not occur, and General Díaz later permitted the church to revitalize its wealth and educational mission and to restore its institutional credibility. His rapprochement with the church made a political ally of a traditional foe and avoided a renewed conflict between liberals and conservatives that would have sidetracked political consolidation and economic development.

POLITICAL CONSOLIDATION

General Porfirio Díaz had fought with distinction for Juárez's liberal cause and used his military prestige as a springboard into national politics, just like his contemporary in the United States, General Ulysses S. Grant. President Juárez's grip on the presidency, however, blocked General Díaz's road to power. Juárez's personal courage and perseverance in defense of Mexico had earned him immense popularity among the Mexican people. Moreover, Juárez was a master political manipulator. Liberal doctrine advocated federalism, democracy, and individual rights, but Juárez abandoned many of these principles in favor of consolidating his control over the presidency. Thus, Juárez increased the authority of the central government, guaranteed electoral victories by stuffing ballot boxes, and enriched liberal landowners through the enforced sale of church land.[5]

President Juárez's decision to run for reelection in 1871 prompted an increasingly frustrated General Díaz to launch a rebellion, which came to be called the Revolution of La Noria. Díaz's support came primarily from his home state of Oaxaca and from disgruntled or opportunistic liberal caudillos elsewhere in Mexico. The rebels were losing on the battlefield when Juárez's sudden death from a heart attack brought the fighting to a halt. Sebastián Lerdo de Tejada, chief justice of the Supreme Court, then became interim president and called for new elections.[6]

Imitating Juárez, Lerdo took advantage of his control of the executive to assure his election. He solidified his position by declaring an amnesty for the rebels of La Noria and by leaving Juaristas in power at the federal, state, and local levels. This later move gained him key political allies, allowed him to influence provincial politics, and sealed his victory.

Four years later, in 1876, General Díaz reemerged as President Lerdo's principal opponent for the presidency. Díaz hoped that Lerdo would not seek another term and dusted off the old liberal rallying cry of no reelection, invoked in 1867 and 1871 against the unbeatable Juárez. When Lerdo remained in the contest, Díaz launched a successful revolutionary movement called the Rebellion of Tuxtepec. General Díaz benefited from experience as well as from an opponent who lacked the support and luster of the legendary Juárez.[7]

Porfirio Díaz won the presidency on the battlefield and soon laid the foundation for political stability and economic prosperity. In this ambitious undertaking, he clearly benefited from the political conjuncture. His most prominent liberal rivals, Juárez and Lerdo, lay dead or vanquished, the conservatives remained politically discredited, and the public yearned for peace after decades of warfare.

As a political pragmatist largely uninfluenced by ideology, President Díaz increased the power of the executive by continuing the centralizing policies of Juárez and Lerdo and by placing his political supporters in key state and municipal offices. For example, Díaz made good use of a constitutional amendment enacted during the Lerdo administration that allowed the federal government to appoint provisional governors and to organize new elections at the state level. The law, intended to bring order to chaotic conditions in the provinces, allowed Díaz to appoint political allies and to influence elections.[8] The president also convinced the national congress to extend the principle of no reelection to state houses, allowing him to promote his supporters, including grateful members of the provincial middle class kept from power by Juárez and Lerdo.[9]

Sweeping political change in the provinces, however, did not take place overnight. Several governors were too powerful or too clever to be dislodged immediately. Díaz therefore negotiated political alliances with these regional strongmen, which provided him with time to erode their local power bases or promote the careers of their rivals. All the liberal kingpins in the countryside—Alvarez in Guerrero, Méndez in Puebla, the Craviotos in Hidalgo—eventually fell from power as a result of Díaz's pressure. Only Luis Terrazas in Chihuahua, buttressed by his immense ranching and banking empire, withstood political co-optation for several years before finally reaching a rapprochement with Díaz.[10]

In selecting governors, President Díaz prized loyalty and administrative competence above other characteristics. Some 70 percent of his gubernatorial appointments went to residents of other states. This increased Díaz's control over provincial politics because outsiders were largely unencumbered by local family, financial, and political entanglements that might compromise their allegiance to the dictator. In the early years of his presidency, a majority of these appointments went to army generals, thus creating closer political ties between the president and the military.[11]

As long as governors remained loyal, Díaz allowed them considerable discretion in the daily management of the states. Ambitious governors took advantage of the dictator's support to create regional political networks *(camarillas)* through graft, patronage, and force and to form partnerships with businessmen (including foreigners) in a variety of lucrative ventures. Governors greased the process by providing tax breaks, insider information, and help with controlling workers. Prominent examples include the Molina-Montes camarilla in the Yucatán and the Terrazas-Creel clan in Chihuahua. Other provincial oligarchs formed less powerful camarillas and jockeyed for political power and wealth. If they failed to reap a fair share of the spoils, their frustration and anger sometimes created politically dangerous feuds among provincial elites.[12]

For most Mexicans, political life rarely went beyond the confines of their home village. Mexico had a long tradition of local political autonomy, in some areas predating the Spanish conquest, that permitted villagers to control certain basic judicial, administrative, and legislative aspects of their daily lives. Villagers prized this independence. Selection of village leaders had democratic trappings, although those selected invariably possessed greater wealth and status within the community. Effective local leadership helped villagers protect land and water rights, contest questionable taxes, and generally survive the uncertainties of a premodern agricultural economy.

Porfirio Díaz recognized better than his predecessors did that effective political control required usurping this traditional village autonomy. Whenever governors possessed sufficient power and administrative skill, the president urged them to seize control of local government by appointing municipal heads *(jefes políticos)* and police chiefs *(comisarios de policía)*. Many of the new appointees were outsiders unknown to villagers, and they proved unfamiliar with and disinterested in local problems. As accusations of graft, extortion, rape, and neglect of office mounted against these petty tyrants, discontented villagers protested and sometimes resorted to violence.[13] The venality of some officials was notorious. For example, the jefes of Azteca, in the state of Morelos, "took advantage of poor girls. If they liked a girl, they got her—they always enjoyed fine women just because of the power they had. One of the caciques died at eighty in the arms of a fifteen-year-old girl."[14]

As Díaz's tentacles of power reached into the countryside, he simultaneously succeeded in gaining control over the national congress and federal judiciary. These centralizing tendencies, already initiated by Juárez, matured under Don Porfirio and remained in place after the Mexican Revolution. Díaz viewed all branches of the federal government as his personal political domain, and his selection of congressional candidates guaranteed their election. In choosing a congressman, he prized loyalty above all other characteristics. Díaz did not insist that a candidate reside in his congressional district. In fact, the anointed candidate might even have difficulty finding his district on a map. For example, Luis Pombo, elected deputy for Colotlán, Jalisco, expressed the wish that "some day I hope to make the acquaintance of the Colotlanenses." Such representatives typically showed little or no interest in the problems of their constituents and increasingly viewed political office as an opportunity to amass wealth through graft, extortion, and patronage. If congressmen proved loyal, then Díaz generally ignored the mounting discontent among the neglected constituents.[15]

The federal judiciary, another theoretically independent branch of government, also became a pawn in the hands of the chess-master president. Díaz appointed and dismissed federal judges based on their loyalty to him and personally nominated candidates for election to the Mexican Supreme Court. Only at the local level did judges retain some degree of independence, but individual levels of competence and honesty varied widely.[16]

The federal bureaucracy grew in size and agencies acquired the trappings of modernity and efficiency—large staffs, impressive buildings, and detailed regulations—but without the anticipated results. Poorly trained and underpaid personnel, with neither the incentive nor knowledge to perform their jobs satisfactorily, demanded bribes to perform minor tasks. They avoided complicated or difficult assignments altogether.

Under the circumstances, it became more effective for executive cabinet officers, under the direct control of the president, to intervene and order compliance, or noncompliance, with laws and regulations.[17]

The process of political consolidation, which took several years to accomplish, was still incomplete when President Díaz temporarily fell victim to his own campaign slogan of no-reelection. As his first term drew to a close in 1880, he found it necessary to step aside. But by no means did he relinquish power. Instead, he handpicked a successor, trusted military and political ally General Manuel González, and made sure González won the election. Díaz remained in the presidential cabinet and played an active role in policymaking. He did not, however, tell González what to do. That was unnecessary because González simply emulated his predecessor's policies. The principal difference between the two was that González failed to match his mentor in effectiveness and charisma. When González's term ended in 1884, Porfirio Díaz was ready to reclaim the presidency and eliminate the politically inconvenient "no reelection principle," a cornerstone of Mexican liberalism.[18] When Díaz returned to the presidency, the pace of political consolidation accelerated. Díaz's allies passed a constitutional amendment that allowed the president to succeed himself, thereby paving the way for twenty-six more years of dictatorship.

The president tightened his control over the countryside by enlarging the size of the rural police corps (the *rurales*), which had been created by Juárez to combat endemic banditry along Mexico's country roads. The rurales cut dashing figures. Outfitted in fancy charro suits, mounted on fine steeds, and flashing modern weapons, they drew praise from foreign visitors and businessmen whose investments they protected. They were, however, a corrupt and inefficient bunch. Some were former bandits themselves. They proved effective in hunting down solitary criminals or helping to suppress striking workers but were less impressive when confronted with the daunting task of bringing physical security to the lives of rural Mexicans, whom they themselves frequently exploited.[19]

The Mexican Army presented President Díaz with another political dilemma. On the one hand, loyal generals such as Manuel González made important administrative contributions to the consolidation of the regime. On the other hand, the president recognized that the Mexican Army (like other Latin American militaries) had produced the vast

FIGURE 5: President Díaz utilized special security forces, the rurales, to patrol Mexico's highways and to suppress peasants and workers. The rural pictured here cut a dashing figure in his fancy outfit.

Source: Rafael Tovar, ed. *México: una nación persistente, Hugo Brehme fotografías* (Mexico City: Instituto Nacional de Bellas Artes, 1995), photograph 5, p. 34.

majority of presidents, usually via coup d'etats. Díaz himself was a prime example. Therefore, the president limited the army's political potential by reducing the number of men in uniform and by professionalizing the officer corps along European lines. Aiming to reduce federal expenditures, Díaz also saw distinct monetary benefits in reducing the size of the

FIGURE 6: Rurales, such as those pictured here, broke up strikes, arrested political dissidents, and shot many accused of fleeing while under arrest (the so-called *ley de fuga*).

Source: Rafael Tovar, ed. *México: una nación persistente, Hugo Brehme fotografías* (Mexico City: Instituto Nacional de Bellas Artes, 1995), photograph 6, p. 35.

military. During the course of his dictatorship, he cut the size of the army from 30,000 to 14,000 men and the number of generals by 25 percent. In addition, the president gradually replaced most military governors. He retained only those who, like General Bernardo Reyes in Nuevo León, combined outstanding administrative skills with unquestioned loyalty to the regime. In a related decision, Díaz also succeeded in trimming the size of state militias, a traditional source of military support for politically ambitious provincial elites. As political maneuvers designed to protect the president's power, all of these reforms worked magnificently. However, a weakened military, largely consisting of conscripted recruits, proved unable to meet its greatest challenge: the Madero rebellion in 1910.[20]

The president proved equally successful in neutralizing another source of potential political conflict—the Catholic Church. Since independence from Spain, Mexican liberals had attacked the church's wealth, special

FIGURE 7: Federal troops positioned on the roof and
bell tower of a church, Xochimilco, c. 1903.

Source: Rafael Tovar, ed. *México: una nación persistente: Hugo Brehme fotografías*
(Mexico City: Instituto Nacional de Bellas Artes, 1995), photograph 1, p. 31.

judicial rights, and conservative policies in an attempt to establish a
modern, secular state. The ensuing civil war in the 1850s, provoked by liberal attacks on the church, tore the country apart. The victorious liberals,
Porfirio Díaz among them, struggled to pick up the pieces. Under the circumstances, making peace with the church involved great political risk.
Die-hard liberals wanted the church subservient to the state and out of the
public arena. Díaz reasoned, however, that open hostility between church
and state increased the likelihood of civil war. Further, such hostility damaged Mexico's relations with Catholic nations—France, for instance—with
surplus capital to invest. Besides, the president, a master political strategist, undoubtedly believed that he could make peace with church leaders
on his own terms.

In effect, Díaz refused to compromise on issues of material and legal
substance. Church lands confiscated during La Reforma remained the
property of wealthy liberal supporters of the regime, and laws restricting

the church's activities and legal status stayed on the books. By contrast, Díaz allowed the clergy to stage public ceremonies, wear religious garb in public, teach catechism in public schools, and administer a variety of social welfare programs. Significantly, these activities had the unanticipated result of increasing the church's credibility and popularity and creating preconditions for its reentry into national politics.[21]

Díaz's second wife, Carmen Romero Rubio de Díaz, is traditionally given credit for reconciling her husband with the church.[22] Unlike the dictator, who was a mestizo from Oaxaca, Carmen Romero came from a wealthy Mexico City family with close ties to the church hierarchy. Díaz was probably influenced by his young wife's views, and he used her as an intermediary. Señora Díaz helped raise funds to purchase an ornate crown for the coronation of the Virgin of Guadalupe, Mexico's patron saint, an event that symbolized the rapprochement between church and state. Of greater importance, the president allowed the archbishop of Mexico, Antonio de Labastida, to return from exile and preside over the Díaz's wedding. The occasion had great political significance because Labastida, as bishop of Puebla, had organized the first conservative rebellion against the liberals in 1855 and had welcomed the French invaders into Mexico City in 1862.[23]

Despite improved relations with the church, General Díaz approved other policies that clearly troubled the bishops. For example, he permitted Protestant missionaries in Mexico and allowed the Mormons to establish polygamous communities in the far north.[24] These openings to other religions, unthinkable in the past, helped define the limits of Díaz's political reconciliation with the Mexican church.

Mending fences with the church helped create political peace (pax porfiriana) unknown since colonial times and established necessary preconditions for the economic modernization of Mexico. Before new investment could occur, however, several foreign policy problems, stemming from recent conflicts with France and the United States, required resolution. France and Britain had lent Mexico's governments, including rebel conservative regimes at midcentury, large sums of money, and merchants from both countries claimed damages incurred during Mexico's numerous civil wars. Presidents Juárez and Lerdo had refused to honor loans made to their conservative usurpers, reasoning that lenders had gambled and lost.

Remembering recent interventions, most Mexicans understandably held strong animosities toward Western Europe. Any diplomatic settlement would require a deft touch.

Mending relations with the United States, which had in Mexicans' recent memory invaded their country and annexed their northern provinces, would also be difficult. Despite cordial relations during the 1860s, when civil wars engulfed both nations, tensions existed. Subsequent incursions into Mexico by U.S. troops and law enforcement agents in pursuit of Apaches and outlaws provoked diplomatic disputes. The border region remained volatile. Both sides remembered that following a skirmish along the Rio Grande in 1846, President Polk had asked Congress to declare war against Mexico, falsely claiming that "American blood had been shed on American soil."[25]

As a means of improving Mexico's diplomatic relations with the United States and Europe and promoting economic growth, Díaz paid the nation's foreign debt. This action created an attractive investment climate for foreigners. Ideally, foreign capitalists and the Mexican people would both profit from the modernization process. In 1888, the minister of the treasury, Manuel Dublán, negotiated an agreement with Britain and Germany designed to retire Mexico's entire foreign debt. Called the Dublán Convention, the accord authorized new bonds worth 10,500,000 pounds sterling at 6 percent interest for thirty-five years. Germans subsequently purchased most of the bonds at 70 percent of their face value. By settling its foreign debt, Mexico restored its credit rating abroad. The government could now contract additional loans and enter into complex business arrangements with overseas corporations.[26]

ECONOMIC DEVELOPMENT

Mexico needed foreign capital to jump-start its economy after fifty years of economic decline. In 1800, toward the end of the colonial period, productivity and per capita income were comparatively high. However, political independence from Spain removed certain economic safeguards provided by the Mother Country, such as the steady supply of cheap mercury required to refine silver ore. Republican regimes, at the same time, retained other imperial policies that retarded development.

Concessions to privileged individuals, internal tariffs, and a high sales tax loomed large among these. In addition, decades of nearly continuous warfare had destroyed crops and livestock, flooded mines, deterred European immigration, and kept officials from implementing institutional changes that might have facilitated economic growth.

Beyond these problems, development required overcoming Mexico's difficult geography. In comparison with the United States, with its network of canals, rivers, and lakes that served as commercial highways, Mexico's mountainous terrain and untamed rivers served as roadblocks. Wagons and mules that moved slowly along poorly maintained roads increased costs, eroded competitive advantage in exports, and retarded development of areas distant from marketplaces.[27]

Benito Juárez and Sebastián Lerdo de Tejada recognized that railroad construction could alleviate the problem and they built a railroad connecting Mexico City with Veracruz, the nation's largest port. Construction of additional railway lines, however, awaited more stable political and financial conditions because of the enormous sums of money required.[28]

With Mexico's finances in order, the Díaz government signed a series of contracts with U.S. firms authorizing construction of privately owned railroads across Mexico. The most important lines linked the Central Plateau and northern mining centers with towns on the U.S. border, bridged the southern Isthmus of Tehuantepec, connecting the Atlantic and Pacific Oceans, and linked Mexico City and Veracruz with a second line. Numerous shorter railways, some of them owned by U.S. mining companies, tied northern mines to rail and refining centers directly across the border. In total, 24,560 kilometers of track were laid between 1880 and 1910.[29]

The Mexican government paid dearly for this communications revolution. In a manner similar to that pursued in the United States, Mexico underwrote much of the cost of construction and gave contractors generous land grants paralleling the new lines. For example, in 1879 the government appropriated 32,000,000 pesos to underwrite the laying of 2,500 miles of track, and in the 1880s it voted subsidies ranging from 7,500 to 15,000 pesos for each new kilometer of track. U.S. railroad magnates also received huge amounts of land in northern Mexico. For example, F. S. Pearson received more than 3.5 million acres in Chihuahua upon completion of the Northwestern Railroad in that state.[30] Railroad

FIGURE 8: Extensive railroad construction, mostly by American firms,
traversed Mexico's difficult terrain. Railroads opened up
new markets, expanded capacity, and increased land values.

Source: Anita Brenner, *The Wind that Swept Mexico: The History of the Mexican
Revolution of 1910–1942,* with 184 historical photographs assembled by
George R. Leighton (Austin: University of Texas Press, 1971), photograph 22.

subsidization added significantly to Mexico's national debt and left
ownership and management in the hands of U.S. companies.

Nevertheless, the transportation revolution fostered political consolidation and economic development. President Díaz could now dispatch
troops more quickly to the countryside to crush upstart caudillos or rebellious peasants and industrial workers. Improved communications with
governors, military commanders, rurales, and other officials also helped
create a modern state. Porfirio Díaz utilized the new technology effec-
tively. This is one reason why he transcends the model of the military

FIGURE 9: Impressive engineering achievements, such as this trestle,
characterized railroad construction in mountainous regions.

Source: Anita Brenner, *The Wind that Swept Mexico: The History of the Mexican
Revolution of 1910–1942*, with 184 historical photographs assembled by
George R. Leighton (Austin: University of Texas Press, 1971), photograph 23.

strongman on horseback. Díaz should be viewed instead as a transitional
figure, bridging the nineteenth and twentieth centuries, in the evolution of
modern dictators.

Railroad construction reaped immediate economic rewards. Shipping
costs dropped a spectacular 90 percent in comparison to the days when
goods traveled slowly via mule trains and covered wagons, and this had a
positive ripple effect throughout the national economy.[31] Railroads
increased land values along newly constructed rail lines, fostered development of agriculture and stock raising in outlying areas, and permitted
shipment of industrial minerals by the ton to refineries on both sides of
the Mexican-American border.[32] On a larger scale, railroads also
contributed to the formation of a global economy by facilitating the

distribution of goods between countries and by funneling surplus capital from industrial nations to developing regions.

The Díaz government also facilitated Mexico's economic transformation by providing corporations and property owners with institutional safeguards. New commercial codes permitted the formation of corporations based on shares; new legislation limited the ability of state governments to tax corporations; new banking laws facilitated lending; commercial treaties with the United States and Western Europe encouraged overseas trade; and new mining codes permitted foreigners to own subsoil rights and acquire land on the border.[33] In another reflection of the Mexican government's commitment to economic development, the Treasury Department, run by the influential José Ives Limantour, received the largest budgetary allocation of any government agency, including the War Department.[34]

Clearly, these institutional safeguards facilitated the transition to a modern capitalist economy. Díaz further enticed investment by offering foreign investors special concessions, tax breaks, and enhanced police protection. Special treatment for big business was not unique to Mexico: witness the U.S. government's support for industry in the Gilded Age. It was more controversial in Mexico, however, because the Mexican government's highly visible hand reached out to help foreign interests and neglected most national firms. Foreign mining companies, for example, benefited from government favors. The French branch of the House of Rothschild, in return for developing massive copper deposits at El Boleo, Baja California, did not pay federal and local taxes for twenty years or export taxes and customs duties for fifty years. Díaz also built docks for the Rothschild's mine at Santa Rosalia, and allowed the family to collect 50 percent of customs revenues.[35]

Colonel William E. Greene, the American who developed the famous copper mines at Cananea, Sonora, received similar concessions. Greene's exemption included taxes on copper production, on the construction and operation of his physical plant, and the importation of building materials. Greene estimated that these special breaks saved him more than one million dollars per year.[36] These types of concessions, routinely granted to major foreign investors, encouraged massive capital investment and promoted development. However, they also facilitated foreign control

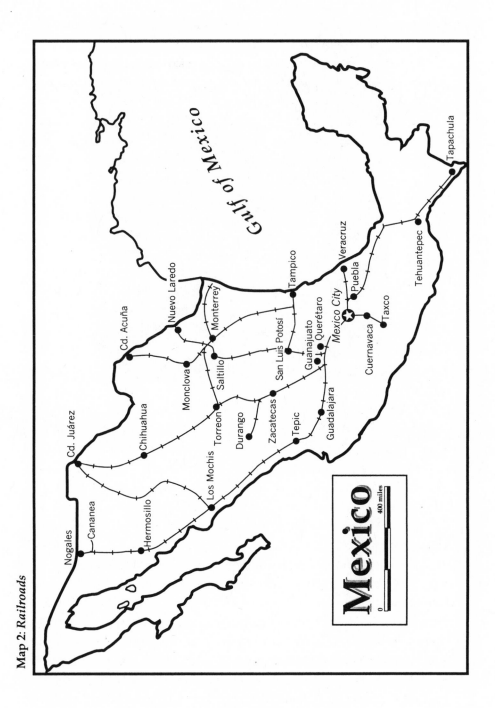

Map 2: Railroads

Gulf of Mexico

Tapachula
Tehuantepec
Veracruz
Puebla
Taxco
Cuernavaca
Mexico City
Querétaro
Guanajuato
Tampico
San Luis Potosí
Nuevo Laredo
Monterrey
Cd. Acuña
Saltillo
Monclova
Zacatecas
Tepic
Guadalajara
Durango
Torreon
Chihuahua
Los Mochis
Cd. Juárez
Hermosillo
Cananea
Nogales

Mexico
400 miles
0

FIGURE 10: José Ives Limantour, President Díaz's minister of the treasury and an architect of Mexico's economic development.

Source: Anita Brenner, *The Wind that Swept Mexico: The History of the Mexican Revolution of 1910–1942,* with 184 historical photographs assembled by George R. Leighton (Austin: University of Texas Press, 1971), photograph 3.

over key sectors of the Mexican economy and eventually provoked a nationalist backlash.

Rapid economic growth in underdeveloped countries characteristically brings unanticipated consequences that governments cannot satisfactorily manage. Investment occurs in products that promise the highest return on capital without much consideration for adverse social consequences. Among the Mexico City governing elite there existed a strong belief that order and progress, based on science and technology, would benefit society as a whole. Elites also believed that what was good for them was good for Mexico. They expressed little concern, for example, that land

FIGURE 11: Colonel William C. Greene developed the vast copper
deposits at Cananea, Sonora. The mine became one of the ten
leading copper producers in the world.

Source: Alicia Ahumada and David Maawad, eds., *Cananea y la Revolución Mexicana*
(Mexico City: Talleres de Litográphica Turmex, S.A., 1987), p. 47.

consolidation and agricultural commercialization might deprive villagers
of economic security and disrupt paternalistic methods of social control.
Few safety nets existed for displaced peasants beyond work as wage
laborers (when they could find it), or the limited charity provided by
church-run institutions in urban areas. Economic growth was driven
primarily by external demand for Mexican agricultural products, metals
and petroleum. Population growth and a growing middle class also
stimulated limited industrial development for expanding internal
markets. While foreign companies dominated the mining, petroleum, and
textiles sectors, Mexican firms held controlling interests in many

agricultural enterprises and several nascent industries, such as beer, matches, soap, and glass.

The foreign invasion of the Mexican economy was by no means a sneak attack. Rather, the government created the institutional foundation, helped pay for railroad construction, and provided special concessions and tax breaks. Despite the importance of foreigners to economic development, however, no one could do business in Mexico without the talents of Mexican lawyers, officials, and intermediaries who got the best deals, cut red tape, and made fortunes in the process.

AGRICULTURE

Mexican businessmen led the way in the transformation of agriculture. Sweeping change occurred as railroads integrated distance provinces with urban markets, overseas demand increased for agricultural products, and banks, merchants, and hacendados poured capital into new ventures. The commercialization of agriculture led to rationalization of production and land consolidation, often to the disadvantage of small producers of foodstuffs (usually Indians and poorer mestizos) who lost land and a niche in the marketplace. In the case of the Maya Indians of southern Mexico, the cultivation of corn also had cultural and religious meaning of pre-Colombian origin. For these people, loss of their corn patches *(milpas)* signified more than a loss of income; it also signified the loss of traditional culture at the altar of commercial capitalism.

Simultaneously, the state contributed to agricultural commercialization through underwriting railroad construction and creating an institutional framework conducive to capitalist development. The Díaz government also facilitated land consolidation through commissioning the survey of public land *(terreno baldío)* to demarcate property lines and transfer so-called idle land into private hands through auction. Significantly, the enormous expanses of "idle" public lands had served as an economic safety net for villagers. In Chihuahua, for example, villagers harvested unbranded cattle on public land. Without access to this resource, many joined the growing numbers of impoverished farmhands who migrated from one harvest to another, and who later swelled the ranks of revolutionary armies.

Without question, the land surveys widened the economic gap between rich and poor in rural Mexico. Between 1878 and 1908, nearly 45,000,000 hectares of public land previously accessible to peasants became the private property of hacendados. This increased property values, brought more land into production, and enriched the surveyors who received one-third of the surplus land they had measured. To some, this appeared an elaborate scheme because most surveyors were also local hacendados.[37]

The state undermined the village economy further through forced disentailment of communal property. In the sixteenth century, the Spanish Crown had attempted to protect the dwindling indigenous population from settlers through the creation of autonomous Indian villages with communal property rights, local government, and the paternal protection of church and state. The crown also wanted to protect its own economic interests, as natives provided essential labor services and paid tribute to the royal treasury.

Communal forms of property ownership survived independence from Spain but came under attack from Mexican liberals at midcentury. Liberals sought to divest the Catholic Church of its vast landholdings and transform communal farmers into independent entrepreneurs. During the administration of Juan Alvarez, Finance Minister Miguel Lerdo de Tejada authored legislation (Ley Lerdo) that confiscated property owned by corporate bodies, such as the Catholic Church. Greedy liberal hacendados and lawyers quickly applied the law to village property, and court battles and firefights erupted across Mexico as peasants and clergy fought to keep their land.

The liberal victory on the battlefield sealed the church's fate, and liberal hacendados eagerly acquired valuable ecclesiastical estates for bargain-basement prices. Some villages withstood the landgrab through determined resistance, or simply because they owned less fertile, poorly watered, or isolated property less attractive to landlords. Village property came under renewed attack in the 1880s, however, as land values rose, commodities prices increased, transportation improved, and new markets opened up at home and abroad. Peasant resistance proved difficult as the federal government consolidated its power and President Díaz brutally suppressed dissent.[38]

The loss of village land placed tremendous pressure on natives.

FIGURE 12: Mexico's rural poor, such as the man pictured here,
did not benefit from the economic progress of the *Porfiriato*.

Source: Rafael Tovar, ed. *México: una nación persistente: Hugo Brehme fotografías*
(Mexico City: Instituto Nacional de Bellas Artes, 1995), photograph 117, p. 103.

Mexico's population had grown from 10,000,000 to 15,000,000 between
1877 and 1900; now remaining land had to be subdivided among more
people.[39] Villagers struggled to sustain their subsistence and generate a
modest surplus, essential for celebrating feast days, supporting priests,
and paying for weddings, burials, and lawsuits over land and water
rights. The wholesale loss of land created an economic as well as a
cultural crisis.

As hacendados accumulated village land, they increased acreage in those crops that promised the highest return on their investment. In many cases, this meant taking land out of food crops, such as corn and wheat, and replacing it with commodities destined for the export market. Thus, rubber, coffee, tobacco, henequen, and sugar production increased, while corn output declined. In the Yucatán Peninsula, for example, between 1845 and 1907 the area dedicated to corn production decreased from 15,000 to 4,500 hectares, while the acreage planted in henequen increased dramatically.[40] Corn was the basic staple of the Mexican diet, and between 1900 and 1905 the average price of corn rose by 38 percent.[41] Moreover, peasants' ability to pay higher prices diminished as agricultural wages stagnated or fell.[42]

Table 1

Selected Commodity Production Increases in Mexico (tons)

COMMODITY	1877	1910
Rubber	27	7,443
Coffee	8,161	28,014
Tobacco	7,504	8,223
Henequen	11,383	128,849
Sugar	629,757	2,503,825
Cotton	16,500*	44,000

*COTTON PRODUCTION IN 1892

Friedrich Katz, "Labor Conditions on Haciendas in Porfirian Mexico: Some Trends and Tendencies," *Hispanic American Historical Review*, 54, no. 1 (Feb. 1974): 15; and William K. Meyers, *Forge of Progress, Crucible of Revolt: The Origins of the Mexican Revolution in La Comarca Lagunera, 1880–1910* (Albuquerque: University of New Mexico Press), 64.

The economic and social impact of agricultural commercialization varied significantly from region to region. In some ways, the most dramatic changes occurred in the Yucatán, located on Mexico's southern periphery and characterized by distinctive historical and cultural features. In the 1840s Yucatán's Maya Indians, angered over land losses to encroaching sugarcane estates and higher taxes, began the protracted Caste War against local elites. Intense fighting for several years gave way to decades of guerrilla warfare and ultimately resulted in the deaths of more than 300,000 Maya—approximately one-half of the state's total population. The reconquest of this proud and ancient people sealed their subordination to a provincial elite determined to maintain premodern social relations based on forced servitude.[43]

Hacendados in the western portion of the peninsula had for some time cultivated the henequen plant, whose fiber could be woven into twine. Demand for hemp skyrocketed in the late nineteenth century with the invention of the McCormick Reaper, which required strong cordage for baling. The Yucatecan elite, given the opportunity to amass fortunes, used their political power to confiscate more village land and compel the Maya to labor under difficult conditions. Approximately 75 to 95 percent of local inhabitants lost their land and became destitute laborers on henequen estates. In many cases, Maya laborers were forced to remain on plantations for long periods of time to repay loans they had received from the landlord (debt peonage).[44] Maya who lived on the verge of starvation accepted a meager wage of corn, water, and a few cents to assure survival.[45]

The state helped planters increase labor supplies by shipping rebellious Yaqui Indians as forced laborers from Sonora to the Yucatán. The U.S.-based Richardson Construction Company and local elites coveted Yaqui land and water rights, and their incursions ignited a rebellion. Government troops engaged in ongoing battles with the natives, and between 1907 and 1910 Díaz deported 16,000 captured Yaquis to the Yucatán. Such deportation amounted to a death sentence. Grueling labor in Yucatán's tropical climate killed most Yaquis within a year of their arrival.

During periods of high prices, planters worked the Yaqui especially hard in order to maximize production and profits.[46] Just as those Caribbean and South American slave owners who imported male African slaves and worked them to death, growers clearly viewed the Yaqui as a renewable resource. Such callous disregard for human life underscores a fundamental contradiction of the Porfiriato: a regime committed to economic modernization without alteration of premodern social relations of production or concepts of justice.

The Díaz government also increased the labor supply by sanctioning the importation of several thousand Chinese and Korean indentured servants. Historians know comparatively little about the Asian experience in the Yucatán, but evidence suggests that "coolies" worked and perished much like the Yaqui.[47] A similar fate reportedly awaited thousands of Central Mexican peasants recruited by labor contractors to plant and harvest henequen. Contemporaries observed that recruits commonly signed work contracts while drunk or under the false assumption that they would receive good wages. Once on the henequen estates, however, they fell victim to debt peonage and labored under harsh conditions.[48]

Approximately thirty prominent planter families—the so-called *casta divina*—produced the bulk of Yucatán's henequen. Given the fact that they virtually monopolized global production, their profits should have climbed in unison with rising prices. Profits were seriously eroded, however, by a secret agreement signed between the U.S.-based International Harvester Company and a planter-merchant named Olegario Molina.

Molina, working in partnership with his son-in-law Avelino Montes, acquired control over a significant portion of henequen production by granting planters loans redeemable in fiber at below market price. Molina also exercised substantial control over the transportation and marketing of henequen through early acquisition of railroads, warehouses, and shipping companies. He methodically invested profits in land, and by the end of the Porfiriato stood as the peninsula's largest landowner.

This success story, laudable by contemporary standards, is tainted by Molina's secret deal with the International Harvester Company in 1902. The terms of the agreement specified that Molina's group would use "every effort within their power to depress the price of sisal fiber" and would "pay only those prices which from time to time are dictated by the International Harvester Company." To facilitate the arrangement, Harvester placed at Molina's disposal ten thousand bales of henequen that he could dump on the market at any time to depress prices. For their services, Molina and Montes "earned a commission of between 0.275 and 0.55 cents (U.S.) on every kilogram of henequen they acquired for Harvester during the decade preceding the Revolution, not to mention the enormous control that . . . [access to foreign capital] . . . gave them over the local elite."[49]

As a result of the agreement, Molina became the wealthiest and most powerful man in Yucatán, and International Harvester acquired an informal economic empire in the Yucatán. The agreement succeeded in driving down the price of henequen from 21.65 cents per kilogram in 1902 to 8.6 cents per kilogram in 1911, while Harvester increased its market share from 80.3 percent in 1903 to 99.8 percent in 1910. In effect, Harvester had succeeded in gaining control over an export industry and dramatically reducing costs without having to purchase land or otherwise risk capital (apart from Molina's commission).[50]

As for Molina, he became a national figure. News of his wealth, power, and acumen reached the presidential palace and Porfirio and Carmen Díaz traveled to the Yucatán to visit him.[51] The trip conveyed great symbolism. Presidents since Independence had avoided Yucatán, long considered an isolated backwater. Mexico's most powerful president, accompanied by his aristocratic wife, wanted to see the fruits of Molina's effort. Díaz was so impressed that he appointed Molina minister of development and brought him into his inner circle.

Molina's career encapsulates the strengths and weaknesses of Mexico's elite. Molina's shrewd understanding of local politics and the regional economy, coupled with lack of federal regulation, allowed him to negotiate the secret deal with International Harvester. In his mind, he was not compromising Mexican economic sovereignty, harming fellow planters, or exploiting laborers. Rather, he was facilitating the linkage between native producers and overseas manufacturers and promoting long-term development by moderating henequen prices and avoiding a boom-and-bust economic climate.[52] Molina's attitude toward labor remained firmly premodern. He may have experienced paternalistic feelings toward his Maya laborers, but he did not believe they deserved political rights, individual or collective freedoms, or higher wages. Nor did he have humanitarian concerns for Yucatán's Asian, Yaqui, and central Mexican workers. In fact, as minister of development, he arranged massive deportations of Yaquis from northern Mexico to the peninsula.

By the end of the Porfiriato, Molina and other cabinet ministers, notably José Ives Limantour, grew leery of foreign control over the Mexican economy and recommended increasing the importance of the public sector. However, it was a classic case of too little, too late.[53] Back home, Molina grew critical of his deal with International Harvester and sold out to his business partner before the revolution reached the Yucatán. Molina subsequently moved to Cuba, safely invested his fortune and—

after Díaz was doomed—supported the revolution from a distance. When Don Olegario died in 1925 the revolutionary government, displaying an incredibly short memory, gave him a hero's burial in the state capital.[54]

Entrepreneurs in other regions also amassed fortunes in the production and sale of agricultural commodities. In the Soconusco Valley in Chiapas, for example, Mexican and German coffee planters increased production to supply expanding markets in the United States and Europe. Hacendados acquired most of the fertile bottomlands and then enlisted the support of Governor Emilio Rabasa in overcoming poor roads and inefficient government. During the 1890s, Rabasa responded by building a new highway, abolishing internal tariffs, removing corrupt officials, and sanctioning the expropriation of village land. He also signed an agreement with a New Jersey–based company to build a railroad that connected the coffee zone with the Gulf of Tehuantepec. For their work, the U.S. company received $10,000 for each mile of track completed. German, Mexican, and North American capital poured into the region. Coffee production doubled from 10,000,000 to 20,000,000 pounds between 1907–1908 and 1909–1910.

With more land planted in coffee, planters required more laborers during harvest time. Maya from nearby Guatemala had been the traditional source of labor, but increased production now compelled planters to send labor contractors into the Chiapas highlands to recruit Maya villagers.[55] The highland Maya's geographic isolation and poor lands had traditionally given them some relief from outside penetration. Recruiters now offered them cash advances to work on the coffee plantations. There, the Maya endured harsh working conditions and became entangled in the web of debt peonage.[56]

Despite these conditions, however, the Maya kept returning to harvest coffee. The explanation lies in their abject poverty, which gave their lives a desperate edge. They struggled to earn the surplus income necessary to pay for festivals, weddings, and burials. Under these circumstances, the opportunity to earn cash wages could not be ignored.

Ricardo Pozas's poignant biography of Juan Pérez Jolote details the tragic life of a highland Maya Indian during this period. As a child, Juan's abusive father compelled him to run away from home. Found and sold into slavery by mestizos, falsely imprisoned as a young man, he was later conscripted into federal and revolutionary armies. Juan never understood the reasons why Mexicans were fighting one another, was wounded and discharged, worked at various jobs, and eventually returned home to marry and lead the life of a subsistence farmer. Venal mestizo officials abused villagers and rapacious mestizo merchants sold them cane alcohol at inflated prices. Alcoholism afflicted the entire adult male population. Given the limitations of the regional economy, Juan's only means of earning extra money—despite the trade skills that he acquired between stints as a soldier—came through harvesting coffee.[57]

Chiapas and the Yucatán, regions of great poverty and social injustice, did not produce indigenous revolutionary movements. The south's geographic isolation serves as a partial explanation, because news of revolutionary movements in northern and central Mexico did not necessarily reach Maya villagers and plantation workers. The social and political implications of the fighting, moreover, may not have been easily understood. Juan Pérez Jolote clearly did not understand the issues at hand, despite his involuntary participation in the fighting. The world outside his village contained violence, death, and disease on a higher order of magnitude, and Juan preferred the familiar poverty of subsistence farming.[58]

Farther south, the Yucatecan Maya had been decimated during the Caste War and were then thoroughly controlled by henequen growers during the Porfiriato. The importation of Asians, Yaquis, and mestizos from central Mexico created a mélange of cultures and languages that inhibited communication and solidarity among laborers and facilitated planters' notoriously harsh methods of social control.

The Maya also remained unlikely to rebel, according to John Tutino, because of their limited economic horizons. Centuries of exploitation and diminishing resources compelled the Maya to concentrate on maintaining their economic subsistence. As long as they did not starve, they did not rebel. Plantation workers received a corn ration as part of their wage, or could buy corn at reasonable prices at the company store. Moreover, the highland Maya retained their village lands and could supplement their income by working in the coffee harvest. Residence in their ancestral villages, despite poverty and political oppression, also provided them with a sense of autonomy and security.[59]

The establishment of a precarious social equilibrium following the commercialization of agriculture in the far south could not be replicated in other parts of Mexico. The upheaval caused by the expansion of the sugar industry in Morelos, for example, gave rise in 1911 to the revolutionary movement led by Emiliano Zapata. Sugarcane had been introduced to the hot, irrigated valleys of Morelos by Hernán Cortés and his collaborators, and during the colonial period planters and ranchers subsequently purchased, occupied, or stole large amounts of village land.[60] The pace of land consolidation in the sugar region accelerated during the Porfiriato in response to rising sugar prices, the growing internal market (particularly in nearby Mexico City), and the political and economic protection afforded planters by the Mexican state.[61]

Plantation expansion had invidious consequences that contributed to violent confrontation between peasants and elites. Hacendados acquired much more land than required to maximize sugar production. For example, Luis García Pimental's estates Santa Clara de Montefalco and Santa Ana Tenango measured 68,181 hectares in 1897, or almost the entire eastern portion of the state of Morelos. Most of this land, about 50,000 hectares, was dry or hilly terrain unsuitable for cane cultivation. Nonetheless, the acquisition of so much land reaped financial rewards for García. He received substantial income from rental and sharecropping agreements with landless peasants, and he (and other planters) made villagers economically dependent by monopolizing arable land and water resources.[62]

Villagers received daily reminders of their economic dependence, political impotence, and social inferiority. Planters seized village irrigation systems dating from pre-Columbian times and, in one case, lined the canals with barbed wire to keep the peasants from the water. Hacienda expansion completely engulfed eighteen villages, while estate lands surrounded some other hamlets. One planter actually ordered a village encircled with a brick wall. While villagers were losing land, the population of Morelos increased from 113,841 to 179,594 between 1850 and 1910. Resulting labor surpluses allowed planters to demand more from sharecroppers, tenants, and plantation workers. Owing to job scarcity, permanent employment was seen as "an act of kindness by the hacendado," and disobedient or unproductive laborers were immediately dismissed and replaced. Workers employed on a permanent basis netted only 37.50 to 50 centavos per day. This wage was not supplemented by a corn ration, a real disadvantage since corn prices rose dramatically during the Porfiriato.[63]

Impressive technical improvements and favorable government policies underpinned planters' progress. Progressive growers incorporated strategies of vertical organization, thus controlling the entire production process. Planters constructed modern mills to process massive amounts of cane quickly and efficiently, built internal rail systems to haul freshly cut cane to the mill, and hired experienced technicians, engineers, agronomists, and administrators to oversee operations. As a result, sugar production quadrupled between 1880 and 1910.[64]

Impressive profits were virtually assured to the sugar planters by the proximity of Mexico City. The population of the capital doubled between 1877 and 1910, increasing from 327,000 to 720,753.[65] Two new railroad lines linked the sugar mills of Morelos with eager consumers in the capital.[66] Strong local demand gave Mexican producers an advantage over foreign competitors who produced primarily for an international market susceptible to violent price swings. When after 1900 overseas sugar prices fell, Porfirio Díaz protected Mexico's sugar planters by doubling the tariff on imported sugar.[67]

The dichotomy between wealthy planters and impoverished peasants created a precarious equilibrium, to which many elites remained virtually oblivious. They flaunted their prosperity by building mansions, living in Mexico City for much of the year, and indulging in wasteful displays of public consumption.[68] Porfirio Díaz aggravated the situation by forcing an unpopular governor, Pablo Escandón, on the people of Morelos. Díaz had announced in 1908, in his famous interview with the North American journalist James Creelman, that he would permit free elections. Mexicans took him seriously. In Morelos a popular local candidate, Patricio Leyva, garnered widespread support. Escandón, conversely, was viewed as an outsider. After Escandón's fraudulent election, he created a political crisis by persecuting Leyvistas, increasing the property taxes of small farmers, and reducing those of planters. Adding insult to injury, he ignored his local responsibilities, instead choosing to spend his time in Mexico City.[69]

The political crisis set into motion a series of events that ended in revo-

FIGURE 13: Emiliano Zapata, photographed 1914, led Morelos's
peasants into battle to recapture the land and liberty that they
had lost during the Porfiriato.

Source: Rafael Tovar, ed. *México: una nación persistente: Hugo Brehme fotografías*
(Mexico City: Instituto Nacional de Bellas Artes, 1995), p. 107.

lution. The unrelenting spread of sugar plantations had shattered
villagers' economic subsistence and political autonomy. Their grievances
against the regime festered, waiting to erupt. Revolutionary leadership
emerged from within these communities whose cohesion "was an established ideal."[70] From the village of Anenecuilco emerged Emiliano
Zapata, a local dignitary whose ancestors had fought the French invaders.
It was Zapata who issued the battle cry of "land and liberty."[71]

In other regions of Mexico, preconditions for revolution also stemmed from rapid commercialization of agriculture but with significant variations. For example, planters in the Laguna region of north central Mexico, bridging the states of Coahuila and Durango, developed prosperous cotton estates through massive irrigation projects, modern technology, and the labor of more than 200,000 migrant laborers and sharecroppers. These were peasants from overcrowded and impoverished regions of central Mexico who sought economic security in the expanding labor market.[72]

The Laguna region developed through both entrepreneurial initiative and government support. New legislation promoted transportation by removing burdensome internal excise taxes and granting railroad concessions. The railroads proved decisive by linking the cotton zone to markets in the United States, improving export capacity, reducing freight rates, and facilitating importation of machinery and workers. The city of Torreón, Durango, emerged as a major rail center and market town with a diverse foreign population of Chinese, Spanish, British, and North American merchants, entrepreneurs, landlords, and speculators. The federal government also assisted planters in overcoming water shortages. The Federal Water Law of 1880 served as implementing legislation for a massive irrigation project that rechanneled the Nazas River and brought hundreds of thousands of hectares of previously untilled land into cultivation. On the margins of the cotton fields, new towns emerged in the former wilderness area.

Most newcomers to the Laguna region migrated from central Mexico, where previously stable village economies had been undermined by land consolidation and population growth. Between 1880 and 1910, the number of permanent rural residents of La Laguna increased from 20,000 to 200,000, and the number of seasonal workers rose to 40,000 during the cotton harvest. These numbers reflected the comparatively high wages paid to cotton workers, who earned up to 1.25 pesos a day. These were the highest agricultural wages in Mexico.

The cotton boom attracted investment from some of Mexico's wealthiest and most powerful families, including Vice President Ramón Corral, Luis García Pimental from Morelos, and presidential advisor José Ives Limantour. The plantations themselves, however, belonged to a handful of families and the British-owned Tlahualilo Company. The Tlahualilo retained direct control over all facets of the production process. Like other modern corporations, it rationalized production by investing in infrastructure and vertical integration. A narrow-gauge railroad, cotton mills, presses for cottonseed oil and cake, a soap factory, and a massive irrigation project (built with the cooperation of President Díaz and Governor Juan N. Flores) created an agro-industrial complex.

Downriver, numerous small and midsized producers planted cotton along the riverbank, while larger estates developed on the fertile alluvial plains in the lower reaches of the valley. The lower region's biggest producers included the Maderos, one the North's wealthiest and most prominent families. With proceeds from their agro-industrial-mining empire, the Maderos purchased 167,000 hectares of prime land. They employed modern technology and management skills.

Despite the general regional prosperity, conflicts arose between Mexican producers and foreign interests over markets, water resources, and government policies. In 1885, the government granted the British-owned Tlahualilo Company rights to unlimited amounts of water, duty-free importation of machinery, and exemption from municipal taxes for ten years. Outraged downriver planters—notably the Maderos—filed lawsuits to limit the amount of water Tlahualilo could draw and influenced passage of a 1895 regulation that significantly reduced the British company's water rights. Tlahualilo lawyers filed countersuits and diplomatic protests in London and Washington, D.C. The dispute continued until the outbreak of the revolution.

The Maderos also clashed with the Rockefeller-owned Continental Rubber Company over the guayule industry. In an amazing windfall, someone discovered that the locally abundant guayule plant, previously considered worthless, could be processed into rubber. Domestic and foreign entrepreneurs began to harvest the shrub in huge quantities and export rubber to the rapidly expanding U.S. market. Continental Rubber quickly cornered most of the industry and attempted to drive the Maderos, its only serious Mexican competitor, from business by merging with the United States Rubber Company and oversupplying the rubber market. This drove the price of rubber down from $1.00 to 25 cents a pound, and put the Maderos in serious financial difficulty. Only a last minute loan from French banks, arranged with the assistance of Treasury

Minister Limantour, kept the Maderos in the rubber business.

Despite the help from Limantour, President Díaz and his inner circle did not favor the Maderos. The dictator never forgave family patriarch Evaristo Madero for failing to support him politically during the Rebellion of Tuxtepec.[73] Díaz's subsequent snubs were both personal and political. Moreover, as a matter of national policy, the president did not grant Mexican firms the same generous concessions and tax breaks that he routinely gave to foreign corporations, including businesses that directly competed with Mexican companies. Díaz apparently reasoned that foreign firms, with their experience, capital resources, and technical expertise, would be the most productive. The Maderos were among a handful of Mexicans who owned and operated smelters in Mexico that competed with foreign firms, notably the Guggenheim-owned American Smelting and Refining Company (ASARCO). When President Díaz granted the Guggenheims generous concessions to build bigger and better smelters in Mexico, he undercut Mexican competitors. The Maderos, who displayed remarkable tenacity, were the only Mexican smelter operators to survive the Guggenheim's juggernaut.[74]

The Maderos fought back in the political arena, a fight that spanned nearly two decades and culminated in Francisco Madero's revolutionary call to arms in 1910. The fight began in 1893 when Evaristo Madero successfully led the effort to remove from office Coahuilan governor José María Garza Galán, who had supported the family's economic rivals. However, Miguel Cárdenas, an ally of General Bernardo Reyes, the pro-Díaz governor of Nuevo León, replaced Garza Galán. When the Maderos failed to prevent Cárdenas's reelection in 1905, they helped organize thirty-seven political clubs that served as the foundation for the anti-Díaz Partido Democrático de Coahuila. Elite politics further fragmented following the economic crisis of 1907–1908 that caused widespread unemployment and falling profits. In 1910, Francisco I. Madero, considered the family eccentric, launched a quixotic campaign for president that ended in revolution.[75]

Further north, in the provinces bordering the United States, the expansion of ranching and mining economies also created a volatile social milieu susceptible to revolutionary currents. In the eighteenth century, the Spanish Crown had sent military colonists to the borderlands to establish Spanish outposts in the midst of hostile Indians. These rugged frontiers-

FIGURE 14: Francisco I. Madero, whose call for revolution against
Porfirio Díaz was answered by peasants, workers, village notables,
and members of the provincial elite.

Source: Anita Brenner, *The Wind that Swept Mexico: The History of the Mexican
Revolution of 1910–1942,* with 184 historical photographs assembled by
George R. Leighton (Austin: University of Texas Press, 1971), photograph 47.

men received land grants, formed village enclaves, and fended off the
tenacious Apaches. They developed a hardy frontier culture forged by
continuous warfare. Superior horsemanship, sharpshooting, and independence characterized townsmen in Chihuahua and elsewhere.
American cowboys from neighboring Texas, Arizona, and other cattle-
raising areas emulated the Mexican vaqueros and adopted their ranching
vocabulary (for example, rodeo, chaps, lasso, lariat, calaboose).

Ranching developed during the colonial era to supply nearby mines with fresh meat, a symbiotic relationship that endured into the modern period. The foundation of new mines, towns, and railheads on both sides of the border increased demand for beef, and profit-consciousness hacendados responded by acquiring more land and cattle. Railroad construction opened up additional markets, and the lightly patrolled international border facilitated illegal exporting and rustling.

In comparison with agricultural workers, cowboys received higher wages and enjoyed greater physical mobility. Haciendas required a core group of vaqueros to maintain herds throughout the year, and additional help during roundups. Vaqueros, however, rarely slipped into debt peonage, unlike agricultural field hands in the South. In contrast to coffee, cotton, and sugar production, ranching did not require large numbers of permanent workers. Furthermore, armed cowboys on horseback were not easily restrained by landowners. The close proximity of the international border also made social control challenging, because young men could easily find work on farms, mines, and railroads throughout the southwestern United States. Therefore, relatively few examples of extreme labor exploitation occurred, particularly in comparison with other regions.[76]

More disruptive of the economic and political order was land consolidation that threatened autonomous village economies and legislation that abolished the right of citizens to chose local officials. In Chihuahua, a 1884 law stated that district administrators would be appointed by the governor, rather than elected by townspeople. This deeply offended fiercely independent Chihuahuans who felt that their cherished political rights, earned through generations of struggle against the Apaches, had been unfairly usurped. Twenty years later, state authorities compounded the offense when they declared that municipal officials would be appointed by the governor, rather than elected by townspeople.

These violations of local autonomy removed community-based leaders who were willing to defend the interests of townsmen and replaced them with retainers of the provincial elite. This paved the way for transference of public land to developers, a process that eroded townspeople's economic safety net and drove a wedge between social classes. In Chihuahua, extensive railroad construction in the 1880s and 1890s created new economic opportunities by increasing land values and opening up new markets. Luis Terrazas and his son-in-law Enrique Creel, the state's leading politicians, added to their immense landholdings and diversified their business interests.

Terrazas, who had been at odds with Díaz, reached a rapprochement with the dictator and returned to the governor's mansion in 1903. The following year he appointed Creel interim governor of Chihuahua, and Creel arranged for a new municipal land law that permitted the sale of underutilized community land to outsiders. This led to an outburst of government-sanctioned transfers of municipal property in what amounted to Chihuahua's Ley Lerdo. Many villagers who had survived the earlier expropriations in the nineteenth century now became landless laborers.[77] In the words of John Tutino, "Rancheros saw their autonomy threatened by legalized actions of a government with obvious class interests. Their protests mounted and became more violent."[78]

Environmental problems further contributed to rancheros' and farmers' distress. Drought and frost caused successive crop failures in 1907, 1908, and 1909, and rising corn and flour prices pushed household economies to the edge. The economic depression of 1907–1908, which hurt both the U.S. and Mexican economies, made it difficult for *norteños* to find temporary employment on either side of the border. Their rising levels of discontent made Chihuahua a center of revolutionary activity.[79]

In Tomochic, Chihuahua, state interference in traditional cultural, religious, and political practices had provoked a popular revolt against the government in 1892. The conflict did not directly blend into revolutionary currents in 1910, but its causes were indicative of the increasing alienation of villagers in western Chihuahua from the Porfirian state. As such, the conflict reveals the types of issues that eventually led many Chihuahuans to take up arms. Tomochicans resented outside meddling in their selection of political officers and observance of religious traditions and turned to local political and spiritual leaders for guidance.[80]

In the nearby state of Sonora, commercial agriculture expanded most rapidly in the Yaqui River valley, whose fertile, well-irrigated lands belonged to the Yaqui Indians. For centuries, the Yaqui had resisted efforts by Spaniards and Mexicans to take their property, and they now faced their strongest challenge. The U.S.-based Richardson Construction Company, backed by the full weight of the Porfirian establishment, laid claim to the Yaqui's ancestral lands. Thousands of natives lost their lives in the ensuing civil war. Thousands more perished while working as captive laborers on Yucatán's henequen plantations. Deep grievances seethed among those Yaqui who survived, and they would join revolutionary armies in large numbers after 1910.[81]

MINING

Although commercial agriculture and cattle ranching enriched hacendados and developers and disrupted the lives of tens of thousands of villagers and natives, settlement of the far north was primarily driven by the search for mineral resources. As early as the mid-sixteenth century, the quest for precious metals loomed large in the minds of explorers and settlers. Discoveries of large deposits of silver in colonial times generated great wealth for miners, merchants, and the crown and led to the foundation of permanent Spanish towns. The silver boom endured for centuries until the wars for independence in the early 1800s caused widespread flooding of mine shafts, capital flight, and political chaos.[82]

The industry did not fully recover until President Díaz took steps to attract foreign capital and develop an infrastructure for capitalist development. New legislation allowed foreigners to own subsoil rights (1892), buy land on the border (1894), form public corporations based on shares (1889), minimize corporate taxes (1884), and receive bank loans more easily (1897).[83] Díaz also granted foreign companies generous tax breaks, additional economic concessions, and police protection.[84]

Such incentives encouraged financiers and corporations to invest millions of dollars in developing northern Mexico's vast silver and copper reserves.[85] The French branch of the House of Rothschild, one of Europe's most famous banking families, organized the Compagnie Du Boleo in the 1880s to develop Baja California's copper fields. The Rothschilds negotiated an investment contract with the Mexican government that saved them millions of dollars a year through tax exemptions and special concessions. The Rothschilds responded by building a modern mine and smelter in the desert, a 33-kilometer railroad linking the mine with the port, and electrical and telephone service. "El Boleo" became Mexico's leading copper producer and realized handsome profits for one of Europe's wealthiest families.[86]

Table 2
Copper Production, Mexico and El Boleo, 1900–1910 (metric tons)

YEAR	(1) MEXICO	(2) EL BOLEO	(2)/(1) PERCENT
1900	22,473	11,297	50.2
1901	33,943	11,510	33.9
1902	36,357	10,473	28.9
1903	46,040	11,291	24.5
1904	51,759	10,706	20.7
1905	65,449	10,350	15.8
1906	61,615	11,000	17.8
1907	57,473	11,150	19.4
1908	38,173	12,600	33.0
1909	57,230	12,425	21.7
1910	48,160	13,000	27.0

Juan Manuel Romero Gil, *El Boleo: Santa Rosalia, Baja California, 1885–1954* (Hermosillo: Universidad de Sonora, 1991), 83; and Marvin Bernstein, *The Mexican Mining Industry, 1890–1950* (Albany: State University of New York, 1964), 51.

Table 3
Profit and Loss at El Boleo, 1887–1910

YEAR	FRANCS	YEAR	FRANCS
1887	-502,000	1899	6,500,000
1888	-587,000	1900	7,624,000
1889	-1,204,000	1901	1,750,000
1890	2,000	1902	1,750,000
1891	743,000	1903	3,474,000
1892	1,016,000	1904	4,204,000
1893	714,000	1905	6,367,000
1894	2,518,000	1906	10,133,000
1895	2,633,000	1907	6,373,000
1896	4,554,000	1908	4,693,000
1897	NA	1909	4,113,000
1898	3,441,000	1910	3,856,000

Juan Manuel Romero Gil, *El Boleo: Santa Rosalia, Baja California, 1885–1954* (Hermosillo: Universidad de Sonora, 1991), 84.

Mining frontiers have traditionally attracted adventurers such as Colonel William C. Greene. The "Colonel" had moved from New York to southern Arizona in the 1890s and engaged in a series of episodes characteristic of the popular image of the Wild West. He fought Indians, raised cattle, shot a man in self-defense, and prospected for gold. In 1899 Greene filed several mining claims around the old silver town of Cananea, Sonora, and rushed off to Wall Street with stories of massive copper deposits. Displaying great skills as a promoter, Greene raised large sums of money from influential New York financiers. Equally important, he negotiated numerous concessions and tax breaks from Mexican authorities worth millions of dollars in savings each year. Greene hired George Mitchell, an experienced mining engineer from Swansea, Wales, to custom-design a modern mine and smelter and oversee the construction of housing, stores, streets, waterworks, and everything else needed to create a town from scratch. Within a couple of years, Cananea was connected by rail with southern Arizona and was shipping massive quantities of copper to El Paso and beyond. In 1905 the *Copper Handbook,* the industry's Bible, reported that the population of Cananea had exploded from 100 to 15,000 persons. It ranked the Greene Consolidated Copper Company as one of the world's ten largest copper companies.[87]

The silver industry experienced a similar bonanza. Demand increased in the United States following passage of the Sherman Silver Purchase Act of 1890, authorizing the U.S. Treasury to issue silver certificates in exchange for bullion. The McKinley Tariff in 1890 placed a steep tax on silver ore with heavy lead content, which encouraged U.S. companies to build refineries in Mexico, so that lead could be removed before it crossed the border.[88]

U.S. firms controlled most of the Mexican mining industry. Seventeen of the largest thirty-one mining companies in Mexico were American-owned. Ten of the remaining firms listed British ownership. The Guggenheim's American Smelting and Refining Company controlled several mines and three major smelters worth an estimated 100,000,000 pesos in 1910, which made it the largest company in Mexico. ASARCO's lone Mexican competitor in the refining business, the Madero's Torreón Metallurgical Company, paled in comparison.[89]

The Guggenheims had carefully arranged for their success. They had acquired unparalleled knowledge of the mining business in the United

States, culminating in the takeover of ASARCO and their subsequent control over North America's lead supply. Daniel Guggenheim subsequently developed a personal rapport with President Díaz, who bestowed concessions and tax breaks that facilitated ASARCO's control over Mexico's refining industry.[90]

The booming mining economy created a highly visible group of foreign capitalists, primarily Americans, who had received special treatment from the Mexican government—treatment unavailable to Mexicans. This troubled Mexican nationals such as the Maderos, who competed in unfair market conditions created by their own government. Eventually, it also troubled other segments of the population, both liberal and conservative, who resented their government's role in helping foreign corporations achieve autonomy, power, and wealth in Mexico.[91]

Table 4

Mexican Silver Production, 1891–1910 (kilograms)

YEAR	SILVER
1891	1,087,261
1895	1,456,773
1900	1,776,410
1903	2,018,652
1905	1,890,970
1908	2,221,137
1909	2,212,983
1910	2,416,669

Marvin Bernstein, *Mexican Mining Industry, 1890–1950* (Albany: State University of New York, 1964), table 2, 51 (adapted).

Mining camps harbored other potential dangers for the Díaz government. Uprooted villagers and miners from home and abroad found themselves thrown together in makeshift towns and camps, sometimes hundreds of miles from the nearest established community. Mexicans had traditionally traveled long distances to earn cash wages, and land consolidation and population growth since midcentury had increased the

FIGURE 15: Thousands of miners migrated within and outside of the
country to large mine sites in isolated locales in northern Mexico.
Pictured here is the Ojuela mine in Durango.

Source: Anita Brenner, *The Wind that Swept Mexico: The History of the Mexican
Revolution of 1910–1942*, with 184 historical photographs assembled by
George R. Leighton (Austin: University of Texas Press, 1971), photograph 27.

pressures to migrate.[92] Cananea, as noted, grew from 100 to 15,000
persons between 1899 and 1902. Other mining towns experienced similar
demographic explosions.[93] Cananea's starting daily wage of 3 pesos,
nearly three times higher than the highest agricultural wage, attracted
workers from Sonora, Sinaloa, Nayarit, Aguascalientes, San Luis Potosí,
and the United States.[94]

Mine owners also hired labor contractors *(enganchadores)* to recruit
laborers from peasant communities and rival mines. El Boleo, for

example, hired Florencio Carrasco from Mazatlán to recruit groups of one hundred men and boys from Sinaloan villages to dig copper for the Rothschilds. The company paid Carrasco a commission of 2 pesos per worker and lent recruits money to bring their families to the mine.[95]

Some historians argue that cash advances, because they created a debt, automatically led to debt peonage.[96] Nevertheless, advances may have been necessary to recruit workers in competitive labor markets, and miners' comparatively high wages would have facilitated repayment of loans. Northerners also enjoyed greater physical and social mobility than other Mexicans did, owing to the structure of the regional economy and settlement patterns. The proximity of the international border and employment opportunities on the other side also made social control difficult. Debt peonage undoubtedly occurred in the mines and elsewhere, but more research is required to determine its perseverance and effectiveness in maintaining stable workforces.

The large number of foreign workers at Mexican mines suggests the heterogeneity and fluidity of the labor market. For example, on 30 July 1902, Cananea employed 1,265 North Americans, 189 Chinese, 132 English, 62 Germans, 52 Irish, as well as several Scots, Canadians, Swedes, French, Italians, Swiss, Russians, and a Hungarian. The ethnic division of labor practiced by foreign managers reflected their racial prejudices against dark-skinned Mexicans, a widespread and divisive feature of foreign-owned enterprise in Mexico.[97] Many upper-class Mexicans, who believed themselves further along the evolutionary chain, shared the racial prejudices of the foreign business community.

In the organization of labor, North Americans and Europeans manned skilled positions both underground and in the smelter, and North Americans monopolized managerial and accounting positions.[98] The Chinese worked on the railroad. The most arduous, dangerous, and lowest-paying work—digging, hauling, and sorting of the ore—went to the Mexicans.[99] Foreign employees received daily reminders of their privileged status. Superior housing, medical care, and food as well as higher wages separated them from native workers. The dual wage scale troubled native workers the most. Regardless of their work record, Mexicans always received substantially lower wages than did foreigners with the same jobs.

Table 5

Daily Wages Paid to Mexican and Foreign Workers at Cananea, 1906 (pesos)

POSITION	FOREIGNERS	MEXICANS
Miner	7.00	3.25
Machinist	7.50	4.00
Machinist's helper	7.00	3.50
Blacksmith	8.00	5.00

Wage Scales, Cananea Company Archive, 1916 Documental 0032.

Furthermore, wage discrepancies were actually greater than they appeared in nominal terms because foreigners received gold dollars and Mexicans silver pesos. The situation reached crisis proportions in 1905 when the silver peso was devalued by 50 percent and the cost of imported goods skyrocketed.[100] Understandably, this dual wage scale stirred up labor unrest.[101]

PETROLEUM

Seas of petroleum awaited discovery beneath the Gulf Coast region from Tampico to Chiapas, and the development of an oil industry entailed economic opportunities and political risks for Díaz. During the Porfiriato, the production of large amounts of heavy crudes characterized Mexico's petroleum industry. Crudes were used primarily in the production of asphalt. Producers also imported and refined lighter crudes into kerosene, gasoline, and lubricants for the Mexican market. The U.S. company Waters-Pierce, which maintained strong ties with Standard Oil, controlled the marketing of petroleum products in Mexico for many years.[102]

The industry changed in 1901 when Californian oil tycoon Edward Doheny, acting on a tip from an American railroad executive in Mexico, began buying land around Tampico and drilling for petroleum. Doheny hired a politically connected Mexico City attorney, Pablo Martínez del Rio, who worked for several foreign firms in Mexico, to help secure major concessions and tax breaks from the Díaz government. Doheny paid Martínez del Rio $300,000 for his services. He then invested millions in pipelines, storage facilities, refineries, and exploration. Doheny's major breakthrough came in 1911 with the discovery of lighter crudes in the Huasteca, 50 miles south of Tampico, which could be exported to the United States. Standard Oil agreed to purchase 2,000,000 barrels per year for five years from Doheny, a deal that contributed to his estimated annual profits of $10,000,000 per year.

Doheny's principal competition in Mexico came from Sir Weetman Pearson, an English engineer responsible for several important construction projects. Pearson enjoyed especially close ties with President Díaz and Treasury Minister Limantour. His success at draining Mexico City's wetlands, dredging Veracruz's harbor, and building a railroad across the Isthmus of Tehuantepec earned him the respect and admiration of Mexico's leaders. Pearson and his wife also cultivated the favor of the national elite by hosting lavish parties and presenting the president and his cabinet members with expensive European antiques.

Limantour and Díaz, who wanted to balance American and European investment in Mexico, welcomed Pearson's interest in Mexican petroleum. In particular, the president wanted to prevent Standard Oil, the giant of the petroleum industry, from acquiring a monopoly position in Mexico. Pearson expected strong financial backing from Díaz, who had already granted Sir Weetman $85,000,000 in public funds to complete the Tehuantepec Railroad and port facilities at Coatzacoalcos. In 1906, Díaz awarded Pearson the largest petroleum concession in Mexican history. He received a fifty-year lease to explore for petroleum on public lands in Veracruz state, duty-free importation of machinery, and free exportation of oil. Federal and state royalties were also limited to 7 and 3 percent, respectively.

Pearson soon founded the Compañía Mexicana del Petróleo El Aguila, S.A., and placed several prominent Mexicans on the company's board of directors. He began exploring for oil around Tampico and imported and retailed petroleum products. In both cases, he intruded onto market space already occupied by major U.S. firms. Pearson's challenge to Water-Pierce's retailing monopoly benefited Mexican consumers by driving down the price of petroleum products and helped local industrial growth by reducing production and maintenance costs. Waters-Pierce, whose price gouging had hurt Mexican consumers, lost market share but

FIGURE 16: Sir Weetman Pearson, named Lord Cowdray, received concessions from the Díaz government and developed Mexico's vast petroleum reserves. Cowdray is seen here on the right walking with Lord Aberdeen.

Source: Anita Brenner, *The Wind that Swept Mexico: The History of the Mexican Revolution of 1910–1942*, with 184 historical photographs assembled by George R. Leighton (Austin: University of Texas Press, 1971), photograph 24.

continued to make a profit. Pearson's returns skyrocketed in 1911 after the discovery of high-grade light crude near Doheny's oil fields.

Sir Weetman Pearson was already a wealthy man when he arrived in Mexico, but his spectacular engineering projects and lucrative business deals forever associated him with that country. After his election to the House of Commons, fellow members referred to him as "the member for Mexico," and Queen Victoria, in recognition of his overseas business career, later named him Lord Cowdray.

The oil boom transformed Veracruz from a state best known for its port into Mexico's second richest state. Despite the harsh climate and difficult work, migrants came from throughout the country, lured by its comparatively high wages. As in mining camps, however, seeds for working-class discontent existed in the dual-wage system for natives and foreigners, abusive foremen, and the power and arrogance of management.

Table 6

Yearly Production of Mexican Oil in the Northern and Southern Fields, 1901–1919

REGION	YEARS	TOTAL (BARRELS)
Northern Fields*	1901–1913	134,073,451
Southern Fields**	1910–1919	400,676,924
Isthmian***	1907–1911	2,241,730

    * Area just west of Tampico and along the Pánuco River
    ** Area just south of Tampico along the Gulf Coast
*** Isthmus of Tehuantepec

Jonathan C. Brown, *Oil and Revolution in Mexico* (Berkeley and Los Angeles: University of California Press, 1993), table 3, 121 (adapted).

INDUSTRY

Success in petroleum, mining, and railroads encouraged investment in manufacturing. Industrial development presented significant obstacles, however, because of the high cost of imported technology, limited domestic markets, low labor productivity, and capital scarcity. Industrialists' success hinged on state intervention, such as tariff protection and tax exemptions, to secure markets and increase profits.[103]

Industrial pioneers included European émigré merchant-financiers who could provide the initial capital outlays unavailable from Mexico's nascent banking industry. These financiers benefited from excellent political connections, developed throughout years of underwriting politicians and government projects.

Manufacturers produced for a relatively small domestic market. More than 90 percent of Mexico's 12,500,000 inhabitants worked as agricultural or menial laborers and earned less than 50 cents a day. Their limited purchasing power restricted consumption to essentials such as clothing, soap, and shoes, or inexpensive luxuries such as cigarettes and beer. Mexico's lone steel mill, the Fundidora Monterrey, produced steel products almost exclusively for railway companies and government public works projects.

Comparatively high production costs also limited industrial growth. Mexico did not have a developed tool dye or machine-making capacity, which forced importation of heavy machinery and equipment at considerable cost. Fully operational modern facilities, moreover, could not operate at full capacity because of limited demand. This reduced production efficiencies and increased the cost of the final product. Labor productivity also suffered from shortages of experienced industrial workers, and the need to employ first-generation workers unfamiliar with manufacturing.

The high cost of Mexican industrial products made them uncompetitive with imports from advanced industrial nations. Domestic producers (both foreign and national), therefore, sought government intervention to guarantee them a competitive market share. The government had granted similar requests to foreign corporations in petroleum and mining, and Díaz responded favorably by raising tariffs, granting tax exemptions, and providing federal subsidies. These policies saved domestic industry, but at the expense of increasing consumer prices.

Some companies received extraordinary support. French financier Augusto Genín and Mexican businessmen Saturnino Sauto and Tomás Reyes Retana formed the Compañía Nacional Mexicana de Dinamita y Explosivos and placed on the board of directors Porfirio Díaz, Jr. (the president's son), Julio Limantour (the treasury minister's son), and Enrique Creel (the secretary of foreign affairs). The Mexican mining industry generated strong demand for dynamite and explosives, the company's principal products, and the Mexican Army always needed ammunition. The market could have accommodated several producers, but the company received what amounted to an official monopoly. It lobbied the government to create an 80 percent tariff on imported dynamite and a steep consumption tax, and then received an exemption from both imposts. This gave the firm a decisive edge over competitors.

Producers employed other anticompetitive tactics to capture market shares. For example, the Compañía Industrial Jabonera de la Laguna, property of English émigré John Brittingham, cornered most of the market for cottonseed oil used to produce soap. Vidriera Monterrey purchased the patent for automated glass-bottle blowing machinery, which allowed that company to produce one million bottles a year. The company enjoyed a virtual monopoly in industrial glass production. Brittingham, who also owned a major share in this company, put the bottles to good use when he acquired the Cervecería Cuauhtemoc brewery.

Several producers also managed to acquire regional monopolies, sometimes aided by the nature of their product. For example, the high cost of shipping cement limited distribution to regional markets, and the highly perishable quality of beer restricted distribution. Textile manufacturers also succeeded in gaining control over retailing networks and restricting competitors' ability to reach consumers.

Despite such effective anticompetitive strategies, most industries did not earn large profits. Among the few that earned a median yearly profit of 10 percent or more were the cigarette manufacturer El Buen Tono and the textile companies Compañía Industrial de Orizaba (CIDOSA) and Compañía Industrial Veracruzana (CIVSA). Each produced low-cost, consumer nondurables that enjoyed relatively large markets. El Buen Tono accounted for 50 percent of all cigarette sales in Mexico. By contrast, producers of higher cost intermediate goods, such as cement and steel, sold to restricted markets and barely made money. According to historian Stephen H. Haber, investors recognized the weak short-term profit potential of heavy industry in Mexico, but they reasoned that the medium-term profits would be high. Their calculation was based on the rapid growth of the Mexican economy from 1880 to 1900, which they believed would continue unabated for many years.

Industrialization was concentrated in selected urban areas that provided access to markets, transportation systems, and sources of capital. The Federal District witnessed the largest concentration of factories, and the cities of Orizaba, Puebla, and Veracruz had several textile plants. Monterrey, located across the border from Texas, rivaled Mexico City in industrial production and became known as Mexico's Pittsburgh. A variety of enterprises ranging from steel mills, glass factories, breweries, and

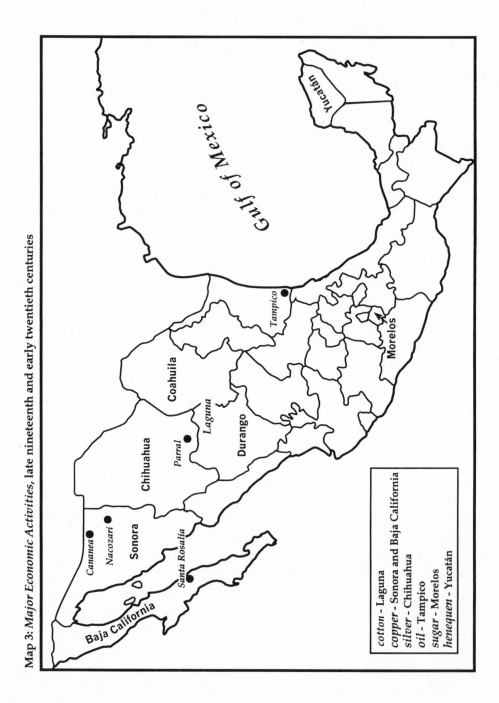

Map 3: *Major Economic Activities*, late nineteenth and early twentieth centuries

Gulf of Mexico

Yucatán

Tampico

Morelos

Coahuila

Laguna

Durango

Chihuahua

Parral

Sonora

Cananea

Nacozari

Santa Rosalía

Baja California

cotton - Laguna
copper - Sonora and Baja California
silver - Chihuahua
oil - Tampico
sugar - Morelos
henequen - Yucatán

smelters prospered and produced an industrial elite composed of Mexicans and émigrés from Spain, Ireland, Britain, and Germany. Their patron was General Bernardo Reyes, governor of Nuevo León from 1889 to 1909. A close associate of President Díaz, Reyes helped businessmen negotiate special deals and tax breaks with Mexico City. He was considered a strong candidate for vice president in 1910 and a likely successor to Díaz.

Mexico's industrial working class remained relatively small and disorganized. Paternalism served as a relatively effective method of social control, and the government helped businessmen suppress unions.[104] Downturns in the economy after 1905, however, resulted in layoffs, falling wages, and inflation, which created tense situations in the workplace.

CONCLUSION

In the eyes of his contemporaries inside and outside of Mexico Porfirio Díaz had achieved the impossible by overseeing the creation of political stability and economic development in a nation that had floundered since Independence. He had tamed the unruly caudillos through force, manipulation, and bribery, gained control over local government by removing elected officials and replacing them with appointees, and ended decades of presidential instability—marked by coup d'etats and changing policies—by holding onto power for more than thirty years.

Díaz also created the institutional infrastructure and legal safeguards required to entice foreigners to invest their money in Mexico's troubled economy. The massive infusion of capital that ensued underwrote the development of key sectors of the national economy, including railroads, silver and copper mining, the petroleum industry, and textiles. Mexican entrepreneurs, by contrast, predominated in agriculture and oversaw the rapid expansion of commercial crops, such as sugar, henequen, and cotton, which contributed significantly to overall economic growth. Still, the causes of discontent lie woven within the very fabric of Porfirian order and progress. Expansion of commercial agriculture came at the expense of peasant landowners, development of mining and industry facilitated foreign control over key sectors of the national economy, and political stability sacrificed local self-determination and alienated villagers and members of the provincial elite.

CRISIS AND REVOLUTION

NO ONE SAW THE REVOLUTION COMING. It began with a bungled political event—the election of 1910. Under Díaz, elections had been merely ceremonial reaffirmations of the president's rule. In 1908, the aged dictator had indicated in a published interview that he might step down from the presidency and permit free elections. Although later events made clear that he did not mean it, elite cliques and interest groups jockeyed for political position by supporting different contenders for Díaz's vice-presidential running mate and likely successor as the election approached. Those seeking important offices formed political organizations, held rallies, lobbied the president, and in the process unleashed democratic sentiments, exposing divisions within the ruling class.

The potential for political unrest was greatest in the countryside, where any suggestion of elite vulnerability increased the likelihood of violence. Some local patriarchs who had been dislodged from office in the consolidation process never forgave the dictator for their loss of prestige, patronage, and power, and they still retained the capacity to mobilize private armies.[1]

Mexicans from all walks of life had grievances against the regime. Some liberals believed that Díaz, through his conciliatory policies toward

FIGURE 17: Many political prisoners, including strike leaders from
Cananea, were incarcerated in the infamous San Juan de Ulua
penitentiary pictured here in 1910.

Source: Rafael Tovar, ed. *México: una nación persistente: Hugo Brehme fotografías*
(Mexico City: Instituto Nacional de Bellas Artes, 1995), photograph 4, p. 33.

the church, had violated the 1857 Constitution. Provincial elites denied
access to public office chafed under the dictator's tight political reins.
Moreover, Mexico's growing number of industrial workers—miners, railroad hands, textile workers—resented receiving half the wages paid
foreign workers for the same work. They also suffered injury, imprisonment, or death at the hands of soldiers and police when they attempted to
form unions or to strike. Mexican workers correctly concluded that the
Díaz government supported the interests of foreign workers and corporations over those of native labor and capital.[2]

Mexico's peasants, however, held the strongest grievances against the
Díaz regime. Tens of thousands of them had lost their land to modernizing estates bent on increasing acreage in highly priced commercial crops

such as sugarcane, cotton, and henequen, while their capacity to grow food crops diminished. Land consolidation and rising food prices, exacerbated by population increases, created great poverty in some regions. Thousands of peasants migrated to work in the mines and on commercial estates, but a majority continued to scratch out a living as seasonal field hands and impoverished farmers.[3] Some modernizing zones, particularly in Morelos and the Laguna region of Coahuila and Durango, became hotbeds of revolutionary activity and produced movements that spread to other parts of Mexico.[4]

ECONOMIC CRISIS

Among the pillars of the Porfirian edifice, the economy appeared particularly strong. The attractions of economic liberalism, helped along by the visible hand of public policy, included commercial and industrial growth, a growing middle class, a wealthy elite (whose businesses created jobs and trickled down the proceeds), and integration into a reconfigured and expanding Atlantic market economy.

Mexico's economic growth had been driven primarily by expansion of the export economy based on strong overseas demand for minerals, cotton, henequen, and other commodities. After the turn of the century, however, falling demand for these products in industrial nations exposed the vulnerability of an economy overly dependent on exports.

Mexico suffered most from the declining market price of silver, its most valuable export, and from the depreciation of the silver-based peso. The peso purchased less in industrial nations with gold-based currencies, and its 1905 devaluation increased inflationary pressures. The skyrocketing price of imports hurt peasants and workers the most.[5]

Moreover, the rising cost of imported foodstuffs and other products could not be easily offset by increased domestic production. The hacendados' decision to boost production of commercial crops, such as cotton, sugarcane, and henequen, decreased acreage in corn, beans, and squash at a time of rising demand. Food shortages resulted in higher prices and the specter of malnutrition, and even starvation, for lower-class Mexicans. The price of a metric ton of corn sold at Veracruz, for instance, increased by 200 percent between 1877 and 1907. At the same time, Mexican per capita corn production fell from 282 to 144 kilograms, a decline of nearly 50 percent.

Beginning in the 1890s, merchants attempted to compensate for falling domestic production by importing large quantities of staple food-stuffs. This increased supplies in some areas, but did not lower prices nor significantly improve consumption patterns. Government efforts to increase food supplies also failed to provide consistent long-term solutions. Stopgap measures included a temporary suspension of import taxes on food products in 1892 and government-subsidized food sales in crisis zones, including the introduction of fifty food outlets in Mexico City in 1905. The state also urged charitable institutions to sell corn and beans at cost. This reactive approach to endemic shortages, however, did not provide a permanent solution. Periodic food riots, including one in Durango involving more than four thousand people, unsettled the social equilibrium in the countryside.[6]

Miners and industrial workers, whose numbers were growing, also suffered from rising food prices, falling real wages, and periodic layoffs. Tensions ran especially high among Mexico's 31,000 textile workers, who worked long hours in modern French-owned factories in Orizaba and in older Mexican-owned mills in Puebla and Mexico City. In 1905 Orizaba's textile workers formed the Gran Círculo de Obreros Libres (GCOL), with an impressive membership of 9,000 to 10,000 workers, and requested a 5 percent wage increase, an end to payment in script redeemable at the company store, and other reforms. The French managers refused to negotiate and, flexing their political muscles, reduced workers' wages.

Faced with similar wage reductions, Puebla's textile workers joined the GCOL, and the union went out on strike. Mexican mill owners, taking a defiant stance, issued a new labor code that increased workers' hours. On December 24, 1906, mill owners led by the French interests declared a national lockout of major textile mills and threw 30,000 workers out of work.

Public opinion strongly sympathized with the displaced workers and their families. Newspapers editorialized against the harsh treatment of Mexican workers by French capitalists, particularly Rio Blanco mill owner Garcín. Veracruz Governor Teodoro Dehesa and President Díaz sought political damage control, and the president took the extraordinary

FIGURE 18: In 1906, workers at Rio Blanco's textile mill complex went
on strike to win job security, higher wages, and the right to join unions.
The French-owned mills refused to negotiate, and President Díaz ordered
troops to suppress strikers. Díaz later commented, "Thank God I can still
kill." The assembled strikers are pictured here.

Source: Anita Brenner, *The Wind that Swept Mexico: The History of the Mexican
Revolution of 1910–1942*, with 184 historical photographs assembled by
George R. Leighton (Austin: University of Texas Press, 1971), photograph 42.

step of summoning management and strike leaders to Mexico City to
present them with a compromise solution.

Garcín and his associates, however, refused to implement the settlement. Frustrated and hungry workers sacked Garcin's company stores.
Díaz, no longer in the mood to compromise, dispatched troops to the
scene, intent on breaking the union. In the days that followed, soldiers
killed between fifty and seventy workers, sent dozens more to work

camps in Quintana Roo, and executed six union leaders. President Díaz remarked, "Thank God I can still kill."[7]

The famous Río Blanco strike underscores a fundamental weakness in Díaz's blueprint for economic development: generous government support for foreign enterprises created an attractive investment climate and encouraged development. However, it also made foreign companies wealthy, powerful, and independent. Garcín ignored the president's compromise plan and could still count on Díaz to crush workers. In effect, the most powerful foreign corporations stood above state regulation.

Unfortunately for the regime, the strike's suppression did not halt the union movement. Rumors circulated that several hundred workers had been killed, which became the popular perception of the event. Moreover, those executed became working-class martyrs, and the anniversary of their deaths a workers' day of remembrance. Nationwide, sixty-five strikes occurred between 1907 and 1909, including several by textile workers. Abusive behavior by foreign foremen, particularly North Americans employed by mills, railroads, and mines, ignited many of these disputes.[8]

Perhaps most disturbing for the regime, the working-class movement contained ideological strains antithetical to Porfirian authoritarianism. Their foundations came from both traditional and contemporary sources. Pope Leo XIII's *Rerum Novarum* encouraged church organization of labor unions and support of pro-labor legislation. The Mexican church responded by forming workers' clubs, a national labor union in 1908 (the Unión Católica Obrera), and advocating labor and social reforms (including higher wages and the abolition of labor contracting). The moderate reforms advocated by the Catholic Church contradicted Díaz's policies, won working-class support for the church, and deeply disturbed liberals inside and outside of the government.[9]

The church hierarchy, however, sometimes underestimated the persistence of anticlericalism. For example, in 1900 the bishop of San Luis Potosí imprudently remarked that the reform laws were a dead letter. In response, Camilo Arriaga, a wealthy mine owner and former liberal politician, called for the organization of liberal clubs throughout Mexico to stem the rising tide of clericalism. Middle-class professionals, including lawyers, doctors, teachers, engineers, and students, quickly formed fifty liberal clubs in thirteen states. At the first national liberal congress, in

February 1901, delegates gave impassioned speeches attacking the church and supporting the reform laws.

Ricardo Flores Magón, a journalist-politician from Oaxaca, led a contingent of radical delegates to the Congress, which was also the site of increasing attacks on the Díaz government. This move, however, went too far for the movement's moderates who understood that criticism of the dictatorship invited repression. Several deserted the liberal movement just before the police closed clubs, destroyed printing presses, and imprisoned several movement members.

Flores Magón and other leaders, including future Zapatista chief Antonio Díaz Soto y Gama, managed to escape to the United States. They continued publishing their newspaper *Regeneración,* eluded U.S. immigration officials, and conferred with American and Spanish anarchists. In 1906 they formed the Partido Liberal Mexicano (PLM) in St. Louis and issued a reform manifesto that advocated a four-year presidential term, a minimum wage, an eight-hour workday, and the end to child labor. Flores Magón and his associates managed to distribute *Regeneración* throughout Mexico and to maintain contact with dozens (perhaps hundreds) of PLM cells.

The PLM's program resonated among Mexico's workers and professional classes. Outbreaks of local-level political violence in 1906 and 1908 have been linked by historians to the PLM, and their pro-labor ideology clearly influenced miners at Cananea and elsewhere.[10] Members of Cananea's two liberal clubs, the Unión Liberal Humanidad and the Club Liberal de Cananea, distributed copies of *Regeneración* around town and spoke of "reclaiming justice" for the wage earner and of resisting the "caciques, the vile lackeys of capitalism." Esteban Baca Calderón, the most militant PLM leader, wanted miners to recognize that "the dictatorship was their worst enemy" and to "feel the desire to overthrow it." Foreign capitalists, he added, treated Mexican workers like "beasts of burden."[11] Such rhetoric unsettled the social and political equilibrium and contributed to labor conflict.

The mineworkers' movement north of the border also influenced Mexican miners. News reached Cananea, located only 45 kilometers south of the Arizona border, of strikes by American miners in Colorado, Idaho, and Arizona. News of the Western Federation of Miners' (WFM)

FIGURE 19: Miners' grievances, including abuses by American foremen and the dual wage scale that paid foreigners twice as much as Mexicans, led to outbreaks of serious strikes. In this photograph, Colonel William C. Greene addresses striking miners at Cananea in 1906.

Source: Alicia Ahumada and David Maawad, eds., *Cananea y la Revolución Mexicana* (Mexico City: Talleres de Litográphica Turmex, S.A., 1987), p. 65.

efforts to establish unions also reached Cananea. The WFM counted 1,500 adherents at Cananea in 1905; they undoubtedly discussed their experiences and beliefs with the local miners. Mexican authorities and company police successfully prevented the establishment of an union at Cananea, but they could not prevent the spread of threatening ideas.[12]

WFM and PLM ideologies helped miners conceptualize their grievances and organize Mexico's most famous strike, which occurred in June 1906. In a manifesto presented to mine owner Colonel William C. Greene, three thousand Mexican miners requested pay increases, the end to the dual pay scale for Mexican and foreign workers, the hiring of Mexican foremen, and an eight-hour workday.[13] Demands for equality in the workplace transcended labor-management issues and represented a nationalist response to business and government policies that favored foreigners over natives.

The subsequent actions of Colonel Greene and Mexican authorities transformed a serious labor dispute into a major political scandal. Greene received guns and ammunition from Phelps-Dodge chief Walter Douglas in Arizona, and he telegraphed Governor Rafael Izábal and the rurales to send troops.[14] In the meantime, he positioned armed company men at strategic locations around town and refused to negotiate with strikers. Deadly clashes soon occurred between roaming mobs of Mexicans and heavily armed North Americans. Miners torched the lumberyard and incinerated two foreign employees. Greene's men retaliated by shooting indiscriminately into crowds and killing at least fifty people.[15]

The next day Greene escalated the conflict by requesting the assistance of two to three hundred Arizona Rangers, a flagrant violation of both international law and the instructions of federal authorities. Governor Izábal rushed to the border, deputized the North Americans, and accompanied them to Cananea. General Torres's federal troops and Colonel Kosterlitzky's rurales were also en route to the mine.

By the afternoon of June 7, the combined Mexican and North American expeditionary forces, consisting of both cavalry and infantry, confronted Cananea's miners, who were armed with picks, shovels, and a few firearms. Company riflemen now made sport of the situation and culled Mexicans from the crowd; cavalry men spurred their horses into miners and trampled them to death. General Torres, having witnessed the hard lesson, gave miners his ultimatum: either return to work or be forced into the army and sent to fight the Yaquis. Miners returned to their jobs without having won any concessions except for the token dismissal of one foreman.[16]

Colonel Greene praised the surgical killings to the Governor of Chihuahua, Enrique C. Creel: "One of the most fortunate circumstances connected with the lamentable occurrences, is that every Mexican who was killed was a striker and nearly everyone was a ringleader. . . . This seems almost providential."[17] Greene also noted that the strike had given authorities the excuse to imprison eighty-seven Mexican activists, including local PLM leaders, and to exile foreign miners suspected of WFM affiliation. Cananea's municipal president and the U.S. vice-consul were also replaced, at Greene's request, for failure to defend company property with sufficient vigor.[18]

For his part, Sonoran Governor Izábal, apparently wishing to address the foreign community, defended his actions in the English-language newspaper the *Mexican Herald*. Cananea's miners, he asserted, lived like members of the "middle class" with houses, furniture, and bank accounts. Their insolent behavior had been dealt with appropriately.[19]

Nevertheless, Izábal and Greene had badly misjudged the public mood. Their decision to invite U.S. gunmen into Mexico to kill Mexicans was protested by conservatives and liberals in terms unsettling for the regime. For example, the pro-clerical daily *El Estandarte* compared the Arizona Rangers' incursion to the U.S. invasion of 1847, and the business and commercial weekly *El Progreso Latino* termed the strike a conflict between abused Mexicans and exploitative North Americans.[20] In Sonora, the Cananea affair also turned members of the local elite against Izábal, Torres, and Vice President Corral (a native son).[21] Francisco Madero, viewing events from Coahuila, considered the strike one of the principal abuses of the Porfiriato.[22]

The Cananea affair got the federal government's attention. As in the Rio Blanco strike, its instructions had been ignored by powerful foreign businessmen. Public outcry called for a response. Cabinet members José Ives Limantour and Olegario Molina expressed concern over the supreme position of North American capital in the Mexican economy and advocated new policies. Limantour won approval in 1907 to begin nationalizing most U.S.-owned railroads; Molina proposed limiting foreign ownership of mines in the border states and increasing government's regulatory power over mining. Molina complained that "foreign trusts" enjoyed more privileges than Mexican companies. He specifically mentioned the Cananea affair as a reason for the proposed mining law.[23]

Unfortunately, these proposals changed very little. Nationalization of the railroads proved slow and expensive; daily management remained in the hands of foreigners. Moreover, the new mining legislation was vigorously opposed by the mining companies, whose lawyers and lobbyists successfully delayed passage for two years. The law that finally emerged changed virtually nothing.[24] In effect, foreign businesses' privileged position in Mexico had been nurtured and fortified to the point that the Díaz government could not reform its own policies.

POLITICAL CRISIS

Economic and social crises clearly strained policymakers' imaginations and revealed weaknesses in the political system. Porfirian authoritarianism had evolved as a solution to nineteenth-century political chaos and economic underdevelopment. Liberal elites prized the benefits of authoritarian rule over participatory democracy. For example, political theorist and jurist Justo Sierra advocated the sacrifice of individual liberty on the altar of political stability, and journalist-intellectual Francisco Cosmes praised "honorable tyranny." For these scientific thinkers, or *científicos,* Díaz's reelections expressed "popular will" within a controlled "constitutional democracy."[25]

By the turn of the century, however, científicos agreed that continued stability required planning for orderly presidential succession. Francisco Bulnes, in his 1903 presidential nominating speech, praised Díaz for saving Mexico from "radical Jacobinism" and providing the country with decades of peace. Mexico was now prepared, Bulnes concluded, for a mature political system based on liberal and conservative parties. Díaz's advancing age added urgency to the discussion and provoked debate among elites over the presidential succession.

Orderly succession, however, required Díaz's cooperation. The president disapproved of political parties. He would only support a constitutional amendment that limited presidential terms to six years.[26] In effect, Díaz reserved the right to name his own successor but refused to suggest candidates. Elites speculated that Díaz's choice for vice president in 1904 would reveal his preference for a successor, especially since the elderly dictator might die in office. Insiders assumed that the next vice president would be a political powerhouse such as Treasury Minister Limantour, favored by European interests and the financial community, or War Minister Bernardo Reyes, backed by the military and powerful regional elites. Instead, Díaz selected Ramón Corral, the unpopular former governor of Sonora. Corral was not associated with a major Mexico City camarilla and owed political allegiance only to the cagey dictator.

Economic and social problems in 1906–1908 increased speculation about the presidential succession. In a 1908 interview with North American journalist James Creelman, representing *Pearson's Magazine,* Díaz further intensified the discussion. He stated that he would not seek reelection in 1910 and that Mexico was ready for a party system.

Díaz's inner circle did not believe him. The interview was only intended for North Americans, Limantour believed, and party regulars started making preparations for the dictator's reelection. But when word of the interview reached Mexico, many Mexicans took Díaz seriously. They began organizing political clubs, writing party platforms critical of the regime, and announcing their candidacies for local, state, and national offices. This spontaneous outburst of enthusiasm at the prospects for free elections must have distressed Díaz and his inner circle, who had lost touch with popular political sentiment. The country was clearly ready for a change.

But what kind of change? Free elections had never been the Mexican tradition. Divisive political clashes, perhaps even armed conflict, might determine the winners. Porfirio Díaz, who had been in power for thirty years, would set the ground rules. If he chose a successor with widespread support, then an election might be a mere formality to a peaceful transition. In the end, however, Díaz decided to stand for reelection. Perhaps Limantour was right—the Creelman interview had been only intended for external consumption.

The political climate remained volatile. Political clubs continued to support alternative candidates for local and regional offices and for the vice presidency. Ramón Corral had not improved his image or political power base, and practically everyone wanted him dropped from the ticket of 1910.

General Bernardo Reyes emerged as a popular alternative candidate for vice president. Reyes had distinguished himself as war minister and governor of Nuevo León, and he enjoyed widespread support among the middle and working classes. Reyes had consistently supported Díaz, and he seemed the ideal transitional figure. His supporters formed the Partido Democrático, six political clubs in Mexico City, and numerous other clubs in Jalisco, Nuevo León, Coahuila, Sonora, Puebla, Veracruz, and elsewhere. Campaign rallies in Guadalajara, Veracruz, Torreón, Monterrey, and Puebla drew thousands of supporters.

All of this, however, made both Díaz and Reyes nervous. Reyes wanted to be vice president (and presumably president), but he had not encouraged big rallies or other forms of popular manifestation. General Reyes was comfortable with Porfirian authoritarianism and uncomfortable with popular democracy. President Díaz had never been influenced by popular manifestations. He viewed Reyes's political popularity as potentially disruptive and divisive. In the end, he disappointed General Reyes, and many Mexicans, by keeping Ramón Corral as his running mate.

Reyes's closest supporters, including his son, urged him to rebel. However, the general refused to take up arms and left for Europe on special presidential assignment. The sentiment for change remained strong among Mexicans, however, and political outsiders sought an alternative standard-bearer. Perhaps someone with the right message could garner enough support to win the election—or at least force Díaz to drop Corral from the ticket.

Someone was waiting in the wings who, at first glance, did not appear threatening to the president. Francisco I. Madero's short stature and slight build hardly corresponded to the image of a dashing caudillo. Madero's belief in communication with the dead through a medium, and unscientific medical remedies also labeled him as something of an eccentric. Nevertheless, Madero's family pedigree gave him credibility among the elite. His managerial skills had earned him a personal fortune. His workers thought highly of him. Further, the Madero family also had accounts to settle with President Díaz because they had been denied political influence in their native Coahuila and the president had granted their foreign competitors special economic concessions and tax breaks.

Francisco Madero emerged as a serious challenger to Díaz because he managed to win the middle ground. All organized threats on the left, such as the Partido Liberal Mexicano, were forced underground by repression and could not participate in the electoral process. Madero, a respectable upper-class challenger with a moderate platform, by contrast, could be tolerated by Díaz. Madero's vast personal fortune bankrolled an impressive electoral campaign. He held rallies throughout central and northern Mexico, published polished campaign literature, and founded numerous political clubs. Madero's book, *The Presidential Succession in 1910,* won support among upper- and middle-class voters by promising democracy without social and economic change. Madero's campaign slogan "Sufragio Efectivo, No-Re-Elección," meant "a real vote and no boss rule," and appealed to those denied a political voice during the dictatorship. By calling his party the "No-Re-Electionist Party," he also cleverly resurrected the old liberal rallying cry used by Díaz himself against Juárez and Lerdo. Madero's choice of issues and symbols, then, fashioned a coalition of centrist supporters, including Reyistas, workers, and professionals, all of whom posed a genuine electoral threat to General Porfirio Díaz.

But only, of course, if the votes were counted. Certainly, Madero understood this as well as anyone. In 1905, he had organized opposition candidates for local offices in Coahuila, only to see the election stolen by the authorities. In the months before the 1910 election, Madero drew crowds of 25,000 and more supporters. The regime had now seen enough. Its thugs disrupted his speeches, destroyed campaign literature, and shut down Madero's newspaper, the *Anti-Re-Elecciónista*. Before election day, Madero went to Díaz with an offer. Madero would withdraw from the campaign if he could run as Díaz's vice president. The dictator turned Madero down and later had him arrested. On election day, the official count gave Porfirio Díaz more than one million votes, and Francisco Madero less than two hundred.[27]

FRANCISCO I. MADERO AND THE MEXICAN REVOLUTION

Released on bail from his dank prison cell in San Luis Potosí, Madero disguised himself as a railway worker, purchased a third-class train ticket to the border, and slipped unnoticed into Texas. Madero made his way north to San Antonio, where he could draw upon the family's local bank account, and met with relatives and political supporters to discuss revolution.

Madero's decision to seek redress through violence clashed with his desire to protect private property and avoid social upheaval. As a result, his call to arms—the Plan de San Luis Potosí—focused on political reform and sidestepped the social and economic concerns of peasants, workers, and nationalists. The plan annulled the recent elections, named Madero provisional president, promised free elections, and proclaimed the no-reelection principle. Land reform, a burning issue for many Mexicans, received only passing reference. Those individuals who had lost their land through illegal application of the pubic lands law, Madero promised, would have their property reinstated.[28] Even this went too far for family patriarch Evaristo Madero, however, who wrote to his friend José Ives Limantour, "I give you my word of honor . . . that we have not contributed a single penny . . . and that far from sympathy with the movement, we repudiate it energetically. To men of business, [a revolution] could only bring harm."[29]

Francisco Madero behaved more like a political reformer than a social revolutionary.[30] He championed the liberal principles of midcentury—the holy trinity of no-reelection, decentralization, and free-market capitalism, rarely honored by liberals but constantly trotted out at election time. Madero's commitment to political stability and administrative efficiency, moreover, revealed his desire to only tinker with the system rather than to overthrow it. Madero's insistence that land disputes should be settled within the courts, rather than through forced redistribution, disappointed land-hungry peasants who demanded immediate redress and unsettled the revolutionary coalition.

THE NATION RESPONDS

Following his electoral defeat, Madero received the support of numerous locally based revolutionary movements whose military victories embarrassed the federal army and weakened the Díaz government. Madero stood as titular head of a revolutionary movement tenuously and temporarily held together by the common goal of overthrowing the dictator. The continued loyalty of revolutionary leaders hinged on his ability to solve local grievances and reward successful military chieftains and their followers.

The first months of the revolution produced few victories. In San Antonio, Madero received Puebla shoemaker Aquiles Serdán, who revealed plans for a revolution in the Puebla-Tlaxcala region. Serdán, a leading Maderista activist during the presidential campaign, planned to occupy Puebla, free political prisoners, and march on Mexico City. Serdán anticipated widespread support from local workers and members of the middle class.

Gustavo Madero was sufficiently impressed with Serdán's plan to bankroll the plot. He slipped 15,000 pesos to Serdán's sister, Carmen. Serdán's history of political activism in support of Madero, however, made him a logical target for police surveillance, and they uncovered enough information to suspect him of subversion. Police raided Serdán's house while the plotters were inside and a firefight ensued. The outnumbered rebels put up a heroic fight, and Serdán managed to kill the hated local police chief. However, at the end of the skirmish twenty revolutionaries lay dead (including Serdán), four others wounded, and the survivors faced stiff prison sentences.[31]

Serdán's failure coincided with other rebel setbacks in small-scale engagements in Coahuila, Durango, and Chihuahua. President Díaz, vengeful in victory, ordered the confiscation of the Madero's property, and family elders advised Francisco to seek permanent exile in Europe. Instead, Madero moved to New Orleans and continued plotting against the regime.[32]

Local movements, largely unconnected with one another, kept the revolution alive. Village-level disturbances over land rights and self-determination proliferated in areas of northern Mexico that had experienced profound change during the Porfiriato. Rancheros and villagers (both mestizo and Indian) joined the struggle in greater numbers than hacienda residents, who received regular wages and had paternalistic relationships with hacendados.

Rebels raided villages, attacked federal troops, and settled old scores. They generally did not formally recognize any central political authority except for a nodding recognition of Madero's existence. From the Durango foothills, village cacique Heraclio de la Rocha—described as "a grizzled, grey-haired old man, with a scrubby beard, huaraches on his feet, [and] a red bandana covering one empty eye-socket"—appeared with an armed retinue that consisted of relatives and a mélange of "dwarves, cranks, wild and beautiful women and brave mountaineers." Equally colorful and terrifying, Calixto Contreras, leader of four thousand rebellious Ocuila Indians from Cuencamé in La Laguna, directed mayhem from a railway car decorated with a beribboned, severed head.[33]

The Partido Liberal Mexicano, divided between anarchist and socialist factions, also maintained an unrelenting propaganda attack on the

Díaz regime. The outbreak of armed rebellion provided its more militant members, including founder Ricardo Flores Magón, with the opportunity to organize workers and to man the barricades. The PLM launched several armed attacks in Baja California, Sonora, and Chihuahua, with its most notable victory coming at Mexicali, Baja California, in January 1911.[34] PLM organizing activities among miners in Sonora and elsewhere also intensified, although most significantly after Díaz's resignation.[35]

Some moderate PLM members supported Madero, but the radical leadership considered him a political opportunist. Ricardo Flores Magón, upset with Madero for arresting a PLM leader, publicly called him a "traitor to the cause of freedom" and "the stunted politician and the vulgar ambitious [one] who wishes to elevate himself on the shoulders of the poor people to collect for supposed services."[36] Magonistas and Maderistas, separated by different political ideologies, tactics, and social class, never forged a workable political alliance.

Revolutionary activity along the border alarmed the Taft administration, which feared for the safety of American citizens and businesses in the region. The U.S. government prosecuted and jailed Ricardo Flores Magón and stationed 20,000 troops on the banks of the Rio Grande. Díaz misinterpreted this as a sign of support. In fact, U.S.-Mexican relations had cooled in recent years because of Díaz's growing independence in foreign affairs and in domestic economic policies. For example, his administration granted French and British interests lucrative concessions coveted by U.S. firms, while denying an American request for a permanent naval base lease at Magdalena Bay, Baja California, and opposing U.S. policy in Nicaragua.[37] The fact that U.S. agents did not initially harass Madero, who had entered the country without a visa, appears to confirm Taft's displeasure with Díaz.

Closer to Mexico City, news of bloody clashes between armed villagers and federal forces in the state of Morelos concerned the government. Villagers sought to reclaim land lost to neighboring sugarcane plantations. They formed a community-based movement supportive of Madero. Article III of the Plan de San Luis Potosí, which promised reinstatement of land illegally acquired by estates, encouraged determined campesinos to support the northern rebel.

Morelense rebels looked to fellow villagers, as opposed to disaffected elites, for leadership. Torres Burgos, their first leader, led angry farmers on raiding expeditions and ambushes before being captured and executed by army troops. The new rebel chief, Emiliano Zapata, hailed from the village of Anenecuilco and would soon emerge as a champion of land reform and as an important leader of the revolution.

The Zapatas occupied a position of importance within their community. They had defended the village against the French in the 1860s, and Emiliano now took up the struggle against the planters. In addition to his pedigree, Zapata's personal qualities made him a natural leader. Villagers admired his horsemanship, machismo, and defiance of authority (which had already involved him in a couple scrapes with the law). Zapata also owned and rented land and raised a fair of amount of livestock, which made him relatively well off and a likely candidate for cogodparenthood and village office.

Zapata's defiance of the powerful owner of the Hacienda del Hospital greatly enhanced his reputation. Anenecuilco had been engaged in an intense struggle with this hacendado over control of land crucial to the village's economic survival. To complicate matters, the hacendado had rented the disputed land to campesinos from the neighboring village of Ayala who had begun to plant corn. When Anenecuilcans complained, the planter replied, "Let them plant in a flower pot." Zapata, who had a personal stake in the disputed property, organized an armed contingent of eighty villagers and forced the Ayalans from the land. The hacendado, startled at Zapata's audacity, did not retaliate.

The agrarian revolution in Morelos gained momentum as rebels raided along the Morelos-Puebla border and formed a tenuous alliance with Ambrosio Figueroa from northern Guerrero.[38] Figueroa's rancheros (mid-sized ranchers and farmers) challenged the hacendados' political authority in their region and seized control over various towns. These rebels were recruited from upwardly mobile rancheros whose families had acquired land from disentailed church and village property a half century earlier and did not share the Zapatistas' commitment to agrarian reform. The two movement's divergent agendas would eventually drive them apart.[39]

Rebel activity in Chihuahua, the mineral-rich province on the northern border, disturbed Díaz even more than the revolts in Morelos. In Guerrero District, rebels led by local notable Pascual Orozco overthrew municipal authorities and posed a military threat to important towns such as Ciudad Juárez on the border. Moreover, political activists, led by Abraham González, embraced the Plan de San Luis Potosí and recognized Madero as their leader.[40]

Energized by this news, Madero rushed to El Paso, Texas, to confer with his Chihuahuan allies. From the onset, however, Madero and Orozco disagreed over military strategy, and the diminutive Coahuilan, who was not battle-tested, chose to launch a raid on Casas Grandes without informing Orozco. The rebels suffered a military setback and Madero, slightly wounded in the arm, nearly fell into the enemy's hands.[41]

Despite this defeat, the revolutionary movement in Chihuahua remained strong. Madero's bravery in battle gained him respect among rebels, and new recruits from mountain villages joined his camp, among them the dashing Francisco Villa who arrived with seven hundred disciplined troops. Revolutionary activity intensified throughout the state, and rebel forces gained control over most of the countryside. In the Chihuahuan cities, relentless criticism of the Terrazas-Creel camarilla and the Díaz government in the pages of *El Correo de Chihuahua* helped turn the middle class against the regime.[42]

At this juncture, a concerned President Díaz made a series of political compromises designed to stop the fighting. He removed several unpopular governors, recalled José Ives Limantour (a friend of the Maderos') from Europe and reappointed him minister of the treasury, recalled Francisco León de la Barra from Washington, D.C. and installed him as minister of foreign relations, and gave Vice President Ramón Corral, whom everyone disliked, an eight-month leave of absence. The president then went before Congress and promised enforcement of the no reelection principle as well as an agrarian reform. Rebels interpreted these maneuvers, however, as a sign of weakness.

As the fighting intensified, Díaz proposed negotiations in New York City. Government representatives met with members of the Madero family in the plush Astor Hotel, while Francisco Madero personally talked with Díaz's emissaries outside of Ciudad Juárez. Orozco was left on the sidelines, however, and his actions would now decisively alter the course of events.

Without consulting Madero, Orozco launched a full-scale assault on Ciudad Juárez and crushed the federal army garrisoned there. The

FIGURE 20: Pancho Villa, pictured here on horseback, organized
the famous "El Dorado" cavalry that swept his opponents from
the battlefields of northern Mexico.

Source: Anita Brenner, *The Wind that Swept Mexico: The History of the Mexican
Revolution of 1910–1942,* with 184 historical photographs assembled by
George R. Leighton (Austin: University of Texas Press, 1971), photograph 86.

supposedly invincible federal troops were also losing ground throughout the country to locally based rebel movements. The regime controlled only five states and elsewhere only held urban areas.[43] When Zapata captured the heavily fortified army garrison at Cuautla, Morelos, manned by the elite quinto de oro corps, he sent Díaz the uniforms of the dead soldiers with a note that read, "Here are the wrappers so that you can send me more tamales."[44]

Madero established a revolutionary government at Ciudad Juárez and named a cabinet that included his brother Gustavo as minister of the treasury and Venustiano Carranza, a fellow Coahuilan, as minister of war. Orozco, outraged over being denied a cabinet post, nearly imprisoned Madero and never forgave him. Meanwhile, rebel victories unleashed a rising tide of social unrest throughout Mexico and hastened the signing of a peace treaty.

The Treaty of Ciudad Juárez, signed on May 17, 1911, changed those in charge but left the old Díaz regime largely in tact. Díaz would be replaced by Francisco León de la Barra, who would serve as interim president, and a new cabinet composed of Porfirians and Maderistas would be installed. The federal army, which had defended the old regime, would remain intact, while the revolutionary forces, which had carried Madero to power, would be disbanded. National elections would be held as soon as possible, and everyone anticipated that Madero would be elected president.

The Treaty of Ciudad Juárez represented a compromise among elite factions, represented by the Maderos and the Porfirians, both increasingly alarmed over the widespread social upheaval that threatened their wealth. In effect, Madero had achieved, with the spilling of some blood, what had been denied him in the previous election. He favored only modest political reforms and cooperated with the old guard to achieve social, economic, and political stability. Madero affirmed that land reform, the underlining cause of rural tension, would have to wait.[45]

Madero's first political appointments pleased Porfirians and alarmed revolutionaries. For León de la Barra's cabinet, Madero selected family members, upper-class Maderistas, and members of Díaz's cabinet. Maderistas included his uncle Ernesto Madero in the treasury, Rafael Hernández (Madero's cousin) in the ministry of justice, Francisco

FIGURE 21: Venustiano Carranza, the bearded man pictured
in the center, became de facto president in 1916.

Source: Anita Brenner, *The Wind that Swept Mexico: The History of the Mexican
Revolution of 1910–1942*, with 184 historical photographs assembled by
George R. Leighton (Austin: University of Texas Press, 1971), photograph 107.

Vásquez-Gómez (Díaz's former personal physician) in education, Emilio Vásquez-Gómez in government, and Manuel Bonilla in communications. León de la Barra, who referred to himself as the "white president," retained his post in foreign relations. Madero also assured that the federal infrastructure remained unchanged by retaining all members of the Supreme Court, Congress, and federal bureaucracies.[46]

Those on both sides of the struggle expressed surprise. A disappointed Venustiano Carranza, who would later emerge as a major revolutionary leader, accused Madero of "delivering to the reactionaries a dead revolution which will have to be fought over again," a statement that proved prophetic.[47] Díaz, upon embarking for exile in Paris, dryly observed that "Madero has unleashed a tiger, let us see if he can control him."[48]

For the moment, however, Madero was a popular hero. News of the signing of the Treaty of Ciudad Juárez had brought thousands of urban Mexicans onto the streets and ignited violent retribution in the countryside. Roving mobs plied the streets of Mexico City shouting "Long Live Madero and Death to Díaz." Madero embarked on a triumphal journey from the border to the capital, and at each stop along the way he was greeted by cheering crowds. As he entered Mexico City, more than 200,000 people applauded him.[49]

Madero viewed popular outbursts of violence that followed the signing of the peace treaty with great concern. In the Bajío and parts of La Laguna, which had experienced economic difficulties, the urban poor took to the streets for an orgy of looting, political retribution, and in one case the slaughter of innocent foreigners. Angry mobs composed of workers and revolutionaries sacked stores, freed prisoners from municipal jails, burned local archives (which contained tax records, police files, and the like), and toppled despised municipal officials. The Spanish and Chinese communities suffered inordinate harm at the hands of the mob, behaviors that reflected xenophobia as well as hatred of prosperous merchants. In Torreón, in one of the worst tragedies of the revolution, 250 Chinese fell victim to rioters. Maderista and federal armies combined to quell these disturbances, much to the relief of merchants, foreigners, and local elites.[50]

Mining camps throughout northern Mexico also experienced widespread conflict.[51] These disputes, mostly related to industrial issues, cannot be divorced from the revolutionary process and the course of political events. The mineworkers' movement had linkages with the Western Federation of Miners and the pro-revolutionary Partido Liberal Mexicano. Following Díaz's resignation, PLM members renewed their efforts to organize miners and press for social change. Miners assumed that the Maderistas would support their struggle with the foreign-owned mines whose managers had favored foreign workers and supported the old regime. They would be sorely disappointed.[52]

At Cananea, Sonora miners welcomed the revolution. Maderista General Juan Cabral entered the town with great fanfare and several hundred workers enlisted in the rebel army. Six months later, in October 1911, PLM organizers Esteban Baca Calderón and Manuel Diéguez, recently released from prison, returned and organized the Unión de Obreros de Cananea. Almost immediately, the union articulated several grievances against the company, including abusive treatment by foreign foremen, and the following year it launched a major strike. Municipal authorities, influenced by socialist and working-class movements, supported strikers. Maderista Acting Governor Ismael Padilla, by contrast, backed management's tough negotiating position and later ordered the arrest of three strike leaders. Maderista officials also restricted union-organizing activities and used the federal army to intimidate miners.[53]

Madero's greatest challenge at social control, however, came in the countryside. Despite the treaty's specification that rebel forces disband, some 60,000 revolutionaries under commanders only tenuously tied to Madero remained in the field. They had been supporting themselves by demanding goods from villagers and merchants and arms from defeated federal troops. Mayors and governors did not want rebel forces billeted in towns and cities, particularly where federal soldiers and rurales remained garrisoned because the odds favored renewed violence between the former enemies.

Simply sending troops home solved little. They had rebelled in the first place, more often than not, to rectify local political and agrarian problems. Despite the transfer of presidential power, those problems remained largely unresolved. The Treaty of Ciudad Juárez froze in place all local and state officials (although some changes still occurred), and Madero wanted land disputes settled in the courts. As a result, tensions ran high and sporadic outbursts of violence unsettled many rural areas.[54]

Madero faced a particularly knotty problem in Morelos. The Zapatistas, a well-organized and focused movement, demanded meaningful and timely land reform. Madero refused to compromise. Instead, he appointed Juan Carreón, a member of the local elite, interim governor of Morelos. He angered and insulted Zapata further by presenting rebels with a list of haciendas that should be protected. Zapata, who had expected more from the democratic revolutionary, requested a meeting with Madero in Mexico City.

Zapata entered the presidential palace well armed and insisted that "the lands be returned to the villages at once, and that the promises of the Revolution be fulfilled." Madero reiterated his position that land reform was an issue for the courts. Zapata reportedly responded with an analogy: If he had stolen Madero's watch at gunpoint, Zapata inquired, would Madero, once armed himself, have the right to reclaim the watch? Madero responded that he would have that right. This, Zapata insisted, corresponds to what has happened with villagers' land in Morelos. Madero then made the mistake of offering Zapata a "good ranch" for his services to the revolution. Enraged, the agrarian leader indignantly rejected the offer. Madero attempted to smooth things over and accepted Zapata's invitation to visit Morelos to learn firsthand about the land problem.[55]

Madero limited his investigation in Morelos, however, to consultation with hacendados critical of the Zapatistas. The Mexico City press, still controlled by Porfirians, provided Madero with daily reinforcement of this viewpoint. For example, *El Imparcial* falsely accused Zapata of raping young girls and branded him the "Modern Attila." Madero ordered Zapata to disarm and blamed him for failure to prevent looting by hungry villagers. Zapata now withdrew into the mountains and prepared to defend himself.[56]

Back in Mexico City, Madero surrounded himself with former Porfirians and federal army officers, with whom he felt socially and politically comfortable. He ignored the villagers whose military victories had brought him to power. Madero brought Porfirian Alberto García Granados into the cabinet to replace Emilio Vásquez-Gómez, who had resigned, and he appointed Zapata's rival Ambrosio Figueroa the provisional governor of Morelos. Finally, in August 1911, Madero ordered

FIGURE 22: Zapatistas.

Source: Anita Brenner, *The Wind that Swept Mexico: The History of the Mexican Revolution of 1910–1942*, with 184 historical photographs assembled by George R. Leighton (Austin: University of Texas Press, 1971), photograph 60.

federal General Victoriano C. Huerta to invade Morelos. He wanted Zapata disarmed.[57]

Madero's hard line with his former allies immediately preceded the October presidential elections. Although everyone expected him to win, the emergence of opposition candidates foreshadowed future political troubles. General Bernardo Reyes, the former governor of Nuevo León, returned from exile and announced his candidacy for president. Madero's candidate for vice president, the little-known Yucatecan José María Pino Suárez, also faced opposition from Interim President Francisco León de la Barra and former cabinet minister Francisco Vásquez-Gómez. In addition, the Catholic Church, which had been waiting its chance to reenter politics, organized a political party and ran candidates for Congress.[58]

FIGURE 23: General Victoriano C. Huerta, on the left conferring with
Emilio Madero and Pancho Villa (with his back to the camera) in 1912,
a year before his overthrow of Francisco Madero.

Source: Friedrich Katz, ed. *Imáges de Pancho Villa* (Mexico City:
Instituto Nacional de Antropología e Historia, 1999), p. 28.

As expected, Madero won by a landslide. The vote for vice president,
however, revealed significant political divisions as Pino Suárez received 53
percent, León de la Barra 29 percent, and Vásquez-Gómez 17 percent.
Madero's Progressive Constitutional Party won a majority of seats in
Congress, but the National Catholic Party carried Jalisco, Querétaro, and
Mexico State, and emerged as a legitimate second party.[59] As expedi-
tiously as possible, Madero now had to address the political, social, and
economic problems that had caused the revolution in the first place.

For his cabinet, Madero appointed conservatives as ministers of foreign relations, development, finance, and justice. These included many holdovers from the León de la Barra government, including his cousin Rafael Hernández in development and his uncle Ernesto in finance. Together, the conservatives would block any initiative put forward by more progressive cabinet ministers, several of whom resigned after a few months in office.[60]

Even before the election, Madero had begun the process of replacing Porfirian governors and local officials. His appointees soon occupied statehouses and most municipal offices. Many of the new officeholders were conservatives who had jumped onto the revolutionary bandwagon at the last moment. They had little sympathy for the plight of the rural masses, and their loyalty to the president was paper-thin. In hindsight, Madero should have rewarded his revolutionary supporters and kept the conservatives at arm's length.[61]

Disappointed and angered by Madero's apparent perfidy, social revolutionaries in Morelos and Chihuahua who had brought Madero to power now sought to overthrow him. Madero's refusal to enact an agrarian reform had placed Zapata, as head of an agrarian revolution, in an impossible position. Moreover, Madero forced a confrontation by ordering federal troops to occupy Morelos and disarm the Zapatistas. Not intimidated, Zapata and his advisors articulated their revolutionary objectives in the "Plan de Ayala." This document accused Madero of betraying the Plan de San Luis Potosí and announced a national campaign to remove him from power. The Zapatistas' battle cry became "land and liberty." They demanded the return of land and water taken from villages by haciendas. They did not advocate expropriation of large estates or the end to private property. Rather, they sought the reestablishment of an economic equilibrium that would permit villagers to survive. Zapata did not assume leadership of the envisioned national movement. He recognized Pascual Orozco, whose relationship with Madero was unraveling, as head of the revolution.[62]

Zapata gained many adherents in Morelos but immediately found himself on the defensive. Columns of federal troops invaded the state. General Juvencio Robles, attempting to demoralize villagers, put crops and homes to the torch and shot unarmed civilians. Zapata, outnumbered and outgunned, chose to retreat into the mountains and launch strategic raids on patrols, outposts, and haciendas. In this way, he maintained a military presence close to Mexico City that made the rich and powerful uncomfortable.[63]

Popular rebellion in Chihuahua posed a more serious threat to Madero. Failure to implement meaningful reforms coupled with mismanagement of political appointments led to widespread discontent. As in 1910, localized revolts would eventually coalesce under the leadership of former Madero supporter Pascual Orozco. Former Maderista Colonel Antonio Rojas won a series of battles against federal troops and forced the resignation of Governor Abraham González and his successor. José Inés Salazar and Emilio Campa, also former Maderistas, captured Casas Grandes and linked up with Rojas to overrun Ciudad Juárez. Salazar, a former PLM member, denounced Madero for his failure to comply with the Plan de San Luis Potosí and for nepotism. A decisive moment came when Pancho Villa, still loyal to the president, attempted to intercept rebel forces converging on Chihuahua City. Pascual Orozco, who had remained neutral to that point, attacked Villa and drove him from the battlefield.

Orozco's estrangement from Madero was long in coming. The two had quarreled over military strategy in 1910 and at Ciudad Juárez Orozco had threatened to detain the Coahuilan. After Díaz's resignation, Orozco became a popular hero throughout the North, and he expected Madero to appoint him governor or to a cabinet post. Instead, Madero asked Orozco to head the rurales in Sinaloa (and later in Chihuahua). He appointed Abraham González, a loyal, middle-class politician, to the governor's mansion. Disappointed and angry, Orozco turned against Madero. With close ties to the campesinos of western Chihuahua, he probably shared their concern over the slow pace of meaningful reforms. To confuse matters, he also received financial and political support from local elites, a fact that tarnishes his image as a social revolutionary and brands Orozco an opportunist.

The Plan Orozquista articulated a progressive program designed to increase popular support for the movement. In addition to freedom of expression and municipal autonomy, Orozco advocated improved wages and conditions for workers, suppression of company stores, restrictions

FIGURE 24: Pancho Villa, pictured here at left, with his men before
the first rebel victory at Ciudad Juárez in 1911.

Source: Friedrich Katz, ed. *Imáges de Pancho Villa* (Mexico City:
Instituto Nacional de Antropología e Historia, 1999), p. 27.

on child labor, and nationalization of the railroads and the labor force.
His pro-worker, nationalist stance reflected PLM and trade union influence among miners, railway workers, and factory hands, who constituted
an important sector of Chihuahuan society with legitimate grievances
against Díaz and Madero.[64]

89

Orozco posed an ideological as well as a military threat to the president. Madero offered to negotiate, but Orozco refused and prepared to march south. At Rellano, Orozco defeated a federal army and threatened Mexico City. The heavily garrisoned capital posed a formidable military obstacle, however, and Orozco decided to return to Chihuahua and gather more men and supplies. Fresh arms proved difficult to acquire because the United States had closed the border to weapons of war. Orozco's decision to put off attacking Mexico City gave federal troops time to organize an expedition under the command of General Huerta, who earlier had harassed the Zapatistas in Morelos. Huerta defeated Orozco at the second battle of Rellano, pursued him relentlessly across Chihuahua, and defeated him again at Ciudad Juárez. For the moment, Madero had survived.[65]

CONCLUSION PART III

The overthrow of General Porfirio Díaz, which ended Latin America's longest dictatorship, started with a bungled election and the unlikely challenge of Francisco I. Madero. The confusing signals given by the dictator in the Creelman interview, competition among elites for the vice-presidential position, and the unanticipated popularity of General Bernardo Reyes and Francisco I. Madero created serious political problems. Díaz's use of tried and proven strong-arm tactics to silence Madero failed, however, only because of the widespread opposition to the regime among peasants, provincial elites, and workers.

Signs of popular discontent had surfaced during the economic crisis of 1905–1907 when food shortages, inflation, currency devaluation, and layoffs provoked strikes and rioting nationwide. In the countryside, anger had been brewing for decades over loss of land and political autonomy. Expanding estates and government-sponsored land surveying companies stripped villages of their land; government-appointed politicians replaced local officials previously selected by villagers; and financial privileges given by the regime to foreign businessmen and workers angered their Mexican counterparts. After Madero's arrest, peasants, workers, and gentry answered his call to revolution in anticipation that he would solve their grievances against the Díaz government.

Once in power, Madero's failure to carry out comprehensive reforms and to sever ties with the Porfirian establishment cost him the support of grassroots revolutionaries. Madero maintained the Porfirian infrastructure, relied on family members, and kept the federal army in tact. When rebel allies deserted him, Madero called on General Huerta to crush Orozco and to drive Zapata into the mountains.

COUNTERREVOLUTION

FRANCISCO I. MADERO's reliance on the federal army made him vulnerable to counterrevolution. Disgruntled elites, hedging their bets and sizing up the opposition, waited for the opportunity to overthrow him. Leading the list of conspirators were General Bernardo Reyes, whose presidential campaign in 1911 had ended in ignominious defeat, and General Félix Díaz, the deposed dictator's nephew who received financial backing and encouragement from exiled Porfirians. These conservative plotters, hoping to return to the policies of the pax porfiriana, now courted military allies who could deliver the men and arms needed to topple the government.

General Victoriano C. Huerta was a likely candidate. Although Huerta had defended Madero on the battlefield, his personal relationship with the president had been rocky and he had political ambitions of his own. When a counterrevolution unfolded in Mexico City, Huerta, as commander of army forces in the capital, was in position to either save or vanquish Madero. He chose to abandon the president, hijack the coup, and seize the presidency.

Huerta's coup should be viewed as a counterrevolution. His backers represented the pillars of Porfirian society and his military reputation rested on his ruthless campaigns against Zapata, Orozco, and rebellious

Indians. Although Huerta kept some of Madero's programs on the books, he did not enforce them. Instead he concentrated on consolidating his personal power and increasing the size, firepower, and influence of the army. Under Huerta, Mexican society became militarized, and political discourse was reduced to assassination, intimidation, and capriciousness.

Huerta's coup divided the country, although not neatly along class lines. The vast majority of Maderista governors and congressmen meekly recognized Huerta as interim president. Support also came from European investors, who helped him gain diplomatic recognition from Great Britain, France, and Germany. His opponents included the same peasant revolutionaries who had opposed Porfirio Díaz as well as intellectuals, workers, and elites drawn from nonconforming ideological and class perspectives. Foreign opposition to the regime also came from the recently elected U.S. President Woodrow Wilson, who championed democracy and refused to recognize Huerta. Wilson's opposition would contribute directly to the dictator's ultimate demise.

THE COUP

Bernardo Reyes's political campaigns had floundered, and an ill-conceived attempt to oust Madero in late 1912 now proved equally disastrous. He only drew a handful of supporters—indicative of a tremendous fall-off in popular support—and he landed in the federal penitentiary in Mexico City. Madero failed to keep a close eye on him, however, and he continued to plot conspiracies from his prison cell.[1]

Meanwhile, an overconfident Félix Díaz, the former dictator's nephew, launched his own counterrevolution in Veracruz. Díaz had received 5,000 pounds sterling from exiled Porfirians living in Paris, and he counted on support from military units in Veracruz and in his home state of Oaxaca. Madero dispatched troops from Mexico City to crush the rebels in Veracruz, and U.S. President Taft sent battleships to protect U.S.-owned oil fields in nearby Tampico. Díaz had made few military preparations on the assumption that local commanders would abandon Madero and support him. He overestimated his popularity, however, and federal forces suppressed the revolt within six hours. Félix Díaz was now sent to the same Mexico City cellblock that held Bernardo Reyes.[2]

Madero's decision to bring the two defeated conspirators to Mexico City, rather than have them executed, hastened his overthrow. Despite their imprisonment, Reyes and Díaz were allowed to receive visitors and continued to conspire against Madero. Generals Manuel Mondragón and Gregorio Ruíz and prominent businessman Cecilio Ocón visited the imprisoned Porfirians and joined the conspiracy. A cunning General Huerta turned down an invitation to join the plot. He used his knowledge of impending events to maneuver himself into position through deceit and murder and to hijack the coup.

Before sunrise on February 9, 1913, rebel troops released Reyes and Díaz from their prison cells (although Díaz, something of a dandy, made them wait while he completed his morning toilet). Things went badly for the conspirators. General Reyes's frontal assault on an entrenched federal position buckled under writhing gunfire, and Reyes's bullet-riddled body lay lifeless in the street. General Díaz, who was more of a storefront general, gathered the survivors and occupied the nearby armory (the Ciudadela), a formidable but poorly guarded structure. General Ruíz, old and portly, arrived late at the National Palace, the scene of an early rebel victory, and found it reconquered by loyal troops. He was immediately arrested and later shot.

Among the leaders only Félix Díaz, holed-up in the Ciudadela with 1,500 troops, remained. Madero, riding on horseback, reached the city center to assess the situation. Along the way, the president encountered General Huerta, who may have been apprised of the president's route. Madero placed Huerta in command of federal forces defending the capital, a decision that would seal his fate.

Loyalists should have won an easy victory. Rebels—surrounded, outnumbered, and short on supplies—could not hold out for long. Victory over rebel troops was not, however, Huerta's objective. He conferred with rebel leader Díaz on several occasions and permitted fresh supplies to enter the Ciudadela. In the meantime, a mock ten-day battle, subsequently called the Decena Trágica, ensued that caused heavy civilian losses without reaching a military conclusion. Artillery exchanges between loyalists and rebels missed military targets and killed many bystanders, and loyalist cavalry charges on fixed rebel machine-gun placements proved suicidal. As the rotting bodies of victims accumulated on

FIGURE 25: Avenida Balderas, Mexico City, showing damage resulting from
fighting during the "Ten Tragic Days" in February 1913, that led to the
overthrow of Francisco Madero by General Victoriano Huerta.

Source: Rafael Tovar, ed. *México: una nación persistente: Hugo Brehme fotografías*
(Mexico City: Instituto Nacional de Bellas Artes, 1995), photograph 9, p. 37.

city streets, the concerned American ambassador, Henry Lane Wilson,
took special interest in resolving the conflict.

Wilson's humanitarianism, however, concealed a stronger desire to
oust Madero in favor of Huerta. Wilson referred to Madero as a
"lunatic" incapable of governing Mexico, and this personal hostility led
him to meddle in Mexico's internal affairs. Wilson, who had strong ties
to U.S. business interests, undoubtedly hoped that a strongman like
Huerta would topple Madero and re-create an economic and political
climate similar to the Porfiriato. The American ambassador's subsequent
roles in overthrowing Madero and in elevating Huerta to power have
earned him a vile reputation among Mexicans.

President Taft opposed U.S. intervention, and the State Department
denied Wilson's request to negotiate a settlement between the loyalists
and rebels. Nevertheless, Wilson disobeyed orders and pursued secret

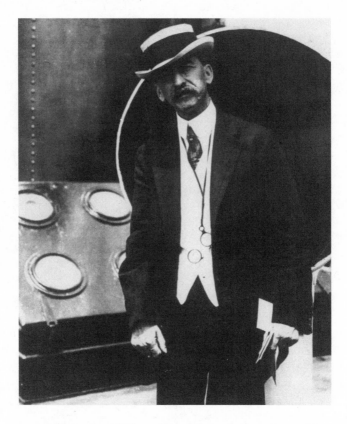

FIGURE 26: Henry Lane Wilson, United States Ambassador to Mexico,
who helped General Huerta overthrow President Madero.

Source: Anita Brenner, *The Wind that Swept Mexico: The History of the Mexican
Revolution of 1910–1942,* with 184 historical photographs assembled by
George R. Leighton (Austin: University of Texas Press, 1971), photograph 20.

negotiations with Félix Díaz and Victoriano Huerta. In a dramatic move,
Wilson also assembled the ambassadors from Britain, Spain, and
Germany and convinced them that Madero should resign. Bernardo
Cólogan, the Spanish ambassador, agreed to carry their recommendation
to Madero. The president, indignant and angry, refused to step down and
complained to Taft about Wilson's outrageous meddling. The State
Department instructed its renegade ambassador to behave appropriately,
but without effect. Wilson, recently informed of Huerta's collaboration in
the coup plot, said nothing to Madero.

Meanwhile, a delegation of twenty-seven congressmen loyal to Félix Díaz (Felicistas), led by Foreign Minister Pedro Lascurán, approached Madero and asked him to resign. The president still enjoyed the support of eighty-nine congressmen, however, and he refused to leave. Then came a crucial moment. Gustavo Madero, Francisco's observant brother, had been given a list of conspirators that included Huerta. He ordered the general's arrest. Gustavo presented both Huerta and the document to his brother. Francisco Madero, who had feuded with Huerta and disliked him intensely, interrogated the tough, battle-tested veteran. Madero was obviously ill suited for the task, however, because he came away from their encounter convinced of Huerta's loyalty. The president upbraided his brother in front of the general and personally gave Huerta back his sidearm.

The next day Huerta overthrew Madero. A contingent of troops, commanded by General Blanquet, stormed into the National Palace and exchanged gunfire with the president's bodyguards. Madero ran into the courtyard and straight into the arms of the waiting Blanquet, who drew his pistol and arrested the dazed president. At the same time, Huerta was lunching with Gustavo Madero, ostensibly burying the hatchet. At one point, he left the room to confirm the coup. When he returned, he placed Gustavo under arrest and turned him over to Félix Díaz.

Two hours before the coup, Henry Lane Wilson had wired the State Department of Madero's overthrow. The American ambassador, who obviously knew about the plot, now contributed to the postrevolutionary settlement. Huerta and Díaz, accompanied by numerous associates and bodyguards, met with Wilson at the U.S. embassy to hammer out the details of an interim government. Wilson, who wanted Huerta president, once again resorted to lies and deception to get his way. Without a quick settlement, he warned, Washington might not be able to prevent a European intervention in Mexico. That threat brought the negotiations to a conclusion. Huerta would become provisional president, and Díaz would be allowed to run for president in upcoming elections. Most cabinet posts, moreover, would go to Felicistas. Those receiving portfolios included as foreign minister the politically flexible Francisco León de la Barra, as war minister the coup originator Manuel Mondragón, and as justice minister, Rodolfo Reyes, Bernardo's son.

FIGURE 27: The counterrevolutionaries who overthrew President Madero. From left to right: Generals Mondragón, Huerta, Félix Díaz, and Blanquet.

Source: Anita Brenner, *The Wind that Swept Mexico: The History of the Mexican Revolution of 1910–1942*, with 184 historical photographs assembled by George R. Leighton (Austin: University of Texas Press, 1971), photograph 76.

Francisco Madero, under house arrest, agreed to resign after receiving assurances of safe passage. Gustavo Madero's fate, however, foretold Francisco's future as well as the character of the new regime. Gustavo had been turned over to Felicista troops at the Ciudadela. The troops ripped out his one good eye, beat him, stabbed him repeatedly, and finished him off with a gunshot.

Francisco, unaware of his brother's savage slaughter, was promised exile. While Huerta dined at the U.S. embassy, two cars took Madero and former vice president Pino Suárez to the federal penitentiary. Accompanied by General Blanquet, coup-plotter Cecilio Ocón, and Major Francisco Cárdenas, Madero and Pino Suárez were forced to stand in the darkened prison courtyard. Major Cárdenas hurled a few well-chosen insults at the fallen leaders and then shot both of them behind the ear with his service revolver.[3]

HUERTA IN POWER

One can imagine General Victoriano C. Huerta, a cigar in one hand and a whiskey in the other, flashing a quick grin as he reviewed the list of foreign and local dignitaries waiting in the anteroom to congratulate him. Huerta had disclaimed any knowledge of the murders of Madero and Pino Suárez and had quickly arranged for an intimidated Congress to proclaim him interim president. His supporters included Porfirian elites, Catholic Party members, wealthy businessmen, and federal officials who assumed that ironed-fisted rule would bring peace and prosperity.

Huerta, born to impoverished Huichol Indian parents in Colotlán, Jalisco, had relied on hard work, intelligence, and ruthlessness to rise rapidly through the ranks of the federal army. Huerta's road to political power rested on winning battles against revolutionaries. This was not an unusual résumé for nineteenth-century Latin American presidents. It was, however, starkly different from his Porfirian supporters who were more skilled and experienced at forming political families (camarillas), stuffing ballot boxes, and conducting political ceremonies. An uneasy political alliance resulted.

The Pact of the Embassy, signed by the anti-Madero conspirators and arranged by U.S. Ambassador Henry Lane Wilson, called for early elections. Felicistas naively assumed that Huerta would allow Félix Díaz to win the presidency, but the wily general proved difficult to dislodge from the presidential palace. An appearance of democratic procedures gave a veneer of legitimacy to Huerta's ascendancy to power. The Congress, controlled by Maderistas and Catholics, recognized Huerta as interim president, a procedure that the Mexican Supreme Court, the final arbitrator of liberal justice, found constitutional.[4]

Appearances proved difficult to maintain, however, when Huerta appointed Generals Mondragón and Blanquet to his cabinet and promoted others implicated in the murders. Had Huerta taken measure of the Maderista elite and decided that they did not have the backbone to oppose him? All but four Maderista governors quickly recognized the general as president, and a significant number of Maderista congressmen openly supported him. These frock-coated liberal politicians, some only recent converts to Maderismo, once again went with the political flow.[5] Huerta viewed civilian politicians with contempt and never trusted them. His viewpoint, not unusual for a military man, was likely reinforced by observing their lack of political courage following Madero's ouster. When popular opposition to Huerta emerged in the North, he removed Maderista governors and replaced them with trusted military officers. This shored up his control over the region, but turned otherwise ambivalent elites against him.[6]

Huerta also attempted to consolidate his position by negotiating with independent rebel factions in the countryside. Although fundamental differences on social policy separated Huerta from peasant revolutionaries, both the dictator and the revolutionaries had fallen out with Madero. Skillful negotiators sometimes fashioned political compromises (transacciones) among strange bedfellows. Although Zapata refused to deal with Huerta, whom he detested for burning villages and killing civilians, Pascual Orozco agreed to negotiate with the dictator.

Orozco's history of changing sides had already influenced the course of the revolution. His populist movement, with roots in the villages of western Chihuahua, had provided decisive military support for Madero's overthrow of Díaz. Orozco's break with Madero in 1912, however, forced the president to choose between seeking support from revolutionaries or relying more heavily on the federal army. Madero chose the later course, and his selection of General Huerta to crush Orozco put Huerta in position to seize power during the Decena Trágica.

Orozco, who had sunk from revolutionary caudillo to political opportunist, now agreed to join forces with Huerta. Orozco saw Huerta's offer as an opportunity, perhaps his last one, to become an important political figure. Since his defeat in 1912, Orozco's reputation had faded, and he could no longer raise an army without outside support. Orozco also received Huerta's endorsement for a future agrarian reform in western Chihuahua, a validation of his revolutionary credentials. It seems unlikely, however, that the dictator, whose reputation had been based on crushing agraristas, would have actually complied. In addition, Orozco received promises from Huerta of extensive material support for his recruits, including weapons, ammunition, salaries, pensions, life insurance, debt payments, and future employment as rurales. Even with these incentives, however, Orozco could only put three to four thousand men in the field. Such disappointing numbers indicate the lack of popular support in Chihuahua for both Orozco and Huerta.[7]

Without powerful allies drawn from ranks of disaffected rebels, Huerta was forced to increase the size of the federal army through a military draft *(la leva)*. He wanted 250,000 men in uniform and 50,000 rurales under arms. He also told hacendados, who were among his strongest supporters, to organize private armies, called Ligas de Defensa Social, to protect their land and to defend the regime.

These measures met with mixed success. The federal army never grew beyond 125,000 soldiers, the Ligas did not provide significant firepower, and Huerta also lost popular support through overzealous implementation of the draft. Local officials, desperate to meet their quotas, kidnapped villagers, enlisted convicts, and rounded up citizens at public events. On one occasion, soldiers conscripted seven hundred men attending a Mexico City bullfight. Such tactics undermined army moral, provoked desertions, and drove the uncommitted into the arms of revolutionaries.[8]

Through training and inclination, Huerta relied more on force and intimidation than political finesse. Nevertheless, politicians and interest groups who had suffered under Madero or who feared radical reform if revolutionaries came to power, openly cooperated with Huerta. Members of the Catholic Party, including the ubiquitous Francisco León de la Barra, were willing to serve in Huerta's cabinet, and Mexican bishops made financial contributions to the regime. In return, Huerta allowed the church to dedicate Mexico to the Sacred Heart of Jesus. Huerta's deals with the church, however, did not significantly strengthen his administration. Peasant revolutionaries, most of them Catholics, remained opposed to the government, and anticlericals fought that much harder.[9]

Huerta received more meaningful support, by contrast, from overseas investors and their governments who looked for a return to the golden days of the Porfiriato. After all, U.S. Ambassador Wilson and his European colleagues had lobbied against Madero and supported Huerta's rise to power. In addition, rising demand for Mexico's mineral and petroleum products with the threat of war in Europe increased competition for new concessions, and foreign investors (and their governments) wanted a strongman in control who could enforce the peace and guarantee production. The outbreak of the First World War in 1914, which pitted Britain and France against Germany, also made access to Mexican resources a national security issue for belligerents.

U.S. policy in Mexico, which had been supportive of Díaz and Huerta, changed significantly during the administration of Woodrow Wilson, who took office in January 1913. Wilson criticized his Republican predecessors Roosevelt and Taft for intervening militarily in Latin America to protect U.S. corporate interests, and he gradually implemented new foreign policy guidelines for the region. Although Wilson wanted to protect U.S. business and security interests (especially after the outbreak of the war), he believed this could be achieved through the exportation of American political ideals as well as capital and troops. This led him to support individuals and movements who appeared comparatively more democratic and capitalistic. Democrats proved difficult to locate in nations without strong democratic traditions, however, and Wilson's political guidelines became increasingly blurred. In Mexico, he repudiated the two most obvious violators of democratic procedures, Ambassador Henry Lane Wilson and General Victoriano C. Huerta, and then struggled to find a consistent policy.[10]

Woodrow Wilson's Mexican policy, for all its limitations, at least represented a more nuanced approach than those of his European counterparts. Western European states, as well as Latin American governments, quickly recognized Huerta as president, giving the regime a semblance of legitimacy. The European diplomatic community in Mexico, led by the British and German ambassadors, steadfastly supported the dictator, and major overseas investors lobbied their governments on Huerta's behalf. Lord Cowdray played a key role in securing British recognition of Huerta and subsequently helped him negotiate a 45,000,000-peso loan from European banks in return for new oil drilling concessions. U.S. investors in Mexico, including major corporations, also backed Huerta but enjoyed comparatively less entree and creditability with their president.[11]

WILSON'S GAMBIT

Woodrow Wilson did not oppose Huerta from the outset. He gradually turned against the dictator, however, after gathering information from special diplomatic envoys. The president sent William Bayard Hale, a trusted personal confidant, to Mexico City with instructions to assess recent political events. Although Hale was not familiar with Mexico, his political experience and detachment allowed him to analyze the complex situation with considerable accuracy. He concluded that Madero had been overthrown by a conspiracy rather than a popular movement. He also concluded that U.S. Ambassador Wilson, in his zeal to support Huerta, had filed false reports with the State Department. Secretary of State William Jennings Bryan accepted Hale's analysis and recalled Ambassador Wilson to Washington, leaving Chargé d'Affairs Nelson O'Shaughnessy in charge of the embassy.

In the meantime, Western European and Latin American nations had already recognized Huerta, and U.S. business interests, who claimed special knowledge of Mexico, recommended the same course to President Wilson. Huerta also applied pressure on President Wilson. He ordered the government-controlled press to editorialize against U.S. nonrecognition policy, and he organized large-scale anti-U.S. demonstrations in Mexico City and elsewhere. Wilson responded by sending John Lind, the former governor of Minnesota, to Mexico City to assess normalizing U.S.-Mexican relations. In the meantime, Wilson allowed Huerta to purchase arms in the United States, while he maintained an arms embargo on his opponents, including Pancho Villa.

Lind arrived in Mexico burdened with controversial proposals and anti-Mexican prejudices. Lind found it impossible to broaden his cultural horizons beyond those gained during his Swedish, Protestant upbringing in Minnesota's lake country. He found Mexico dirty, priest-ridden, and chaotic, and this attitude undercut his ability to negotiate objectively. Lind's proposals, moreover, proved untenable. The envoy proposed an armistice, early elections, and U.S. recognition of the winner. But he insisted that Huerta not be a candidate. Predictably, the dictator rejected the plan and accused Wilson of unwarranted intervention in Mexico's internal affairs. Huerta once again organized anti-U.S. demonstrations, and Lind retreated to Veracruz to issue reports increasingly critical of the regime.

Wilson's opposition to Huerta, however, did not extend to political conservatives more generally. For example, Secretary of State William Jennings Bryan stated that either Catholic Party leader Federico Gamboa or Félix Díaz would be acceptable to the administration, despite Díaz's overt role in Madero's overthrow. Wilson's willingness to accept Díaz and his increasingly heavy-handed involvement in Mexican politics suggest the limits of his democratic vision.

In the meantime, Huerta refused to budge. He announced his candidacy for president and named General Blanquet as his running mate. Wilson responded by placing an arms embargo on Mexico and pressuring Britain to withdraw its support for Huerta. Although the dictator still found all the arms he needed in Europe and Japan, U.S. policy eventually weakened his regime.[12]

Huerta's relentless suppression of his political opponents cost him supporters both at home and abroad. The dictator abandoned his attempts at maintaining a facade of democratic procedures and ordered assassinations of political dissenters, arrests of journalists critical of his regime, and closures or takeovers of opposition newspapers. The most notorious incident, which caused serious political fallout, was the assassination of Senator Belisario Domínguez from Chiapas.

Theoretically, the Mexican Congress represented an independent branch of government with the right to disagree with the president over policy. Elected representatives from several different political affiliations, notably Catholics, Maderistas, and Felicistas, could not be expected to rubber-stamp all presidential initiatives. Domínguez had emerged as the most outspoken critic of the regime. His attacks on Huerta in the Congress showed more courage than prudence, and his friends warned him to moderate his comments. Instead, he sharpened them. Foreign Minister Francisco León de la Barra, appearing before the Senate to criticize the non-recognition policy of the United States, bristled as Domínguez shouted, "How can the United States recognize the government stained with the blood of President Madero and Vice President Pino Suárez?" Apparently emboldened by his initial verbal attack, Domínguez condemned Huerta in the congressional record for ordering assassinations, muzzling the press, and failing to restore peace. Huerta, he concluded, was a traitor and an assassin who should be ousted from power.

Having accurately assessed the dictator's record, Domínguez should have anticipated a reprisal. However, he showed neither fear nor common sense. He asked the Senate to pass a resolution demanding Huerta's resignation, which health-conscious senators refused to endorse. Domínguez nonetheless continued attacking Huerta on the Senate floor and shortly discovered the limit of the dictator's patience. On the morning of October 8, 1913, four Mexico City policemen, including Huerta's son-in-law, broke into Domínguez's hotel room, forced him into a waiting car, and drove him to a nearby cemetery. A freshly dug grave had already been prepared. Two of Mexico City's finest, including the dictator's kin, then murdered the senator and buried his body.

Domínguez's disappearance alarmed a suddenly defiant Congress. When the government claimed no knowledge of Domínguez's whereabouts, Congress vowed to investigate and publish its findings. If similar incidents occurred, an outraged Congress warned, it would disband and reconvene somewhere outside of Huerta's military control.

The growing split between Congress and Huerta surfaced elsewhere as well. Shortly before the Domínguez affair, Congress had rejected Huerta's nomination of Catholic Party member Eduardo Tamariz as minister of education. Congressmen accused Huerta of clericalism, and Maderistas and Felicistas combined to block the appointment.

Huerta had seen enough. Against the advice of several cabinet ministers, he issued a decree abolishing Congress and ordering the arrest of all deputies he considered enemies of the government. Troops surrounded Congress and eventually rounded up 101 deputies and incarcerated them in the federal penitentiary. In the weeks that followed, Huerta also ordered arrests of minor officials, journalists, union members, and others opposed to his regime. Some of those illegally detained were subsequently shot.[13]

This brutal repression served as the immediate backdrop to the October elections. National elections had been discussed for months and several political factions, including Felicistas, Catholics, and Maderistas, announced candidates for the presidency. Huerta viewed the elections, however, as a ceremonial exercise to legitimize his government. The dictator reasoned that, given the chaotic conditions, voter turnout would not reach the 51 percent required by law and he would remain interim president. Huerta did what he could, moreover, to assure this outcome. He dispatched his principal opponent, Félix Díaz, to Japan to thank the emperor for sending a delegation to Mexico's centennial celebration in 1910. Díaz's prolonged sea voyage prevented him from campaigning and nearly kept him from returning by election day. According to Mexican election laws, that would have automatically disqualified him from the race. Not surprisingly, official results gave Huerta the most votes. Rather than a mandate, however, the election caused embarrassment. Diplomatic representatives reported widespread stuffing of ballot boxes and voter turnout fell short of legal requirements, which nullified the election and left the dictator in charge.[14]

The electoral farce did nothing to enhance Huerta's reputation as a legitimate president. The dictator subsequently shut down what remained of the opposition press and arrested the leader of the Catholic Party. Félix Díaz, who had collaborated with Huerta in plotting Madero's demise, now feared for his own life. Díaz disbanded his political party, gained asylum in the U.S. consulate in Veracruz, and went into exile.[15]

Huerta still drew strength from diehard supporters among the clergy, the army officer corps, and large landowners, all of whom sought a return to the Porfiriato. Huerta was also supported by Great Britain, a superpower with massive investments and colonies in the region. Great Britain wanted more Mexican petroleum as well as a limit on U.S. expansion in the Gulf-Caribbean Basin. Britain showed little or no interest in instilling democratic ideals or procedures in the Mexican political process. On the contrary, the British ambassador to Mexico, Sir Lionel Carden, had encouraged Huerta's dissolution of Congress and cancellation of concessions to U.S. companies. The principal British investor in Mexico, Lord Cowdray, later arranged a timely loan for Huerta from European banks. In exchange, Cowdray received more petroleum concessions.

Despite this support, however, the regime began to crumble under pressure from Mexican revolutionaries and a determined Woodrow Wilson. In late October, the U.S. president, in a dramatic speech in Mobile, Alabama, accused Europe of seeking to subvert Latin American nations through control over their economies. This was a thinly veiled reference to British policy in Mexico and an attempt by Wilson, in the spirit of the Monroe Doctrine, to increase U.S. influence in the region. The following month, Sir William Tyrrell, British undersecretary of state, met with Wilson and

Secretary of State Bryan in Washington. Britain's Mexican policy, Bryan told Tyrrell, had been reduced to serving the interests of "oil barons" and gaining access to petroleum. In a dramatic policy reversal, Tyrrell intimated that Britain would withdraw its support for Huerta and allow the United States to assume a preeminent position in the region.

. Britain abandoned Huerta in favor of closer ties with the United States for two primary reasons. First, Britain's deteriorating relations with Germany dictated that London focus on Europe and cultivate harmonious relations with likely allies. Second, the United States had already surpassed Britain as the leading investor in the Caribbean, Central America, and Mexico and had intervened militarily on several occasions to protect its interests. It did not appear likely that Britain could halt the American juggernaut in the region.

The Wilson administration eased the transition to U.S. preeminence in the area by pledging to uphold concessions granted to British petroleum and mining companies by Porfirio Díaz and by reducing tolls charged foreign ships passing through the Panama Canal. U.S. oil magnate Edward Doheny also agreed to sell Britain large quantities of the high-quality petroleum desperately needed by the Admiralty. It seems that Lord Cowdray's oil fields now yielded only inferior crudes unsuitable for ocean-going vessels. Ironically, Britain's petroleum requirements ultimately reduced Lord Cowdray's influence at Whitehall and helped make Huerta dispensable.[16]

With British support for Huerta wavering, Wilson approached Venustiano Carranza, the political leader of the anti-Huertista Constitutionalist movement, with plans for an armed U.S. intervention to topple the dictator.[17] Wilson proposed an American blockade of Mexican ports, followed by the occupation of major cities by U.S. troops "to protect the lives and property of foreigners." Wilson also wanted Carranza to declare Mexico's northern provinces independent from the rest of the country, an idea first proposed to Wilson by U.S. military advisors. An interventionist policy also received strong endorsement from some U.S. business interests in Mexico, who abandoned Huerta under pressure from Wilson.

The success of Wilson's policy hinged on Carranza's cooperation. Otherwise, U.S. intervention would be widely viewed as a unilateral military invasion and could draw severe criticism from inside and outside of Mexico. The Constitutionalist leader strongly opposed any U.S. intervention in Mexico, however, and refused to consider a declaration of independence for northern Mexico. Wilson clearly had underestimated Carranza, who was determined to oust Huerta without entering into unholy alliances with the United States.

Wilson remained determined, however, to increase U.S. influence through forging closer ties with the rebel leader. In February 1914, at the urging of Carranza's agent Luis Cabrera, Wilson lifted the arms embargo on Mexico and recognized the Carranza-led Constitutionalists as cobelligerents. This strengthened the revolutionary armies and gave Carranza more political legitimacy and prestige. Wilson and Bryan wrongly assumed that, in return, a grateful Carranza would be more receptive to U.S. policy.

The U.S. president, displaying a stubborn resolve, forged ahead with plans for a military intervention. Wilson's policy, initially wrapped in vague democratic principles, increasingly resembled a unilateral attempt to increase U.S. influence at the expense of Huerta and Great Britain. In April 1914, a seemingly minor incident gave Wilson an excuse to send in the troops. The president had already ordered the U.S. fleet to Tampico to protect U.S. interests, a potentially provocative act similar to Polk's decision to send soldiers to the Texas-Mexico border in 1846. Mexican troops in Tampico, claiming that a state of emergency had been declared, detained a small contingent of U.S. sailors sent ashore to buy fuel. The local Huertista commander, when informed of the incident two hours later, ordered the sailors released.

Under normal conditions, that would have put an end to the affair. However, Wilson and Huerta both attempted to use the incident to their advantage. The U.S. commander of the fleet, Admiral Henry T. Mayo, demanded a formal apology, the arrest of the Mexican officer responsible for the sailors' detention, and a twenty-one gun salute to the U.S. flag. The Mexican commander insisted, however, that he could not comply with the last demand without Huerta's permission. The dictator suggested a compromise solution: both sides would simultaneously salute one another's flags, and the International Court of Justice at the Hague would arbitrate the dispute. Wilson refused the deal, however, and received congressional approval to invade Mexico.

The president ordered more ships to the Gulf and planned to occupy Veracruz, Tampico, and Mexico City. Attention focused on Veracruz, however, when Wilson learned that a large shipment of arms for Huerta, aboard the German steamer *Ypiranga,* was about to arrive. American battleships shelled the port and its environs, inflicting heavy civilian casualties, and the marines charged ashore. The local Huertista commander, outgunned and somehow surprised, beat a hasty retreat. However, young cadets from the Mexican naval academy, as well as individual soldiers and civilians, put up a spirited resistance for several hours. By the next day, American troops controlled the city, the harbor, and its customs house. The *Ypiranga* steamed farther south and unloaded its shipment elsewhere, but the United States now occupied Mexico's principal port and could deny Huerta the customs revenues that sustained his government. Moreover, shiploads of arms soon began arriving and warehouses filled with modern weaponry, seemingly in anticipation of a lengthy stay and a widening military campaign.[18]

The U.S. invasion drew widespread criticism from both Mexicans and Americans. Carranza, who had not been informed in advance of the action, demanded an immediate withdrawal of U.S. troops and threatened military retaliation. Spontaneous demonstrations condemning the occupation and the shelling of innocent civilians occurred throughout Mexico, and U.S. trade unions, peace organizations, and church associations sent written protests to Wilson. Huerta encouraged the popular outrage in his country against the United States, and large numbers of new recruits enlisted in the federal army to fight the Yankee invaders.

Opposition to the invasion, however, was not unanimous. Pancho Villa, Carranza's principal military ally in the struggle against Huerta, refused to condemn the occupation. This demonstrated the growing split between the two leaders and limited the rebels' military and diplomatic options. The two rebel chiefs announced that they would not attempt to recapture Veracruz but would defend rebel-held territory and continue their advance on Mexico City.

In the meantime, Wilson attempted to leverage Huerta's ouster through the use of outside mediators. The United States convinced Argentina, Brazil, and Chile, the most diplomatically influential South American nations, to mediate the Mexican crisis at a hastily convened international conference at Niagara Falls. At first, Huerta appeared willing to step down if a broadly based, stable government could be assembled to succeed him. His position hardened, however, at the urging of the British ambassador to Mexico, Sir Lionel Carden, and Lord Cowdray, who propped up the regime with large cash donations funneled through his petroleum and utility companies.

The principal obstacle to U.S. policy, however, remained Carranza. The first chief steadfastly refused to accept any U.S. proposal, even if it supported his objectives. Wilson now reimposed an arms embargo on Mexico, somehow hoping that this would make Carranza more pliable. In fact, it only increased his resolve to resist a peace settlement imposed by the United States. The Niagara Conference collapsed on July 5, 1914, having achieved nothing.[19] U.S. forces soon withdrew from Veracruz leaving behind their vast arms cache, which Constitutionalist forces gladly confiscated to use against Huerta.[20]

CONCLUSION

Francisco I. Madero's loss of rebel support and his reliance on the federal army made him vulnerable to counterrevolutionaries. Generals Bernardo Reyes and Félix Díaz launched short-lived revolts that failed to garner popular support. Madero kept them alive, however, and the two generals continued to conspire against the president from their Mexico City prison cells. When Huerta sided with Díaz and Reyes, Madero was doomed.

U.S. Ambassador Henry Lane Wilson, acting without the approval of the Taft administration, supported the coup and helped to secure the interim presidency for Huerta. Wilson believed that Huerta would support U.S. interests in Mexico, and he pressured Félix Díaz into settling for an early election and cabinet posts for his supporters. The brutal murders of Madero and Pino Suárez brought to a tragic close the first phase of the Mexican Revolution.

U.S. President Woodrow Wilson's occupation of Veracruz did not prevent Huerta from receiving German arms, nor did it topple the regime. Nevertheless, Wilson's aggressive foreign policy increased U.S. influence in the region at Britain's expense and weakened Huerta by denying him important customs revenues. Wilson also influenced the course of the revolution by inadvertently enhancing Venustiano Carranza's political reputation. Carranza's condemnation of U.S. intervention in Mexico, and his consistent refusal to accept Wilson's diplomatic overtures, boosted his popularity and demonstrated impressive diplomatic skills in defense of national sovereignty.

CHAPTER FOUR

NORTHERN REVOLUTIONARIES
AND THE FALL OF HUERTA

VIEWING A MAP OF NORTHERN MEXICO General Victoriano C. Huerta would have winced over recent military setbacks in towns and rail centers that linked important mining and commercial regions in Chihuahua, Coahuila, Durango, and Sonora. The rebels who controlled these areas rustled cattle from hacendados sympathetic to the Huerta regime and taxed wealthy foreign mining companies, providing revolutionaries with money to buy arms and supplies from U.S. merchants all along the border.

Huerta, who grew up dirt poor in an Indian village, owed his remarkable professional and political advance to the Porfirian army. He favored political and social stability and allied with conservative elites, foreign business interests, and the hierarchy of the Catholic Church. To defeat the rebels, Huerta increasingly resorted to harsh and abusive measures, such as wholesale burning of Morelean villages, to demoralize the opposition. Such tactics failed to vanquish villagers, however, who joined forces with newly formed revolutionary armies from the northern provinces. These armies, which grew into the tens of thousands and benefited from superior leadership, eventually defeated Huerta and his allies.

Despite the opposition of most Mexicans, Huerta nearly succeeded in securing the presidency. Following Madero's assassination, only four Maderista governors had refused to recognize him as interim president. Even the most prominent Maderista loyalists, Governors Venustiano Carranza in Coahuila and José María Maytorena in Sonora, hesitated before rebelling. Most elites valued political stability and protection of private property over the uncertainty of reform and social change. Pressure for revolutionary change came from those with the least to lose and the most to win. Huerta's opponents included the same social revolutionaries who had earlier opposed Porfirio Díaz as well as Maderistas committed to political reform. Hatred of Huerta initially united revolutionaries from diverse social, cultural, economic, and political backgrounds, but fundamental disagreements over the specifics of reform programs were aggravated by class differences that eventually drove anti-Huerta allies apart.

VENUSTIANO CARRANZA AND THE CONSTITUTIONALIST MOVEMENT

Venustiano Carranza, born into a wealthy landowning family in Cuatro Ciénagas, Coahuila, emerged as the political leader (or "first chief") of the Constitutionalist movement. His father Jesús had supported Benito Juárez and fought against the conservatives and the French at midcentury. Juárez rewarded Don Jesús by granting him land confiscated from conservative landowners. This land became the core of the family patrimony of more than 80,000 hectares. After Jesús's death, his sons Venustiano and Emilio divided the property, and subsequently acquired additional estates in the hinterland of Cuatro Ciénagas.

The Carranza brothers, born with impeccable liberal pedigrees, held a variety of public posts during the Díaz dictatorship. Beginning in 1894 Venustiano Carranza served three successive terms as jefe político of Cuatro Ciénagas and later became a federal deputy and senator from Coahuila. Don Venustiano, like many future Maderistas from the region, belonged to the camarilla of General Bernardo Reyes, the powerful governor of nearby Nuevo León. During the 1890s the Carranzas helped General Reyes oust the unpopular Coahuilan Governor José María Garza

Galán, and supported Reyes's selection of Miguel Cárdenas as governor. In return, Cárdenas granted Venustiano Carranza land confiscated from local villages and significantly reduced his property taxes.

In 1908, Carranza resigned as senator and accepted the nomination for governor of Coahuila, which had been arranged for him by Reyes. For the proud Coahuilan hacendado this was to be the crowning achievement of his public career. Carranza's political future as a Porfirista, however, unraveled the following year as Díaz, concerned over Reyes's growing popularity, sent the general packing and purged his camarilla. Although Carranza's hopes of becoming governor had now vanished, he stubbornly remained in the race and suffered a preordained defeat.[1]

Carranza never forgot this personal humiliation and in 1910 he joined other Reyistas in supporting the presidential candidacy of fellow Coahuilan Francisco Madero. Madero's defeat sealed Carranza's fate as a political outcast and left him little choice but to follow his vanquished leader into exile in San Antonio. Carranza served in Madero's revolutionary junta and, despite his preference for wearing a general's uniform, avoided the battlefield throughout the revolution, concentrating instead on politics.

Díaz's military defeat, primarily attributable to Pascual Orozco and Emiliano Zapata, launched Carranza's revolutionary career as Maderista governor of Coahuila. There he auditioned policies that he later advocated as a national leader, including social and educational reforms. For example, he improved public health by initiating inspections of water supplies and food preparation in restaurants. He also attempted to improve public morality by regulating gambling, public drinking, and prostitution and by closing businesses on Sundays. Carranza also supported the improvement of public education by budgeting 400,000 pesos for the renovation of schools. All of these reforms resembled policies advocated earlier by progressive Porfirian reformers.[2]

Carranza's political behavior also revealed a firm grounding in the practices of the old regime. When Madero called for general elections, Carranza stuffed ballot boxes and consolidated his position by appointing political associates to key positions. Carranza's social policies reflected his hacendado background and were undistinguishable from his Porfirian predecessors. For example, he took firm stands against striking miners and supported fellow hacendados in their disputes with peasants over land rights.

Despite these continuities with Porfirian times, however, Carranza's revolutionary nationalism distinguished him from old regime politicians. Most notably, he placed more restrictions on foreign companies investing in Coahuila and significantly increased their taxes.[3]

Madero's revolution had provided a vehicle to power for Carranza and other provincial elites who had been denied access to high office by Díaz. Following Madero's arrest, most Maderista officials cooperated with Huerta rather than risk losing their positions and lives. Even Carranza was initially inclined to support Huerta. But the dictator had driven him into the active opposition by sending federal troops into Coahuila and by ordering Madero's assassination.[4]

In the Mexican tradition, Carranza issued a revolutionary pronouncement, the Plan de Guadalupe, which rejected the Huerta government and proclaimed his own political legitimacy. This plan disputed the constitutionality of Huerta's ascension to power and declared Carranza "first chief" of the "Constitutionalist" army and interim president of Mexico until national elections could be held.[5] The plan's narrow political agenda and silence on social reforms restricted its appeal among discontented peasants and miners, however, and made it difficult for Carranza to raise an army. As a result, federal troops drove the Constitutionalists from Coahuila and across the northern desert into Sonora, where an anti-Huertista movement was forming.[6]

THE SONORANS

At first glance, the state of Sonora appeared an unlikely hotbed of political upheaval. Located in the far northwestern corner of the country and covered by desert and mountain landscapes, Sonora had been traditionally isolated from the rest of Mexico. Beginning in the late nineteenth century, however, foreign investment, mostly from the neighboring United States, triggered an economic boom in mining and commercial agriculture that integrated Sonora's economy into national and international markets.[7]

As the local elite grew wealthier, they chafed under the tight political control of General Luis Torres, Rafael Izábal, and Ramón Corral, who dominated state politics throughout the Porfiriato. Discontented

Sonorans, like many upwardly mobile northerners, backed General Bernardo Reyes's vice-presidential bid in 1910 and later supported Madero for president after the overthrow of Díaz. In Guaymas, Reyista Club Verde members included future Maderista governors José María Maytorena and Carlos Randall, as well as future presidents Plutarco Elías Calles and Adolfo de la Huerta.[8]

Social discontent ran deep among Sonora's copper miners, whose strike at Cananea in 1906 had attracted national attention, as well as among the Yaqui Indians who had been brutally repressed by Díaz. Miners wanted a union and increased political representation, while the Yaquis refused to yield their ancestral lands to North American and Sonoran developers. The Porfirian state suppressed union-organizing activities and launched a bloody war against the Yaqui.

The goals of Sonora's revolutionary leaders differed dramatically from those of local miners and peasants. Peasants and workers supported the Maderistas on the assumption that politicians cloaked in democratic principles would implement social and economic reforms. Sonora's revolutionary leaders, however, wanted power and wealth and eschewed reforms that might disrupt the prosperous regional economy. For example, Maderista leader José María Maytorena, a wealthy landowner with impeccable liberal credentials, never seriously advocated land reform or workers' rights. He rebelled because the dominant Torres-Izábal-Corral political alliance had denied him a significant political voice and had kept him from participating in land development schemes near his estates.[9]

Sonora's emerging middle classes, as well as those on the fringes of upper-class respectability, also produced Maderista leaders. Adolfo de la Huerta, for example, managed the tannery and hacienda of Don Francisco Fourcade, one of Sonora's wealthiest men, and rubbed elbows with other elites. De la Huerta, an attractive bachelor with an excellent tenor voice, received invitations from local matrons to sing at lavish parties, but never gained full acceptance into upper-class society.

Alvaro Obregón, who would become the revolution's greatest general, epitomized the frontier spirit of Sonora's aggressive middle class. In the small town of Huatabampo, Obregón raised chickpeas on a 150-hectare farm, became an expert mechanic, and patented a harvester. Obregón also benefited from political and family connections. His brother José

FIGURE 28: General Alvaro Obregón, seated in the center, served as
president of Mexico from 1920 to 1924. At Obregón's right is
General Plutarco Elías Calles, who became president in 1924 and
dominated Mexican politics for the next ten years.

Source: Anita Brenner, *The Wind that Swept Mexico: The History of the Mexican
Revolution of 1910–1942,* with 184 historical photographs assembled by
George R. Leighton (Austin: University of Texas Press, 1971), photograph 122.

controlled local politics in Huatabampo and his mother's upper-crust
family, the Salidos, pioneered large-scale irrigated agriculture in the Mayo
River valley.[10] A future president, Obregón once made the cynical observation that no Mexican general could "withstand a cannon ball of fifty
thousand pesos."[11]

Plutarco Elías Calles, who would dominate Mexican politics from 1924
to 1934, also lived on the fringes of upper-class respectability. The illegitimate son of prominent hacendado Plutarco Elías Lucero, Calles worked
as a schoolteacher, government clerk, flourmill manager, and administra-
tor of his father's estates. Calles was never accepted into his father's social
circle, however, and his drinking problem suggested psychological distress.
Resolution came through rejection of the traditional order, including

Catholicism and Porfirian politics, and advocacy of puritanical reforms, public education, and, as president, an institutionalized revolution controlled from above.

Other prominent Sonoran Maderistas, such as Juan Cabral, Salvador Alvarado, and Francisco Serrano, came from middle-class backgrounds and had felt their ambitions constrained by the Porfirian elite. Few among them favored the socialist and anarchist ideas advocated by Manuel M. Diéguez and Esteban Baca Calderón, PLM members and labor activists from Cananea.[12]

When Madero issued his call to revolution, most Sonorans had preferred to let Orozco and Zapata do the fighting. Obregón admitted, for example, that he had been an "inactive Maderista" during 1910–1911.[13] By contrast, José María Maytorena, a man with ambitious political objectives, proved an exception and invested much of his personal fortune in raising an army to support Madero. In Las Cruces, for example, he had paid each recruit 500 pesos for enlisting. This helped to establish the precedent of a well-paid professional army that distinguished the Sonorans from other revolutionary and federal forces during the revolution. Sonora's troops, under the command of the brilliant General Obregón, would have the edge over federal forces composed of conscripted recruits, as well as over other revolutionary armies recruited among peasants and free-spirited vaqueros.[14]

In the months following Díaz's resignation, Sonora's Maderistas assumed leadership positions without seriously disrupting normal economic and social discourse. After a brief interlude, Maytorena occupied the statehouse and made a series of pronouncements designed to reassure foreign investors and wealthy Sonorans that he planned to maintain the status quo. For example, the governor renewed concessions granted to foreign firms by Díaz and gave additional concessions to U.S. companies.[15] Governor Maytorena also retained Porfirian bureaucrats at full pay.[16]

The overthrow of Díaz evoked spontaneous democratic outbursts at the local level, however, that could not be completely controlled from above. When General Juan Cabral entered Cananea, for example, thousands of joyous miners poured into the streets to greet him and seven hundred volunteered to join the revolutionary army.[17] Throughout the state, townsmen formed militia units to protect themselves during the political and military uncertainties. Sonora's frontier experience, characterized by generations of constant struggle against Yaqui and Mayo Indians, as well as the demands of overcoming the harsh desert environment, had galvanized communities into tightly knit social units with a tradition of self-defense. These towns had benefited from the economic development of recent decades, and they wanted political autonomy, material progress, and social order.

The revolutionary leaders who emerged from Sonora's settlements, such as Obregón and Calles, represented a frontier culture that valued entrepreneurship, public education, and limited democracy and resisted the centralizing tendencies of old Mexico as represented by Porfirian politics and the Catholic Church. However, land reform and social justice for Native Americans, issues that motivated peasant revolutionaries in central Mexico, failed to resonate with Sonoran farmers whose land and water had been acquired at the expense of the Yaqui and Mayo Indians.[18]

In fact, the place of Indians and miners in the revolutionary process posed an ideological and political dilemma for Sonora's revolutionary leaders. The aspirations of marginalized groups, who assumed that revolutionary leaders would break with Porfirian policy, conflicted with Maderista economic and social conservatism. Before long, miners, railroad workers, and peasants grew restless and provoked a series of conflicts with employers over wages and working conditions that forced Sonora's Maderista leaders to take sides between labor and capital.[19]

The copper mines at Cananea, the site of the major industrial dispute in 1906, once again emerged as the center of strike activity. PLM leaders Esteban Baca Calderón and Manuel Diéguez, released from prison by Madero, returned to Cananea in October 1911 and, according to the U.S. consul, proceeded to "create discontent among the workmen and . . . arouse anti-American feeling."[20] Their arrival also coincided with the formation of the Unión de Obreros de Cananea, which they undoubtedly had a hand in creating.

The union presented management with a list of grievances that included the abusive behavior by foremen, curtailment of hospital services for workers, and a required seven-day workweek. When management refused to negotiate, municipal authorities arrested abusive foremen and held them under a 12,000-peso bond. This aggressive action by local officials in support of miners represented a radical shift in politics and underscores the grassroots nature of the revolutionary process in Sonora.[21] By contrast, Governor Maytorena's actions are equally instructive in underscoring the enduring conservatism of Maderista leaders. In response to miners' actions, the governor asked Mexico City to dispatch three hundred federal troops to occupy Cananea, thus helping management end the strike after a five-day shutdown.[22]

During 1912, the Maderista leadership continued to support Cananea's managers. Prefect Benjamin Hill, an important local official, intervened aggressively to limit union activities and provide management with increased security. For example, Hill supervised miners, declared strikes illegal, prohibited union meetings, and forced two union officers to resign. Cananea's owners, increasingly comfortable with the new revolutionary government, then invested millions of dollars in smelter renovations and development of newly discovered copper deposits.[23]

Government support of owners, however, failed to dissolve the union movement. When management summarily fired six miners in December 1912, workers struck in solidarity closing down the mine. The union then increased the stakes, moreover, by demanding a 20 percent increase in wages, a reduction in the workday from nine to eight hours, and official recognition of the union. Strike leaders also threatened to call a "general strike" and to sack the company store for food and clothing.[24]

Despite the threats, management refused to negotiate and asked Maderista leaders to intervene. Prefect Hill warned strikers against blocking others from entering the workplace and Sonora's Acting Governor Ismael Padilla, in charge while Maytorena visited Mexico City, rushed to Cananea. Padilla openly sided with management and, at the company's request, ordered the deportation of three union supporters, including a schoolteacher and the mayor's assistant.[25]

By January 1913, Sonora's Maderista leadership had succeeded in consolidating its political control without altering the social and economic status quo. Madero's assassination and Huerta's seizure of power, however, presented the new leadership with a political and moral dilemma. They could avenge their leader's overthrow, which would be the honorable choice, or they could cooperate with Huerta, who would likely preserve the economic and social status quo.

Sonora's political leaders vacillated over recognition of Huerta. Precisely when they required strong leadership, moreover, Governor Maytorena took a six-month leave of absence in the United States ostensibly because of illness. His replacement, Ignacio Pesqueira, a wealthy landowner with strong ties to U.S. companies, also failed to take a clear position. Instead, he informed the U.S. consul that he would recognize Huerta, if the majority of governors chose to do so.[26]

Such thinking did not reflect the attitude, however, of Sonora's miners and townspeople. When news of Madero's assassination reached the U.S.-owned copper mines at Pilares de Nacozari and Moctezuma, riotous mobs demanded Huerta's arrest and Prefect Pedro Bracamonte mobilized 420 armed miners to fight against "military dictatorship." At Cananea, municipal president Manuel Diéguez distributed rifles to political allies and called a public meeting to learn "the people's opinion." The assembly, reportedly attended by miners, workers, and merchants, denounced "the recent crimes in Mexico" and demanded that the state government listen to their views.

Shortly after receiving word of miners' militancy, Acting Governor Pesqueira asked the state legislature to denounce Huerta. He explained that it would not be necessary to send Sonorans into battle, but merely to maintain the state's political independence until changes could occur in Mexico City. General Salvador Alvarado, one of Sonora's grassroots militia leaders, grew weary of the legislative debate and stormed into the chamber with a contingent of troops to deliver the ultimatum: "If you recognize Huerta we will denounce both you and Huerta."[27]

Alvarado's actions illustrate divisions within the Maderista movement over revolutionary objectives. Rank-in-file members, represented by miners, townsmen, ranchers, and militia leaders, sought municipal autonomy, economic opportunity, and social mobility; Maderista civilian leaders, represented by the provincial elite, wanted to preserve political gains and maintain the social and economic status quo.

Pesqueira denounced Huerta, joined Carranza's fledgling Constitutionalist movement, and prepared to oust federal troops from the state. The acting governor appointed Alvaro Obregón, who had distinguished himself in the campaign against the Orozquistas in 1912, head of military operations. Throughout the state, revolutionary sentiment swelled the ranks of Obregón's army, and talented local leaders, such as Plutarco Elías Calles and Adolfo de la Huerta, grew politically influential.

Pesqueira and his allies understood that the Constitutionalist victory in Sonora hinged on a steady flow of revenues to pay and equip Obregón's army. Taxes paid by the copper companies and cattle confiscated from Huertista hacendados—and then sold across the U.S. border for $15 a head—constituted the most important sources of government income. Smuggling of cattle and arms also generated personal income for the Pesqueira family, Calles, de la Huerta, and others dubbed "brokers fronterizos" by Héctor Aguilar Camín. Needless to say, merchants on the other side of the border also made fortunes.[28]

The importance of tax revenues to the state's budget encouraged Pesqueira to cultivate good relations with the big copper companies, all of them American-owned. He notified the U.S. consul at Hermosillo that U.S. interests would be protected, and he sent troops to Cananea to control unruly miners who had struck over recent layoffs. Ignacio Pesqueira, whose cousin Roberto served as the company's attorney, ordered the army to feed unemployed workers and transport them out of town. Within a month, the mines returned to production. One million dollars worth of copper crossed the border in a single shipment.[29]

Fortified with revenues from taxes and smuggling, General Obregón raised a professional army and drove the federal forces from Sonora. This military victory, however, intensified political in-fighting among revolutionary leaders. In May 1913, José María Maytorena announced that he was ready to resume his job as governor. Maytorena still counted many supporters among the Maderista elite, and he also benefited from the growing split between Pesqueira and Obregón.[30]

Before the in-fighting intensified, Venustiano Carranza, first chief of the Constitutionalist movement, intervened and brokered a fragile settlement. Maytorena returned as governor, Obregón remained army chief, and Pesqueira was given a post in Carranza's cabinet. The first chief gained considerable prestige by settling the dispute, and he stayed in Sonora to meet with rebel supporters.[31] Among them was Señora Ramona Flores, chief of staff to Sinaloan rebel leader Juan Carrasco, "a stout, red-haired woman in a black satin princess dress embroidered with

FIGURE 29: Constitutionalist troops, including many women,
posing before the taking of Nogales, Sonora, in 1913.

Source: Alicia Ahumada and David Maawad, eds., *Cananea y la Revolución Mexicana*
(Mexico City: Talleres de Litográphica Turmex, S.A., 1987), p. 92.

jet and with a sword at her side," who carried two gold ingots with which
to purchase arms and supplies.[32]

Carranza's Sonoran compromise, however, soon began to unravel.
Maytorena attempted to consolidate his political position by prohibiting
the sale of real estate to foreigners (except the mining companies), estab-
lishing a special war tax against "enemies of the revolution," and inviting
back to Sonora hacendados who had fled after losing their livestock.
Maytorena overplayed his hand, however, when he insisted that Carranza
support his political consolidation by relieving the popular Obregón of
his military command. When the first chief refused, Maytorena made
political overtures to the disgruntled Constitutionalist general from
Chihuahua, the flamboyant Francisco Villa.[33]

PANCHO VILLA, ABRAHAM GONZÁLEZ, AND THE
REVOLUTION IN CHIHUAHUA

Holding together a variety of revolutionary factions under the
Constitutionalist banner proved difficult for Carranza, whose patrician

manner and conservative social policies clashed with rough-hewed vaqueros and peasants determined to seize the lands of wealthy elite families. Hatred of Huerta bound together diverse social groups under Carranza's political leadership, but only for the moment. The first chief logically concentrated on maintaining alliances with the most powerful factions, and Obregón's loyalty would eventually prove decisive in securing Carranza's political supremacy by 1916. Huerta's military defeat in 1913–1914, though, hinged on the firepower of Chihuahua's revolutionary forces led by Pancho Villa. A temporary alliance of convenience united Villa, the dashing cavalryman, former bandit, and popular leader, with Carranza, the shrewd politician with the skill and experience required to fashion a winning political strategy.

Chihuahua's revolution, popular and dynamic, emerged from widespread discontent among gentry, townsmen, rancheros, and peasants over centralization of political and economic control during the Porfiriato. Governor Enrique Creel's attack on village land and self-government destroyed any remaining paternal bond tying Chihuahua's peasants to the local elite and unleashed a cycle of industrial disputes and revolutionary activity. In 1906 and 1908, Partido Liberal Mexicano agitation contributed to outbreaks of strikes among railway workers, and municipal-level discontent soon surfaced in the western province of Guerrero, home to Pascual Orozco and Abraham González.

Orozco's military exploits contributed significantly to Madero's victory in 1911, and González became an important Maderista political organizer and presidential advisor. González, a member of the gentry who had lost land during the Porfiriato, supported Madero's presidential bid in 1910, served in his revolutionary junta, and recruited Orozco and Pancho Villa to the cause. In recognition of these contributions, Madero appointed González governor of Chihuahua.

González's reforms won him widespread support among ranchers, workers, and small businessmen. For example, he created arbitration boards to settle labor disputes, transformed company towns into municipal districts, abolished company stores and script wages, exempted small businessmen from unpaid municipal and state taxes, and eliminated the jefe político law of 1887 that undermined local municipal autonomy. The governor also attempted to control gambling, drinking, and prostitution through raiding the most notorious casinos in Ciudad Juárez. Like the Sonorans, González increased revenues through the confiscation and sale of cattle belonging to Porfirian hacendados, including the state's largest landowner, Luis Terrazas.

The governor attempted to consolidate Maderista political control without further disrupting the provincial economy. For example, he rejected the militant labor policy advocated by the PLM, maintained the special concessions granted to foreign corporations by Díaz, and demobilized rebel forces. As compensation for their services, the governor paid Orozco and Villa fifty thousand pesos and ten thousand pesos, respectively. However, he only gave enlisted men a paltry 1.5 to 25 pesos, and he refused to grant land to Villa's men.

After a brief tenure as minister of the interior, González returned to the governorship and faced serious political problems. Pascual Orozco and Francisco Vásquez-Gómez (a Porfirian turned Maderista), having been denied important political roles by President Madero, launched separate conspiracies. Orozco's 1912 rebellion, supported by Terrazas and Creel, threatened to topple Madero and drove González into hiding.

General Huerta's subsequent victory over Orozco increased the general's prestige and power at the expense of Governor González and President Madero. González mobilized militia units to counterbalance the federal army's influence, and clashed with Huerta over his lackluster pursuit of Orozquistas and his attempt to eliminate González's friend Pancho Villa.

Villa had quarreled with both Huerta and Orozco during 1911–1912, and Huerta decided to charge Villa with stealing a horse, a seemingly trivial criminal offense when compared with the well-known systematic theft of wages and supplies by federal officers. Nevertheless, Villa was sentenced to death by Huerta's judges and transported to a federal prison in Mexico City. If the sentence had been carried out, it would have changed the course of the Mexican Revolution.

Villa had remained loyal to Madero since the outbreak of hostilities in 1911, but President Madero now let his northern champion rot in jail. From prison, Villa issued proclamations of loyalty to the president and implored Madero to release him. The president waffled between executing or pardoning this loyal ally. He finally intervened and ordered Villa's release from prison. Needless to say, the incident only served to intensify Villa's and González's hatred of Huerta.[34]

Following Madero's overthrow, Governor González refused to recognize Huerta but was unable to raise an army or to link up with other revolutionary movements. Federal troops still controlled Chihuahua, and the governor was soon arrested on trumped-up charges. Before his trial, a squad of soldiers took González from his cell into the desert and executed him. General Huerta denied any involvement. However, the general later rewarded González's executioner with a European diplomatic post.[35]

The revolution in Chihuahua did not die, however, with González's execution. Francisco Villa emerged from hiding and fashioned a formidable army of vaqueros and peasants capable of driving federal troops from the state. Villa rebelled for various reasons. He was already marked for death by Huerta, and González's execution only increased his hatred of the dictator. Villa also represented a groundswell of social protest against the old regime. Although he did not have a well-developed revolutionary platform, he advocated an egalitarian society based on the redistribution of land among his soldiers and the establishment of new military colonies similar to those that had flourished in pre-Porfirian times. By contrast, Villa did not express strong nationalistic views. In areas that he later controlled, Villa protected U.S. and British enterprises from sacking and did not increase their taxes. This contrasted with the nationalistic policies of Constitutionalist leader Venustiano Carranza who advocated restrictions on foreign investment and stiff tax increases for foreign enterprises. Villa's protection of American and British interests, however, did not extend to other nationalities. He persecuted the Chinese in outbursts of visceral xenophobia and racism and aggressively confiscated the property of prosperous Spaniards in seeming retribution for the sins of all gachupines.[36]

Villa's humble origins as a muleteer, miner, and bandit in rural Durango helped him form a close bond with his men. Born Doroteo Arango, he had changed his name before the revolution to avoid detection by the police. He fought for a few years in the shadow of others, but became Mexico's most famous commander.

Villa collected colorful lieutenants based on their ability to fight. He did not pay much attention, however, to their political views or previous allegiances. General Felipe Angeles, for example, had been in the federal army and, as a Maderista, had fought against the Zapatistas in Morelos. But Villa still valued him as an excellent artillery officer. Most Villista commanders came from the same modest backgrounds as their troops, which contributed to the army's camaraderie. For example, the American journalist John Reed, who rode with Villa, described Villista General Toribio Ortega in admiring terms.

> [Ortega is] a lean dark Mexican who is called the honorable and most brave by his soldiers. He is by far the most simplehearted and disinterested soldier in Mexico. He never kills his prisoners. He has refused to take a cent from the Revolution beyond his meager salary. Villa respects and trusts him perhaps beyond all his generals.[37]

Other Villista leaders, by contrast, evoked more fear than admiration. General Tomás Urbina, the "Lion of the Sierras," took over the town of Las Nieves and lived like a feudal lord. Reed's unflattering physical description of Urbina depicts an unsettling presence. "[Urbina is] a broad, medium-sized man of dark mahogany complexion, with a sparse black beard up to his cheek-bones, that didn't hide the wide, thin, expressionless mouth, the gaping nostrils, and shiny, small, humorous animal eyes."[38] Rodolfo Fierro, Villa's personal bodyguard, also inspired fear in friend and foe alike based on his penchant for killing people in cold blood.[39]

Despite their rough edges, Villa and his generals displayed considerable organizational skills. Villa's army of 20,000 men was organized into fighting units, outfitted with horses, arms, and ammunition, paid regularly, and fed beef and tortillas prepared by thousands of women who accompanied them on the march. Villa also maintained a field hospital of sixty railroad cars staffed with doctors and nurses, which impressed John Reed. The money for all of this came from Chihuahua's vast cattle herds, including those belonging to Luis Terrazas, which Villa confiscated and sold across the border in the United States. Mexican cattle, taken in the name of the revolution, made its way to Chicago's slaughterhouses and to dinner tables throughout the United States. Rather than divide the haciendas among his men, Villa turned the estates over to generals or other loyal political allies. By maintaining larger scales of production, Chihuahua's

FIGURE 30: Women and children accompanied revolutionary
armies. Entire families are pictured on top of a railroad car,
a common mode of transportation.

Source: Anita Brenner, *The Wind that Swept Mexico: The History of the Mexican
Revolution of 1910–1942*, with 184 historical photographs assembled by
George R. Leighton (Austin: University of Texas Press, 1971), photograph 92.

haciendas generated more revenue and kept the army moving forward.
Villa's commitment to agrarian reform remained a promise that would
have to wait for the shooting to stop.⁴⁰

As Villa's men swept across Chihuahua, driving the federal troops
before them, they developed certain rules of war that targeted specific
social groups and individuals for punishment. Victims of collective retribution included innocent minorities associated with the old regime as well
as others whose only sin was economic success. Northern Mexico's prosperous Chinese community suffered numerous atrocities at the hands of

Villa's men, including murder and theft, and the Spanish and Mormon communities, particularly prominent merchants and landowners, suffered for their presumed arrogance and exploitative ways. Villa also executed captured army officers without trial. By contrast, captured common soldiers were allowed to return home, although sometimes with their ears cut off. General Urbina earned a reputation for meting out particularly harsh reprisals. For example, following the capture of Durango his troops, joined by opportunistic townspeople, looted businesses and homes, and then kidnapped members of the local elite. Urbina ransomed them for 500 pesos each, except for the archbishop who fetched 7,000 pesos.[41]

Villa's army drove Huerta's forces from the north-central provinces in a series of stunning military victories. Federal forces abandoned rural areas, where they had little popular support, and occupied provincial capitals and rail centers. Many elites and foreigners fled across the border into the United States.

Villa's army moved quickly across northern Mexico in confiscated rail cars and then launched massive cavalry charges, coordinated with artillery fire, on the perimeter defenses of cities. Once troops broke through into the streets, fighting became less organized with small contingents of troops engaged in close combat. Villa's victories at Durango, Gómez Palacios, Ciudad Juárez, and Torreón made Huerta's position untenable.[42] Villa's capture of Torreón, a key rail center on the edge of the central plateau, greatly increased Villa's prestige, assured rebels control over a vast expanse of territory, and opened the door to Mexico City.[43]

As Villa grew stronger militarily, his relations with Carranza deteriorated. Villa's unmatched military strength made him virtually independent from outside political control, and he openly opposed Carranza on important issues. For example, Villa threatened to kill Carranza's choice for governor of Chihuahua, former schoolmaster Manuel Chao, who only survived by grudgingly supporting Villa's appointment as Constitutionalist military commander of Chihuahua and Durango. Villa also ignored Carranza's directives to stop confiscating haciendas, which outraged this former hacendado from Coahuila.

The shooting of British hacendado William Benton, moreover, further chilled relations between the two leaders. Benton, who owned Los Remedios hacienda in Chihuahua, had feuded with neighboring villagers over grazing rights, fenced off the disputed land, and stood down the peasants. When Villa emerged victorious in the region, he gave villagers access to the contested pasture without consulting Benton. The British landlord, accustomed to getting his way, stormed into Villa's headquarters in Ciudad Juárez and insulted Villa in the presence of his men. A heated argument followed and Benton was killed. One plausible version of events has it that Benton, having worked up a sweat, reached into an inner pocket for a handkerchief to wipe his brow. Bodyguard Rodolfo Fierro, thinking that the Benton might be drawing a gun on Villa, shot him dead.

For the record, Villa announced that Benton had been formally convicted of a capital crime and executed. The British government, however, demanded a formal inquiry. Lord Cowdray and Ambassador Carden used the incident to attack the revolutionaries. Washington welcomed Britain's appeal for assistance as an affirmation of the Roosevelt Corollary to the Monroe Doctrine, which had proclaimed the right of the United States to enforce Latin American nations' compliance with international law. Carranza assumed control over defusing the crisis, much to Villa's relief, and steadfastly opposed any foreign intervention in Mexican affairs. The Benton affair eventually subsided, and Carranza's defiance of foreign intervention in Mexico enhanced his prestige at Villa's expense.[44]

In addition to his conflict with Villa, Carranza also struggled for control over other revolutionary leaders, particularly those directing agrarian movements. For example, Emiliano Zapata, in open rebellion against Huerta, refused to join the Constitutionalists and subordinate himself to Carranza. Their goals differed. Agrarian reform drove the Morelean revolution, and Carranza, a large landowner himself, opposed the wholesale redistribution of land to the peasantry. Zapata and Carranza also came from vastly different social and cultural backgrounds and found communication difficult.

Zapata certainly could have used some outside assistance. Huertista General Robles, intent on bringing the Zapatistas to their knees, resorted to burning villages and deporting peasants suspected of rebel leanings. Huerta informed an audience of Morelean planters assembled to honor him that "he would have recourse . . . to extreme measures, for the government is going, so to speak, to depopulate the state, and will send to your haciendas other workers." General Robles explained his tactics in similar terms to an American hotel owner in Cuernavaca: "Why, I am trying to clean up your beautiful Morelos for you. What a nice place it will be once we get rid of the Morelenses! If they resist me, I shall hang them like earrings to the trees." Huerta put things even more bluntly to the U.S. ambassador: "The best means to handle the rebel chiefs is an 18 cents rope wherefrom to hang them."[45]

Robles's draconian methods initially put Zapata on the defensive. When the United States occupied Veracruz in April 1914, however, Huerta transferred troops from Morelos to Puebla and Mexico City. The Zapatistas then descended from their mountain hideaways and occupied the villages below. Significantly, the loss of so many men through fighting and deportations now forced the women of Morelos to assume a larger combat role.

In Puente de Ixtla the widows, wives, daughters, sisters of rebels formed their own battalion and revolted "to avenge the dead." Under the command of a husky ex-tortilla maker called La China, they raided wildly through Tetecala district. Some in rags, some in plundered finery, wearing silk stockings and dresses, sandals, straw hats, and gun belts, these women became the terrors of the region.[46]

With the Zapatistas now controlling Morelos in the South, and the Villistas bearing down from the North, Huerta was caught in a pincers movement.

With the Huerta regime on the verge of collapsing, representatives of Carranza and Villa met in Torreón to discuss the transition of political power in Mexico. They agreed, following Huerta's ouster, to convene a convention of revolutionary armies to discuss a reform program and to set a date for elections. Nevertheless, Carranza would not discuss a formula for selecting delegates to the convention, nor would he endorse agrarian, labor, and anticlerical reforms.

In the meantime, Villa sealed Huerta's fate by attacking the last federal stronghold, Zacatecas. Villa crushed the 12,000 federal troops defending the city and closed off all avenues of retreat. Six thousand defenders perished and most of the survivors fell prisoner. Among the few hundred who escaped were many who had torn off their uniforms and disguised themselves as peasants. The battle's decisiveness ended all conservative hope, both at home and abroad, for the restoration of the old regime.

Rather than march on Mexico City, however, Villa remained in Chihuahua and consolidated his social and political base among the lower and middle classes. Villa promised land to his men, lowered the price of beef through confiscation and slaughter of hacendados' herds, and maintained order in the cities, much to the relief of the middle class. When he chose to push southward, his progress was stalled by Carranza's failure to send him promised coal shipments, and by President Woodrow Wilson's decision to renew the arms embargo on Mexico.[47]

Villa's failure to press his initial military advantage opened the door for General Alvaro Obregón, whose 18,000-man army had been methodically pushing through Jalisco, to reach the capital first. On August 12, 1914, Obregón signed the armistice with federal officials that formally ended hostilities, and he immediately positioned his troops in the Federal District. As part of the settlement, he insisted that federal forces on the southern perimeter hold their positions until they could be relieved by his troops. This prevented the Zapatistas, whom Obregón distrusted, from pushing northward from Morelos into Mexico City.

A few days earlier, General Huerta had boarded a train headed for the port of Veracruz where the German battle cruiser *Dresden* waited to take him to Jamaica. After a brief stay in the Caribbean, Huerta stopped over in England before settling in Barcelona. The wily general, however, closely followed the course of the revolution and received well wishers from home and abroad with ideas for restoring him to power.[48]

POWER STRUGGLE

HUERTA'S DEFEAT created the opportunity for a political settlement that could have spared the country from further bloodshed. However, success hinged on the ability of revolutionary leaders with different political agendas to resolve intractable social and economic problems and to determine a peaceful method of political succession. Recent military and political victories had also swelled the chests of revolutionary leaders, which made it difficult for them to surrender authority, particularly to individuals whom, in some cases, they profoundly disliked and distrusted.

The struggle against Huerta had produced alliances of convenience. Zapata and Villa came from humble social backgrounds and favored agrarian reform and regional autonomy under a loose national confederation. Carranza and Obregón, by contrast, grew up in comparative comfort and wanted a strong central government committed to economic modernization. Carranza and Obregón both had strong political ambitions. Carranza was also an ardent nationalist who favored restrictions on foreign investment and influence over the national economy. Villa, by contrast, protected foreign capital in areas that he controlled. None of the other revolutionaries matched Zapata's uncompromising zeal for agrarian reform.

These differences condemned to failure the revolutionary Convention of Aguascalientes, which was convened in the months following Huerta's defeat. Carranza's political intransigence was matched by Villa's military posturing, and Obregón's self-serving attempts at political compromise failed to produce a realistic framework for peace. In the end, Villa and Zapata formed a loose military alliance, Obregón remained loyal to Carranza, and the two sides chose to fight, sinking Mexico into a new round of bloodshed and destruction.

General Obregón's decisive victories over Villa in 1915 assured that Carranza, Obregón, and their political descendants would shape the political and ideological direction of the Mexican state. Nevertheless, Villismo and Zapatismo remained essential parts of the revolutionary ethos for decades, and Villa and Zapata remained politically influential in their home provinces until their deaths. Villa proved particularly difficult to subdue and managed to revitalize his movement during 1916 by invading the United States and creating diplomatic problems for Carranza. Villa mistakenly believed that Carranza had made a secret deal with Washington that would compromise Mexican sovereignty. Villa succeeded in provoking a major diplomatic incident that strengthened his movement, but his actions also gave Carranza the opportunity to showcase his diplomatic skills and nationalist credentials.

THE CONVENTION OF AGUASCALIENTES

After the battle of Zacatecas, which sealed Huerta's demise, Villa and Obregón met to discuss the framework for a possible political settlement. Mutual distrust and Carranza's dubious support of the negotiations, however, poisoned the talks and put both men on edge. The talks took place in Villa's camp. The tough general, famous for his raging temper and violent outbursts, twice lost control and ordered Obregón's execution, only to change his mind at the last minute. Carranza prompted one of the incidents when, in the middle of the talks and without warning, he isolated Villa's army by terminating railroad service between Aguascalientes and Torreón. Obregón emerged from these close encounters with death hating Villa and with a growing distrust of Carranza.[1]

Despite the failure of the Obregón-Villa talks, revolutionary leaders pressed for a peace conference and Carranza reluctantly sanctioned a planning meeting in Mexico City, which he then controlled. The discussions produced frank disagreements among participants, including among Carrancistas, over who should be allowed to attend a proposed peace conference. General Obregón caustically reminded Luis Cabrera, Carranza's brilliant political advisor, that the army had driven Díaz from office only to see civilians collect the spoils and lose power to Huerta. The revolutionary army, Obregón continued, also reflected the sentiments and interests of the common man more accurately than did civilian politicians, an observation that rang true. Obregón's impressive insights, however, probably swayed fewer representatives than did the power of his army. Planners agreed that delegates to the convention would be limited to revolutionary generals and governors, or their representatives. To exclude any last minute converts to the cause, moreover, delegates had to document a revolutionary record antedating the decisive battle of Zacatecas.[2]

The Convention of Aguascalientes, in the minds of the delegates who attended, had the legitimacy and authority to establish a government independent of any revolutionary leader. Villa, Carranza, and Zapata all sent delegations but did not personally attend the meeting. A majority of the 150 delegates considered themselves independents, rather than representatives of a particular leader. Zapata initially refused to send a delegation, and only changed his mind after a visit from the silver-tongued Villista General Felipe Angeles. Presumably Angeles convinced the peasant leader that a convention without Zapatistas, the most important revolutionary movement in the South, would undermine the chances of a national settlement.[3]

The convention format provided delegations with the opportunity to present their proposals within a seemingly democratic setting. Power politics and the threat of violence, however, poisoned much of the discussion. For example, General Pánfilo Natera, ostensibly neutral, had his forces occupy Aguascalientes and guaranteed the security of the delegates. Everyone knew, however, that Natera owed Villa a personal debt for rescuing his army at the battle of Zacatecas, and Villa's own army maintained a menacing presence only a short train ride away.[4]

On the convention floor, however, the Villistas did not dictate the proceedings. Villa's thirty-seven delegates did not outnumber independents, and

FIGURE 31: General Felipe Angeles, Villa's brilliant artillery officer.
In 1915, Angeles advised Villa against marching south and
engaging General Alvaro Obregón.

Source: Friedrich Katz, ed. *Imáges de Pancho Villa* (Mexico City:
Instituto Nacional de Antropología e Historia, 1999), p. 36.

Zapata's twenty-six representatives remained narrowly focused on the
issue of agrarian reform. Some civilian delegates claiming military experience also acquired credentials, which undoubtedly displeased both Villa
and Obregón.[5]

Carranza's machinations to maintain his supreme status as first chief
caused a serious problem. The first chief rightfully concluded that the
assembled delegates would not name him president of a new revolutionary government. Carranza, therefore, insisted that the convention did not
have the authority to declare itself a sovereign body and launched a

vicious press campaign against the proceedings. In response, delegates requested the first chief's resignation. The wily Coahuilan, however, replied that he would comply only if Villa and Zapata also retired. The convention, seeking a compromise solution, removed Carranza as first chief and rescinded Villa's military command. Although Carranza refused to accept this decision, Villa agreed and added (on Angeles's advice) that both he and Carranza should be executed in the interests of peace.[6]

Villa did not face a firing squad, but his bravado and political maneuvering won him allies among the Zapatistas. A critical moment in the proceedings came when Zapatista delegate Antonio Díaz Soto de Gama mounted the rostrum and demanded that the convention accept the Plan de Ayala. Now in his early thirties, Díaz had already passed through several ideological phases, including a phase as a PLM socialist, a moderate reformer (under Madero), an advocate for Mexico City's workers, and finally a champion of agrarian reform and Indian rights.[7] The convention provided a perfect medium for Díaz who, as Robert E. Quirk observes, "knew nothing of the battlefield; his forte was the quintain of parliamentary oratory."[8]

Díaz Soto de Gama proclaimed the Zapatistas the only true revolutionaries and launched into a vitriolic attack on those who would not accept the Plan de Ayala. He took the Mexican flag mounted on the stage, which delegates had signed in solidarity, crumpled it up and threw it to the floor. This rag, he roared, only symbolized the triumph of clerical reaction in 1821. As delegates shouted their disapproval, some reached for their guns and Díaz came close to being shot. Seemingly oblivious to the danger, however, Díaz continued to heap abuse on the audience. He found northerners incapable of understanding natives' aspirations, insulted the respected revolutionary leader Eulalio Gutiérrez, excoriated Carranza, and, for the delegate's edification, provided a rambling summary of world history highlighted by references to Buddha, Marx, and Zapata. The British minister, revealing something of his own character, commented, "[T]he convention at Aguascalientes . . . appears closely to resemble the parliament of monkeys described by Kipling in the *Jungle Book*."[9]

Díaz's tongue-lashing divided the convention further and outraged many delegates, including the powerful Obregón. By making the Plan de Ayala the centerpiece of his presentation, however, Díaz drew attention to the importance of agrarian reform. Roque González Garza, head of the Villista delegation, supported the plan in dramatic fashion. When Obregón questioned González's authority to speak for the Villistas, every Villista delegate at the convention rose in support of the Plan de Ayala. This dramatic gesture foreshadowed a military alliance between Villistas and Zapatistas and demonstrated to Obregón the political centrality of agrarian reform.[10]

Revolutionary independents attempted to bridge the divisions separating the Carrancistas and Villistas. Delegates elected Eulalio Gutiérrez, a well-liked provincial commander who did not have a large army, to serve as provisional president of Mexico. Everyone understood, however, that Gutiérrez was an "accidental president," and that the real power still resided with the biggest armies. Carranza, in a letter to the convention, refused to recognize Gutiérrez and began to mobilize his supporters.[11] Obregón now made a last-minute, self-serving attempt to avert bloodshed. He suggested that Villa and Carranza both renounce any claim to the presidency and leave the country, which would have left Obregón as the most powerful man in Mexico.[12] At this crucial juncture, however, Villa undermined hope of a workable compromise by marching on Mexico City and removing officials appointed by Carranza. Villa and Carranza were on a collision course. Villa did not need Obregón's allegiance to win battles, but Carranza certainly did. Obregón hated Villa for nearly executing him on two occasions, while Obregón merely disliked and distrusted Carranza for his underhanded political machinations. Obregón, whose mother came from the Sonoran elite, may have also felt closer social ties with the first chief. Carranza, moreover, could also offer Obregón something Villa could not: control over his home state of Sonora. On November 19, 1914, Obregón announced in the Mexico City press a formal declaration of war against Villa.[13]

HOSTILITIES

From the end of 1914 until spring 1915, Villa and Carranza worked to expand their political and military bases in preparation for a decisive confrontation. Carranza and Obregón, displaying superior political and organizational skills, developed a clear political strategy centered around nationalism and social reformism calculated to win the support of work-

FIGURE 32: Revolutionary, c. 1915.

Source: Rafael Tovar, ed. *México: una nación persistente: Hugo Brehme fotografías*
(Mexico City: Instituto Nacional de Bellas Artes, 1995), photograph 52, p. 66.

ers, peasants, and the middle classes. Villa remained a charismatic leader committed to distributing land to his soldiers, a position that appealed to peasants and ranchers in the northern provinces, but he failed to articulate a revolutionary platform or style of administration that would allow him to expand his political base in other areas.

As leaders, Villa and Carranza represented social extremes and radically different political backgrounds. Villa emerged from the back roads and mining camps of Durango and Chihuahua and had been in and out trouble with the law for years. Carranza, by contrast, came from the Coahuilan liberal elite and had broken with the old regime only after he had been denied the governorship. Villa retained a regional focus and suffered from lack of political experience and formal education, while Carranza drew on his extensive experience in regional and national politics and learned from the mistakes of Madero, Reyes, and other failed liberal reformers.

FIGURE 33: A young family caught up in the Revolution.

Source: Anita Brenner, *The Wind that Swept Mexico: The History of the Mexican Revolution of 1910–1942*, with 184 historical photographs assembled by George R. Leighton (Austin: University of Texas Press, 1971), photograph 93.

Despite his patrician manners and thinly veiled elitism, Carranza expanded his political base by promising peasants and workers land, higher wages, and a political voice and by unifying Mexicans through a revolutionary nationalism that focused on the condemnation of U.S. imperialism. Carranza also showed his liberal credentials by insisting on a clear separation of church and state, while Villa and Zapata left the church alone. Villa expressed a personal antipathy toward priests, whom he believed exploited poor peasants, but he did not close churches, and instead actually reopened several that had been shut down by

FIGURE 34: A child revolutionary.

Source: Anita Brenner, *The Wind that Swept Mexico: The History of the Mexican Revolution of 1910–1942*, with 184 historical photographs assembled by George R. Leighton (Austin: University of Texas Press, 1971), photograph 95.

Carrancistas. The Zapatistas were more orthodox still, marching into battle with images of the Virgin of Guadalupe sewn on their hats.[14]

By successfully selling a revolutionary agenda with something for everyone, Carranza and Obregón succeeded in swelling the Constitutionalist ranks with peasants, workers, and members of the middle class. Both Constitutionalist and Villista movements, therefore, included Mexicans from similar social and economic backgrounds, despite the yawning class division that separated the opposing leaders.

Following the Convention of Aguascalientes, where he was deposed,

FIGURE 35: Emiliano Zapata and Pancho Villa, pictured here in the center of the photograph, led their troops into Mexico City in 1914.

Source: Rafael Tovar, ed. *México: una nación persistente: Hugo Brehme fotografías* (Mexico City: Instituto Nacional de Bellas Artes, 1995), p. 44.

Carranza fled the capital for Veracruz, taking with him everything of value that his troops could pile onto railroad cars.[15] The Gulf port, only recently evacuated by U.S. troops, provided Carranza with a temporary safe haven as well as a steady source of hard currency from its customs house. Occupation of Veracruz, located just south of Mexico's prosperous oil fields, also provided Carranza with access to petroleum reserves and therefore potential leverage over the big foreign-owned oil companies.

FIGURE 36: Pancho Villa and Emiliano Zapata in the presidential
palace following their ouster of the dictator Victoriano Huerta.
Villa is seated in the president's chair.

Source: Anita Brenner, *The Wind that Swept Mexico: The History of the Mexican
Revolution of 1910–1942,* with 184 historical photographs assembled by
George R. Leighton (Austin: University of Texas Press, 1971), photograph 108.

Carranza could not match Villa's military strength, however, and most
foreign observers believed that the former first chief would be quickly
overwhelmed. Rather than press the advantage afforded by Carranza's
withdrawal to Veracruz, however, Villa wasted valuable time with a cele-
bratory occupation of Mexico City, followed by a series of military
campaigns designed to consolidate his control over the northern
provinces.

Villa's turbulent stay in the capital provided him with the opportunity
to parlay with Zapata and to ignore Eulalio Gutiérrez, whose true status
as a storefront president became obvious to everyone. The meeting
between Villa and Zapata proved awkward and did not produce a clear

FIGURE 37: Emiliano Zapata, seated in the center, with key
advisers before his meeting with Pancho Villa in 1914.

Source: Friedrich Katz, ed. *Imáges de Pancho Villa* (Mexico City:
Instituto Nacional de Antropología e Historia, 1999), p. 50.

military strategy for defeating the Constitutionalists. The two leaders,
despite their mutual concern for the masses, represented dissimilar
movements with distinctive regional characteristics and unclear political
strategies.

According to an observer, Villa and Zapata sat "in an embarrassed
silence, occasionally broken by some insignificant remark, like two country sweethearts." The tension only lifted when the two leaders started
criticizing Carranza, whom Villa called "high and mighty" and Zapata

called "a son of a bitch."[16] Villa promised Zapata artillery, Zapata agreed to occupy Puebla, and they identified two hundred political prisoners to be shot. They did not, however, sign a formal military alliance or fashion a coordinated strategy to defeat the Constitutionalists.

While their leaders deliberated, the two armies of occupation behaved quite differently. Zapata's peasant soldiers "roamed the streets like lost children," refrained from looting and raping, and treated middle-class inhabitants with deference. Zapata himself insisted on staying in a second-class hotel near the railroad station so that he could return home at the drop of a hat. By contrast, the Villistas, who were accustomed to sacking towns, broke into stores and private residences, assaulted women, and shot innocent bystanders.[17]

The Villistas' behavior cost them supporters in the capital, including convention president Eulalio Gutiérrez, who was ignored and humiliated by both Villa and Zapata. After the two revolutionary chiefs had departed, Gutiérrez dismantled Mexico City's waterworks (which further angered residents), resigned the presidency, and linked up with Carranza.[18] The convention's legislature continued to meet in Mexico City, but it had little impact on the subsequent course of the revolution.

The Villistas, having ravaged the capital, now turned north to secure contested provinces and the international border. While these regions, near and dear to Villa's heart, held strategic value and contained valuable natural resources, a quick strike at Carranza and Obregón in Veracruz before they could regroup and rearm would have been a sounder strategy.

Villa's troops fanned out into western, northern, and northeastern Mexico, overwhelming pockets of Constitutionalist resistance. General Felipe Angeles secured most of the border region. Villista troops overran Carranza's home state of Coahuila and gained access to its extensive coal reserves. Other regions, however, proved difficult to subdue. For example, Constitutionalists in Sonora led by Plutarco Elías Calles held out against Villista convert José Maria Maytorena, and Constitutionalist General Manuel Diéguez, the former labor leader from Cananea, fiercely contested control of Jalisco. Villa's most serious setback occurred in the Tampico region, however, when General Tomás Urbina failed to capture the oil fields at El Ebano. Urbina stumbled against General Jacinto Treviño, a recent graduate of the national military academy who used military intelligence gathered from reconnaissance flights to deploy his troops and artillery.[19]

While Villa dispersed his troops across the northern landscape, General Obregón raised and outfitted a new army. Traveling throughout Constitutionalist-held territory in the center-east and center-west, he recruited fresh troops, bolstered morale, and made careful notations of transportation networks and terrain. By January 1915, Obregón was ready to depart Veracruz for Puebla and Mexico City.[20]

The city of Puebla, site of famous battles in Mexican history, had been recently occupied by the Zapatistas without much resistance. However, the Zapatistas felt uncomfortable outside of Morelos and their relationship with Villa had recently deteriorated. Zapata had heard rumors that prominent Villistas, who now included former Madero supporters, considered him a "savage" who would have to be "eliminated." Villa's actions, moreover, lent credence to the rumor. He delayed sending Zapata promised artillery, and news arrived that Paulino Martínez, a prominent Zapatista political advisor, had been assassinated by Villistas. Zapata evacuated Puebla and terminated his alliance with Villa. For the remainder of the revolution, Zapata would let Villa fight the big battles, while he concentrated on maintaining control over his home state of Morelos.[21]

Nothing could now stop Obregón from occupying both Puebla and Mexico City. Although the capital had little military value, its occupation symbolized the Constitutionalist resurgence and allowed Obregón to incorporate Mexico City's workers into his power base. The industrialization of Mexico City during the Porfiriato had created a proletariat eager to improve its working and living conditions, as promised by the rhetoric of revolutionary leaders. Workers had supported Madero, organized mutual aid societies and unions, and launched strikes aimed at winning higher wages and correcting abuses. They did not seek to overthrow the capitalist system. Rather, they aimed to win a more secure niche within the developing economy and changing political landscape and to enjoy upward mobility.

During the Madero presidency, the Casa del Obrero Mundial emerged as a workers' organization dedicated to the promotion of education, unions, and direct action. The Casa, forced underground during Huerta's counterrevolution, reemerged to energize a flurry of organizational and strike activity from 1914–1916.

Pancho Villa had not envisioned Mexico City's proletarians as potential allies, and his marauding troops repelled workers and their families during his infamous occupation. By contrast, General Obregón now pursued pro-labor policies that reaped valuable rewards. When workers struck the Mexican Telegraph and Telephone Company, for example, Obregón allowed strikers to seize control of the firm and assume managerial positions. The general also cultivated the support of the Casa del Obrero Mundial and gave the powerful labor organization confiscated church buildings. These actions earned Obregón the support of thousands of workers and established a precedent for state intervention on labor's behalf. The Casa, through its acceptance of illegally seized church property, also associated itself with the anticlerical policies of the Constitutionalists.

Obregón requested a formal alliance between the Casa del Obrero Mundial and the Constitutionalists. A majority of the Casa's leaders consented, and five thousand union members volunteered for Obregón's army. They soon formed the famous "Red Battalions," which later distinguished themselves in battle.[22]

From Veracruz, Carranza also helped Obregón win recruits by issuing a series of proclamations that promised labor reforms, equitable taxes, and increased state regulation of foreign corporations. Constitutionalist governors, such as Diéguez in Jalisco and de la Huerta in Sonora, also issued similar decrees. These promises, coupled with established policies of anticlericalism and anti-imperialism, created a political platform with widespread appeal.

Obregón and Carranza were accomplished politicians, but popular opinion believed Villa unbeatable on the battlefield. As spring approached, Obregón decided to test the theory. He ordered his army northward into the Bajío region of central Mexico in an attempt to force a decisive military confrontation. General Felipe Angeles advised Villa to let Obregón march farther northward and away from his supply lines in Mexico City and Veracruz. Obregón had observed, however, that it was not in Villa's nature to maintain a defensive position and surrender territory. Villa's pattern of reckless aggression, Obregón believed, was his Achilles' heel.

Against Angeles's advice, Villa ordered his troops southward to halt Obregón's advance. Villa asked Zapata, who had occupied Mexico City following the Constitutionalists' departure, to intercept supply trains leaving Veracruz to supply Obregón's forces. Zapata's subsequent inability to comply allowed fresh supplies and reinforcements to reach the enemy. Obregón's army of six thousand cavalry and five thousand infantry, equipped with eighty-six machine guns and thirteen field pieces, had reached the town of Celaya. Across the agricultural plain at Irapuato, Villa's army of approximately fifteen thousand troops eagerly awaited combat.

During the course of the next four months, clashes between these two armies shaped the outcome of the revolution. Villa should have adopted a more defensive posture and bolstered his supplies of ammunition. However, he succumbed to overconfidence based on his underestimation of Obregón (whom he called "El Perfumado," or the sissy), his string of victories that created an aura of invincibility, and his machismo.

The first battle of Celaya began when Obregón's advance cavalry stumbled into the main body of Villa's army. Obregón's men, badly outnumbered and outfought, beat a hasty retreat to Celaya. Well aware of Villa's confidence in cavalry charges, Obregón shrewdly ordered his army to dig in behind a barrier of irrigation canals that crisscrossed the agricultural plain. The next morning, the Villista cavalry fiercely charged Obregón's entrenched position. These bold attacks by brave vaqueros, however, were not supported by infantry and suffered from poorly aimed supporting artillery fire. By noon the Obregónistas had repulsed thirty separate assaults, and the tide of the battle began to turn. The Villistas had exhausted most of their ammunition, and fallen men and horses littered the battlefield, which made further forays impossible. At this juncture, Obregónista cavalry attacked Villa's exhausted flanks and drove the enemy from the battlefield.

At Celaya Villa lost two thousand men as well as the aura of invincibility. Still, during the next six days, he received a steady stream of reinforcements and ammunition from the North, largely financed with confiscated cattle. At the same time, Obregón welcomed two contingents of Red Battalions from Mexico City as well as fresh troops from Michoacán and supplies from Veracruz. By April 13, Villa's forces numbered twenty thousand men, while Obregón commanded fifteen thousand.

In the renewed battle, both sides employed nearly identical strategies as before with similar results. Obregón's line withstood Villa's cavalry charges and Villa's artillery overshot enemy lines and bombarded the town. Obregón, who anticipated Villa's tactics, had withheld six thousand cavalry and thousands of infantrymen for an afternoon counteroffensive, which successfully pushed Villa from the battlefield. Obregón held little regard for Villa as a strategist and after the battle wired Carranza that "fortunately, Villa [had] directed the battle personally."

Villa, who had suffered his first major defeat, retreated northward and regrouped near the town of León. Fresh troops and supplies arrived daily from the border, and by early May approximately thirty-five thousand men had been assembled. Obregón, his own army replenished with supplies from Veracruz, arrived in the area, ready for battle. Villa had the option of fortifying his position, much like Obregón had done at Celaya, or launching another offensive. Predictably, he chose to attack.

The ensuing battle of León, or Trinidad, lasted more than one month and involved a series of encounters that ultimately decimated the bulk of Villa's army. After an initial clash with Villista cavalry, Obregón retreated and formed a defensive square around the train station at Trinidad. Out on the perimeter, Obregón also concealed hundreds of snipers at strategic positions, who surprised Villa's cavalry with a barrage of rifle and machine-gun fire. According to an eyewitness, a Villista fell every second during the first five minutes.

Successive Villista onslaughts resulted in heavy casualties on both sides and led to a temporary stalemate. Obregón had an end game in mind, however, and Villa did not. If Constitutionalist troops could hold the Hacienda Santa Ana, located at a strategic point along his line, then Obregón would launch a counteroffensive with his best men.

Obregón and his staff, visiting the hacienda to finalize plans, suddenly came under artillery fire. A shell severed Obregón's arm. The general, bleeding profusely and believing the wound fatal, drew his service revolver and attempted to shoot himself. The night before, however, Obregón's adjutant had cleaned the gun and removed the bullets. His men now rushed their commander to the field hospital and the surgeon's table.

Despite the temporary loss of their charismatic leader, Obregón's staff, composed of battle-tested professionals, proceeded with the battle plan.

On June 5, 1915, General Benjamín Hill, Obregón cousin and the second-in-command, ordered the decisive counteroffensive. General Murguía's cavalry rolled back Villa's right flank, while General Diéguez's infantry simultaneously attacked the left. Villa's army broke and ran from the battlefield, leaving behind ten thousand dead, three thousand rifles, three hundred thousand cartridges, twenty machine guns, and six field guns. The Constitutionalists, who lost two thousand men, quickly occupied the important towns of León, Silao, and Guanajuato.

The following month, General Obregón, once again riding at the head of his army, delivered the coup de grace at Aguascalientes. General Villa, still commanding a large and well-equipped army, maintained a well-fortified position that would have been difficult to dislodge. And once again Villa chose to take the offensive and launch a series of predictable cavalry charges against Obregón's carefully planned defenses. Obregón's perimeter withstood the thrusts, and Hill and Murguía's fresh troops forced Villa's exhausted cavalry to retreat. General Villa's golden cavalry, once the most powerful army in Mexico, dispersed and never reassembled at its former strength.[23]

Obregón's brilliant military victories over the legendary Villa virtually assured that the Constitutionalists would govern Mexico. Obregón had displaced Villa as Mexico's greatest warrior and greatly increased his own chances of someday becoming president. The Constitutionalist army now attempted to enforce a peace over war-torn provinces and headstrong revolutionary caudillos.

Leading the list of difficult cases remained the redoubtable Villa. He vanished into Chihuahua's mountains and reverted to guerrilla warfare, hoping to expand his military and political base into neighboring Sonora. Nevertheless, Villa's recent defeats had exhausted his resources, turned his currency into worthless paper, and cost him crucial support at home and abroad. Despite his continuing popular appeal, Villa's troops were reduced to stealing from defenseless villagers and foreigners. New recruits would not enlist without a guaranteed paycheck. Moreover, trusted lieutenants, such as Tomás Urbina, deserted the army and reverted to free-lance banditry, which provoked an outraged Villa to order their executions. By September 1915, many in Villa's inner circle of advisors, including intellectuals and those with upper-class pedigrees, had deserted him.[24]

Villa's comeback hinged on linking up with supporters, particularly with José Maria Maytorena in neighboring Sonora. Through determination and resiliency, Villa managed to reassemble an army of fourteen thousand men and invade Sonora with its vast cattle ranches and prosperous mines. Villa believed that by securing control over two northern provinces (Chihuahua and Sonora) with extensive U.S. investments he would demonstrate that Carranza was incapable of controlling Mexico and force Wilson to reconsider his support of the first chief.[25]

Constitutionalist forces, led by Plutarco Elías Calles, maintained a fortified position at Agua Prieta along the international border. Unknown to Villa, Calles had been reinforced with troops and supplies transported, with the permission of the Wilson administration, through U.S. territory. Villa's frontal attacks failed to dislodge Calles, and the Chihuahuan retreated into the province's interior. Villa, outraged over Wilson's support of Carranza, vented his anger on U.S. citizens and companies. He extorted cash from mine managers at El Tigre and Nacozari and stole nearly 100,000 silver pesos from the Cananea mining company. In the town and environs of Cananea, moreover, Villa's army looted stores, rustled cattle valued at 138,909.54 silver pesos, raped several women, kidnapped two U.S. surgeons, and killed a U.S. mining engineer.

Now resupplied, Villa departed Cananea on November 20, 1915, for the provincial capital of Hermosillo. General Manuel Diéguez, one of Obregón's best commanders, marched north from Jalisco and confronted Villa on the outskirts of town. Diéguez inflicted another defeat on the Villistas, who fought a disorganized retreat across Sonora, losing encounters at Naco and Nogales before slipping into the foothills of western Chihuahua.[26]

Wilson's de facto recognition of Carranza, which isolated Villa, represented a U.S. policy reversal. Previously, State Department officials had perceived Villa as capable of bringing order to Mexico and protecting U.S. business interests. Villa's behavior had seemed to confirm this assessment. He had not condemned the U.S. occupation of Veracruz and had treated the big U.S. mining companies in Chihuahua cautiously. By contrast, Carranza was constantly at loggerheads with U.S. interests. For example, Carranza bitterly opposed the U.S. occupation of Veracruz, refused to cooperate with the U.S.-sponsored Niagara Peace Conference, and annulled the special concessions and tax breaks granted to U.S. firms by Porfirio Díaz.[27] Under the circumstances, Wilson had not rushed to embrace Carranza, but waited until Obregón had crushed Villa before deciding to go with the winner.

The Villista movement appeared dead. Carranza and Obregón offered Villistas a general amnesty that included mustering out pay plus 10 gold pesos. The bulk of the División del Norte, once Mexico's largest army, surrendered. This included 40 generals, 5,046 officers, and 11,128 soldiers. Only a few hundred of Villa's closest followers, mostly members of the elite "El Dorado" cavalry, remained at his side. According to Friedrich Katz, Villa could not sustain a popular following because he had failed to carry out an extensive agrarian reform. A massive transference of land from the rich to the poor would have created a permanent political bond between Villa and Chihuahua's peasantry, similar to the one that Zapata had forged with the villagers of Morelos. Instead, Villa kept Chihuahua's haciendas in tact. They produced cattle that he sold across the border in the United States for the cash he needed to wage war. Villa's army became a professional fighting force whose existence hinged on the payment of regular salaries, rather than loyalty to a charismatic leader with a reform agenda. Once Villa suffered defeat and his economic resources disappeared the majority of his troops went home.[28]

Despite the odds against him, Villa refused to surrender, seek exile, or otherwise go away. He had old scores to settle and believed that many norteños, given the chance, would still favor him over the aristocratic Carranza. Villa now resorted to predatory banditry, including the killing of innocent civilians, to punish his enemies and damage the rapprochement between Wilson and Carranza.

Villa's raiding activities occurred along the international border, a line that had been continuously crossed by revolutionaries to purchase arms and supplies from U.S. merchants, ranchers, and bankers. This contraband trade had contributed to economic prosperity on the U.S. side, but continuous warfare on the Mexican side had resulted in falling agricultural production, livestock depletion, unemployment, and a mass exodus of refugees to the United States. At Cananea, Sonora, for example, 3,000 miners had lost their jobs and many barely "eked out a existence" through hunting, hauling wood, and prospecting. According to the U.S.

consul, some 2,500 men, women, and children were "destitute."[29]

To a certain extent, Mexicans on both sides of the border blamed this on the United States. Many U.S.-owned mines, such as those at Cananea, had shut down, thus causing widespread poverty. Bitterness lingered over the U.S. intervention at Veracruz. Moreover, a group of Mexican Americans in Texas published the Plan de San Diego that called for the return of the southwestern United States to Mexico. Although plan supporters posed no military threat to the United States, they provoked an Anglo backlash that resulted in the slaughter of one hundred innocent Mexican Americans. The lingering antipathy between Mexican Americans and Anglos in Texas contributed to the volatility of the border region.[30]

Francisco Villa directed his anger at the Wilson administration, U.S. citizens residing in Mexico, and former associates who had betrayed him. On January 17, 1916, Villista troops commanded by Pablo López stopped a train near Santa Isabel, Chihuahua, and discovered among the passengers sixteen U.S. mining engineers. López ordered the men shot in cold blood. Although Villa was not present, the crime reflected his emerging anti-Americanism and public opinion blamed him for the incident. That same month Villa pillaged the Hacienda Babicora, owned by U.S. newspaper magnate William Randolph Hearst, whose property Villa had previously spared.[31]

Villa took his anger to another level when his men raided the small border town of Columbus, New Mexico. Villa sought to provoke an international incident that would create political problems for Carranza and Wilson. Felix Sommerfeld, a German spy in Villa's entourage, may have encouraged Villa to invade Columbus to distract the Wilson administration from the European war. Villa was primarily motivated, however, by the mistaken belief that Carranza had signed a secret pact with Wilson that would have ceded northern Mexico to the United States, granted the United States a ninety-nine-year lease over Magdalena Bay, the Isthmus of Tehuantepec, and an unnamed oil region. In exchange, Carranza would receive $500,000,000 and rights to send troops through U.S. territory. Given Carranza's nationalist credentials, the agreement seemed highly implausible. But Villa himself had been offered similar deals by U.S. agents, and his rabid anti-Americanism and hatred of Carranza led him to irrational conclusions.

Despite his flawed logic, Villa's incursion into New Mexico temporarily revived his movement. Wilson's decision to order a punitive expedition into Mexico to capture Villa badly backfired. U.S. troops failed to defeat the Villistas and clashed with the Carrancistas. The intervention increased Villa's popularity, fanned anti-Americanism, and damaged diplomatic relations between Carranza and Wilson.[32]

Villa targeted Columbus, New Mexico, for several reasons. The town was ripe for looting. It had an ample supply of horses, supplies, and money, owing to the presence of a U.S. Army garrison. Villa also held grudges against a local merchant, Sam Rabel, whom Villa believed had cheated him on a business deal, and against the Columbus State Bank, which had informed Villa that his account had been overdrawn. The Villistas killed seventeen U.S. citizens, raped Mrs. J. J. Moore (after killing her husband and baby), and stole horses and supplies.[33] Local residents and troops, however, inflicted heavy losses on the invaders. More than one hundred Villistas died in the fire fight.[34]

Wilson's numerous military interventions in Latin America, including his recent occupation of Veracruz, virtually assured an armed response. Villa presumably had calculated that a U.S. military incursion would disrupt Carranza's rapprochement with Wilson and trigger an anti-U.S. backlash in Mexico that would work in his favor.[35] The crudity of U.S. gunboat diplomacy left little room for political subtlety, which made its practitioners potentially vulnerable to popular leaders like Villa and clever politicians like Carranza, capable of using public opinion to bolster their positions.

Repeated military interventions in Latin America by Wilson and his Republican predecessors conditioned the American public to expect an armed response. The president's advisors warned that to do otherwise would mean losing the upcoming elections as well as respect in Europe. Nevertheless, the Veracruz intervention had demonstrated the complexity of the Mexican situation, and sending green American troops into the unfamiliar mountains and deserts of northern Mexico to battle heavily armed and battle-tested revolutionaries entailed certain risks. Therefore, Wilson sought Carranza's approval before attacking Villa, and U.S. and Mexican diplomats exchanged several communications regarding the matter. Carranza mentioned an 1880s agreement that had given both

FIGURE 38: General "Black Jack" Pershing, pictured here with his troops, was ordered by United States President Woodrow Wilson to invade Mexico and capture Pancho Villa. Villa, who had recently invaded Columbus, New Mexico, feared that Carranza had secretly agreed to cede northern Mexico to the United States.

Source: Anita Brenner, *The Wind that Swept Mexico: The History of the Mexican Revolution of 1910–1942*, with 184 historical photographs assembled by George R. Leighton (Austin: University of Texas Press, 1971), photograph 111.

nations the right to pursue Indians and bandits across their international border. Wilson may have interpreted this as tacit approval for an invasion, which may have been Carranza's intention. However, the Mexican leader stopped short of giving his formal consent, which gave him rights of denial and more maneuverability in case things went wrong.[36]

In March 1916, one week after Villa's raid on Columbus, New Mexico, an expeditionary force of 4,800 men commanded by General

John J. "Black Jack" Pershing entered Mexico with orders to drive the Villistas from the border and capture their leader. Pershing's punitive force eventually grew to 10,000 men and remained in Mexico for nearly a year. The Americans doggedly chased the elusive Villistas around Chihuahua but failed to capture Villa, secure the border, or increase U.S. influence in Mexico.[37]

Pershing believed that he could encircle the enemy and strike quickly, but he soon became frustrated by Villa's evasive tactics. Villa's troops were veterans of guerrilla warfare and knew the terrain intimately. They easily slipped into the mountains of western Chihuahua. Pershing pursued the revolutionaries into the cradle of Villismo, the hilltop villages and isolated ranches of the sierra, where the charismatic leader remained the local hero. In towns like Namiquipa uncooperative locals refused to sell Pershing food, fodder, and information. Pershing's gilded offer of $50,000 for information leading to Villa's capture found no takers, even among impoverished farmhands and callused caudillos.

Pershing's invasion provoked large-scale anti-American demonstrations in Monterrey, Saltillo, Puebla, Mexico City, and Durango.[38] In Cananea, the American mine manager reported that locals "were very bitter toward the American nation and were expressing regret that it seemed to be impossible to draw [the Americans] into a fight; that they, the Mexicans, were bound to have [a fight] even if it should be necessary to attack the Americans on their own soil."[39] The waves of anti-Americanism contributed to a revival of Villismo, and the Villistas regained the offensive and fanned out into neighboring provinces. Pershing, confined to Chihuahua by Wilson's orders, could only watch as Villa's Golden Cavalry swept through Zacatecas, Durango, Coahuila, and parts of Chihuahua, briefly holding Torreón and Chihuahua City. Villa's resurgence caused grave concern within the Carrancista camp, and Carranza now insisted that the Americans leave.

Wilson refused to withdraw U.S. forces, however, until Carranza agreed to several concessions. Pershing would remain in Mexico, Wilson warned, until Carranza promised that foreign lives and property would be protected and a Mixed Claims Commission be formed to compensate American firms and citizens for their property losses. In addition, Wilson wanted Carranza to help the poor and starving and guarantee religious tolerance. These demands clearly violated the stated purpose for Pershing's expedition—capturing Villa—and an outraged Carranza refused to bargain.

With negotiations at an impasse, increased tensions between Wilson and Carranza raised the possibility of a wider conflict. A clash between Americans and Carrancistas near the mining community of Parral, Chihuahua, resulted in the death of two U.S. soldiers and several Mexicans and alarmed both sides. Wilson now ordered Pershing to halt operations and sent General Hugh Scott to the border to confer with General Obregón.

Pancho Villa, undoubtedly pleased with Carranza's problems, attempted to exacerbate the situation by raiding Glenn Springs, Texas, and fleeing across the border with U.S. soldiers in hot pursuit. An alarmed Carranza renewed his insistence that Pershing leave Mexico and warned that any troop movement, except toward the border, would be contested. Carranza also ordered the Carrancista press to savage the United States and stood by while more anti-American demonstrations broke out. General Scott, viewing events from the border, warned Wilson that war could break out between the United States and Mexico, and the president ordered the mobilization of the militia.

As long as Pershing remained in Mexico, the odds favored another bloody clash between Americans and Carrancistas that might ignite a larger war. Neither side wanted this. The potential catalyst occurred at Carrizal, 50 miles south of Ciudad Juárez, when U.S. troops attempted to shoot their way past a Carrancista garrison. Several Americans died, others fell prisoner, and the survivors retreated. Wilson now consented to Carranza's demand and ordered the unconditional withdrawal of U.S. troops from Mexico.

As Pershing marched toward the border, he had little to show for his efforts. The expedition, which had been intended to punish Villa, actually increased Villa's popularity and damaged Washington's relationship with Carranza.

Villistas and Carrancistas continued their struggle for another two years, with Carranza enjoying a major advantage. As de facto head of state, he could collect taxes, receive loans, and pay for fresh supplies and men. Villa, by contrast, was forced to live off a countryside and people

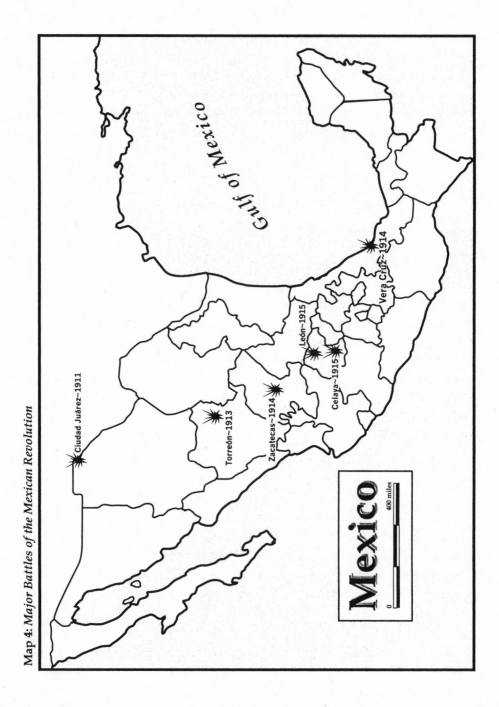

Map 4: *Major Battles of the Mexican Revolution*

Gulf of Mexico

Ciudad Juárez~1911

Torreón~1913

Zacatecas~1914

León~1915

Celaya~1915

Vera Cruz~1914

Mexico

0   400 miles

exhausted from nearly a decade of continuous warfare. Villa's diminished army could no longer sustain an offensive or maintain control over towns and rail centers. As the conflict continued, both sides resorted to wholesale executions of prisoners, and Villa lost key personnel including the invaluable General Felipe Angeles. By 1919, the Villistas began exchanging rifles for ploughs and their great leader returned to the foothills of Chihuahua, never again to challenge for control over Mexico.[40]

CARRANZA IN POWER

AFTER HIS VISIT TO THE CARRANCISTA CAMP IN LATE 1913, the radical American journalist John Reed wrote an unflattering portrait of Don Venustiano Carranza, the first chief of the Constitutionalist movement. Reed, fresh from his hair-raising experiences covering the Villista General Tomás Urbina, and convinced that Villa embodied the concerns of the common Mexican, found Carranza's patrician manners, reticence, and eccentric behavior an unattractive comparison. The first chief, holed up in the border town of Nogales, Sonora, refused to answer Reed's questions and spent most of his time in a cramped hotel room, a setting that to Reed seemed as odd as the first chief himself.

> Carranza rose to meet us, a towering figure, seven feet tall it seemed. I noticed with a kind of shock that in that dark room he wore smoked glasses, and, although ruddy and full-cheeked, I felt that he was not well—the thing you feel about tuberculosis patients. That tiny, dark room, where the first chief of the revolution slept and ate and worked, and from which he hardly ever emerged, seemed too small—like a cell.[1]

Many people underestimated the first chief who never led a cavalry charge and looked like the ex-Porfirian hacendado that he was. But his unhealthy appearance and flowing gray beard belied an inner strength that allowed him to endure long journeys on horseback across northern Mexico, and his odd manner and pretentiousness did not diminish his political and diplomatic skills. Alvaro Obregón may have won the major battles for the Constitutionalists, but Venustiano Carranza held the political reins and organized the first postrevolutionary government.

By the end of 1916, the Constitutionalist movement had grown to include revolutionaries of diverse social origins and political programs, all eager to be associated with the winning side. They included Maderista congressmen *(renovadores)* who did not resign following Madero's assassination, soldiers and labor leaders more loyal to Obregón than Carranza, and local leaders primarily concerned with personal and regional agendas. None of these groups could afford to ignore the inequalities that had compelled their countrymen to rebel, and the Constitutionalist leadership wanted to consolidate its victory by returning to civilian rule and constitutional government.

Political consolidation with legitimacy required, in Carranza's mind, writing a new constitution and holding elections. Carranza's decree of September 14, 1916, authorized the selection of delegates to a constitutional convention. Municipal, state, and national elections followed throughout the next several months.[2]

Political consolidation also involved, according to revolutionary realpolitik, eliminating old rivals at the point of a gun or with an attractive bribe. General Pablo González, who had difficulty winning battles, managed to assassinate Emiliano Zapata, and Carranza dispatched troops to the Yucatán, with its history of political independence and henequen wealth, to bring the province more firmly into the Constitutionalist camp.

Throughout his years in power—1916 to 1920—Venustiano Carranza made a series of policy decisions, few uniformly in compliance with the new constitution, which helped shape the future direction of the Mexican state. Carranza's economic nationalism resulted in new limitations placed on foreign ownership of property, the abolition of special concessions granted to overseas firms, and an increase in business taxes. Nevertheless, Carranza, the die-hard liberal and former hacendado, opposed an extensive agrarian reform and had an uneasy relationship with organized labor. These departures from the revolutionary credo, as codified in the new constitution, created opportunities for Carranza's rivals within the Constitutionalist leadership, particularly General Obregón and his Sonoran allies, to increase their popular base by promising Mexicans more than they would ever deliver.

THE CONSTITUTIONAL CONVENTION

When Carranza issued his decree calling for the election of delegates to write a new constitution, the country lay exhausted from years of continuous warfare, and most Mexicans expressed more concern over finding their next meal than with writing a new constitution. Voter turnout was also limited by continued fighting, especially in Morelos and Chihuahua, and by Carranza's refusal to allow his opponents to stand for election. As a result, voter turnout did not exceed 30 percent, a weak endorsement of the new political process.

The final list of convention delegates reflected the political heterogeneity of the Constitutionalist movement as well as the middle-class origins of its national leadership. In contrast to the Convention of Aguascalientes, which had been dominated by army leaders, only 30 percent of the 220 delegates held military rank. An estimated 85 percent of the delegates were white-collar professionals, including sixty-two lawyers, eighteen teachers, sixteen engineers, sixteen physicians, and fourteen journalists.[3]

Carranza presented delegates with a draft for a new constitution written by moderates, including prominent renovadores. The document recommended various political, electoral, and judicial reforms, while reiterating many of the basic principles embodied in the liberal Constitution of 1857, such as separation of church and state. Notably absent, however, were articles specifying agrarian and labor reform. When the constitutional convention convened on September 14, 1916, in the provincial capital of Querétaro, Carranza addressed delegates, urging them to adopt his recommendations and imposing a deadline of February 1, 1917, for completion of their work. By insisting on this time frame, the first chief restricted the opportunity for debate and increased the odds the convention would rubber-stamp his draft constitution.

From the beginning of the deliberations, however, serious political and philosophical differences divided delegates and virtually assured spirited exchanges. According to E. V. Niemeyer, who has written the most comprehensive study of the proceedings, two discernible factions, each composed of fifty to sixty delegates, can be identified. Moderate liberals, or *liberales carrancistas,* held mildly anticlerical views, believed in individual rights, and wanted to preserve the spirit of the Constitution of 1857. This group, which included the renovadores, supported Carranza's draft constitution. The other group, the progressive liberals, or *jacobinos,* were staunchly anticlerical, advocated state intervention to correct social and economic inequalities, and stressed societal rights over individual liberties. This faction was loosely associated with General Obregón. Obregón did not, however, orchestrate their activities and was otherwise occupied running the Ministry of War. Francisco Múgica and Pastor Rouaix emerged as the jacobinos' most effective floor leaders. They shepherded through historic articles on church-state relations, property rights, and labor reform.[4]

Convention organizers, all Carranza loyalists, attempted to speed up the decision-making process by constituting small committees charged with considering key reforms. Although intended to facilitate ratification of Carranza's draft, articulate leftists frequently succeeded in getting their versions of key articles through committee and onto the convention floor.

Church-state relations stood at the heart of the reordering of Mexican society and successful implementation of a new political order. Both liberals and progressives favored restricting the activities of the Catholic Church, and Carranza's draft recommended secular education and government regulation of ecclesiastical affairs. For jacobinos, however, this did not go far enough. The church represented conservatism and colonial privilege, and it had supported Victoriano Huerta's counterrevolution. Moreover, the church's pervasive influence, based on its monopoly over religion and education for three centuries, gave it the power to challenge revolutionary initiatives. The new constitution represented an opportunity to codify state control over the church and assure preservation of the new revolutionary order.

Bitter disagreements divided delegates before they finally settled on wide-ranging ecclesiastical reforms that approached anticlericalism. Among other things, Article 130 gave the federal government the power to intervene in religious affairs, stripped religious organizations of judicial rights, allowed state legislatures to set the number of priests within their jurisdictions, prohibited clergy from criticizing the government, declared marriage a civil ceremony, and restricted resident clergy to native-born Mexicans. These provisions represented the harshest attack on the Catholic Church since the mid-nineteenth century and set the stage for future conflict between church and state.

Debate over property rights, especially agrarian reform and the national patrimony, resulted in equally radical reforms. Carranza's draft, which followed the 1857 Constitution, empowered the federal government to confiscate private property in the interest of the general public. Liberal presidents from Juárez to Díaz, however, had not used this authority to help the landless. Rather, they had used it to take land from Indian communities and the church and sell it to their supporters.

Progressives now argued that the state should take land from hacendados, the pillars of the old regime, and redistribute it to the landless foot soldiers of the revolution. Jacobinos also reasoned that the revolutionary state, in the tradition of the Spanish Crown, should retain ownership of subsoil rights and safeguard the national patrimony. Mineral and petroleum reserves constituted the principal sources of national wealth and powerful foreign corporations controlled these sectors of the economy. Progressives argued that government should redefine the terms for exploiting natural resources and gain more leverage over foreign capital in the process. These proposals, subsequently embodied in Article 27 of the new constitution, empowered government to redress social and economic inequities and laid a building block in the foundation of the leviathan state.

The Constitutionalists had cultivated working-class support throughout the revolution, and the specific concerns of the proletariat could not be ignored in the writing of the new constitution. Although Carranza's draft said little about labor reform, he recommended legislative approval of his progressive 1915 Labor Code. Carranza's closest supporters, realizing that jacobinos would not settle for legislative promises, took the initiative and recommended putting pro-labor reforms directly into the constitution.

Article 123, which closely followed Carranza's 1915 Labor Code, proclaimed the state's right to intervene on workers' behalf. The article guaranteed workers' rights to sanitary working conditions, one day of rest per week, a just wage, workmen's compensation, and social welfare for the ill, crippled, and homeless. The article also endorsed boards of conciliation and arbitration to negotiate labor disputes and recognized the rights of workers to strike as long as they refrained from violence. The constitution also condemned debt peonage, which bound penniless peons to estates, and advocated the cancellation of their debts. In effect, Article 123 empowered the government to help workers achieve a reasonable living with dignity in an economic environment that had been traditionally dominated by capital.

The constitutional convention, despite the significant splits it revealed among the Constitutionalists, produced a progressive document that empowered the revolutionary state to carry out meaningful reforms potentially beneficial to the majority of Mexicans. Revolutionary leaders still faced the challenge of creating the political and bureaucratic infrastructure required to enforce the constitution, as well as mustering the political courage to make socioeconomic reform the nation's first priority.

SETTLING OLD SCORES

The Constitutionalists' commitment to peasants and workers, it should be stressed, only extended to their political supporters. In February 1917, when Carranza signed the new document, Zapatistas and Villistas still roamed the mountains and valleys of Morelos and Chihuahua and some peripheral regions remained politically insecure. The Constitutionalist leadership, despite their recent proclamations on the rights of man, remained revolutionary pragmatists determined to eliminate, exile, or co-opt the opposition.

Emiliano Zapata, the peasant leader from Morelos, remained a thorn in Carranza's side despite having been driven into hiding on more than one occasion. The proximity of Morelos to Mexico City, Zapata's enduring popularity, and the power of his "land and liberty" message made him difficult to ignore. Following his recent military setbacks, Zapata devoted increasing attention to forging alliances with revolutionary chiefs outside of the Constitutionalist circle. For example, when General Obregón resigned from Carranza's cabinet following the constitutional convention,

Zapata encouraged him to rebel against the first chief. Zapata also instructed his chief political advisor, Gildardo Magaña, to enter into discussions with the exiled Maderista Vásquez Gómez brothers and more tentatively with supporters of Félix Díaz.[5] The fact that Zapata, the champion of agrarian reform, would contemplate political alliances with conservatives and counterrevolutionaries shows his willingness to compromise ideological purity for realpolitik and perhaps his realization that he could not survive in isolation.

In September 1917, Zapata's "Manifesto to the Nation" denounced both the Carrancistas and the Felicistas, and reaffirmed his commitment to the Plan de Ayala. Carranza responded by ordering Pablo González, a general with presidential ambitions, to invade Morelos and to crush Zapata once and for all. González benefited from the outbreak of Spanish influenza that swept through Morelos and decimated villagers weakened by constant warfare, food shortages, and inadequate health care. The Zapatista leadership, recognizing that its ragtag army was no match for González's 11,000 northerners, retreated into mountain hideaways, while their soldiers blended into the village population.[6]

The Zapatistas, who had always stood together, now began to suffer internal divisions. Zapata's brother Eufemio, known for his drunken outbursts, beat a fellow villager, who later returned with a gun and killed him. When they needed allies the most, Zapatistas, placing personal animus over political expediency, shot prominent Tlaxcalan agrarian leader Domingo Arenas. Zapata displayed Arenas's body like a trophy. Zapatismo also lost some of its thunder with the passage of Article 27, which promised land reform and returned subsoil ownership to the nation. People understood that the Constitutionalists had the political and military power to enforce reforms and the Zapatistas did not.[7]

According to John Womack, Carranza wanted Zapata dead because the peasant leader represented a "moral challenge" to his authority. But Zapata also represented a lingering political threat. His negotiations with conservatives had culminated in recognition of Francisco Vásquez-Gómez as provisional head of the revolutionary state, and a broadly based coalition of anti-Constitutionalist movements remained a possibility. The Constitutionalists had also invested considerable men and supplies in an effort to crush Zapata, who now appeared particularly vulnerable.

Although General González had difficulty winning battles, his political acumen gained him a foothold in the inner circle of the Constitutionalist leadership. If he could not defeat Zapata in a fight, perhaps he could arrange his assassination. A golden opportunity presented itself in the form of Colonel Jesús Guajardo. The colonel, who years earlier had overseen the massacre of five hundred unarmed Zapatista villagers, had been recently arrested by González for disobeying orders. Zapata secretly wrote Guajardo and invited him to join his cause. González intercepted the letter and accused Guajardo of treason. The price of forgiveness was Zapata's life.

Following González's instructions, Guajardo agreed to negotiate with Zapata. He sweetened the deal by offering to deliver men and supplies. The possibility of a trap occurred to Zapata, who had himself plotted some ambushes. Fearing betrayal, he took along 150 men. After some false starts, the meeting took place on a hacienda near Zapata's home village of Anenecuilco. While most of Zapata's men lay resting under shade trees along side the road, their leader approached the main house where Guajardo awaited him. Two lines of Guajardo's soldiers outside of the building saluted Zapata with rifle volleys aimed skyward. They then leveled their weapons and murdered the local hero.[8] Carranza's assassination of Zapata eliminated a troublesome rival. Zapata's dedication to agrarian reform, however, secured him a place in the future pantheon of revolutionary gods whose programs and sacrifices would remind Mexicans of why their forefathers had rebelled.

SONORANS IN THE YUCATÁN

Despite Zapata's assassination, several political problems continued to plague the first chief. Important ideological differences divided revolutionaries, as illustrated by the heated deliberations of the constitutional convention. Moreover, an increasingly independent General Obregón represented a major challenge to Carranza's authority, and the loyalty of provincial revolutionary leaders frequently hinged on who could offer them the best deal.

The Yucatán, which had attempted to form an independent state in 1849, resurfaced as a trouble spot for Carranza. Yucatecan elites had lived like feudal lords on their henequen plantations during the Porfiriato, and talk of agrarian reform, social justice, and economic nationalism threatened everything they prized.

The breaking point came in January 1915, when Carranza ordered Yucatecan planters and merchants to loan him a large sum of money for the Constitutionalist cause. Ex-Huertista Colonel Abel Ortiz Argumedo, urged on by alarmed elites, overthrew the Constitutionalist governor, declared an independent state, and asked the United States for money, arms, and protectorate status.

The first chief immediately ordered General Salvador Alvarado, a talented military commander from Sonora, to invade the Yucatán and bring the province back into the Constitutionalist fold. Alvarado and his seven thousand battle-tested northerners quickly overpowered the poorly led Yucatecans and occupied the peninsula with the intention of using the province as a revolutionary laboratory.

Alvarado's program mirrored reforms supported by progressives at the Constitutionalist convention, and the application of his policies demonstrated a skillful use of both patronage and force. Alvarado mobilized popular support and forged cross-class coalitions for the Constitutionalist cause by associating labor and agrarian reforms with his personal patronage and the revolutionary government. His policies and tactics anticipated those of fellow Sonorans and future presidents Alvaro Obregón and Plutarco Elías Calles.

Following his military victory, General Alvarado focused on consolidating Constitutionalist political control and pursuing economic and social reforms. Although he punished the coup organizers and removed thirty-seven Porfirian-era officials, he did not arrest planters and merchants among the conspirators since they were needed to maintain the export economy. Alvarado, who served both as governor of Yucatán and military commander of the Southeast, founded the Partido Socialista de Yucatán to make political appointments and dispense patronage and Ligas de Resistencia to mobilize and control the local peasantry.

The general's dismantling of the henequen marketing agreement between Olegario Molina and International Harvester, forged during the Porfiriato, represented his greatest success. Alvarado literally forced planters to sell their henequen to the government-operated marketing agency (the Reguladora), which gained him a near monopoly over henequen sales. Wartime prices on the world market soared 400 percent between 1915 and 1918, thus netting the Reguladora record profits and giving Alvarado the money he needed to placate planters (who received 42 percent of the earnings, or $81,900,569), finance local reforms, and support the Constitutionalist war effort in the North.

Alvarado's vision for the Yucatán included freeing Maya laborers from their bondage on the henequen plantations and mobilizing worker support for the revolution through the creation of government-controlled unions. His programs had mixed results. Although the general announced the Constitutionalist decree abolishing debt peonage, not much change resulted. Maya laborers had few alternative means of employment, planters continued to manage their own estates, and Alvarado rejected aggressive government intervention that would have disrupted production and jeopardized henequen revenues. The general's decision to import 21,000 contract laborers from central Mexico underscores the limits of his reforming zeal. These outsiders were forcibly recruited from urban areas and suffered greatly not only because of the Yucatán's harsh climate but also from back-breaking work and stern vigilance of foremen and planters accustomed to abusing Maya laborers.

Alvarado's advocacy of local urban workers, by contrast, resulted in the creation of government-sponsored unions and special tribunals designed to adjudicate labor disputes. These organizations gave workers bargaining rights and a political voice that had been denied them during the Porfiriato. Alvarado's support of workers' rights, however, hinged on the formal linkage of organized labor to the new regime. He opposed independent trade unions and the workers' right to strike. Nongovernmental unions might serve as potential breeding grounds for oppositionist political activity, and strikes threatened to decrease production, reduce state revenues, and disrupt the revolutionary order.

Alvarado shared with other Constitutionalist leaders a vision of a modern, secular Mexico purged of vices rooted in popular culture and Catholicism. Alvarado's views reflected his Sonoran background, where the church was weak and U.S. cultural influences were strong, as well as his antipathy to the old regime and traditional Mexico. The general's commitment to public education stemmed from his opposition to parochial education and from his admiration of the North American experience. Alvarado invested henequen profits in the construction of one thousand public schools and one hundred municipal libraries and—in a daring display of avant-garde values—sponsored Mexico's first feminist congress.

Alvarado went too far, however, when he attempted to stamp out popular diversions and vices that offended his Sonoran Puritanism. Stiffer penalties for public drunkenness, gambling, and prostitution only succeeded in upsetting practitioners whose habits did not change. Moreover, Alvarado's attempts to stop blood sports, such as cock fighting and bull fighting, were unpopular among the masses.

General Alvarado also offended local cultural and religious sensibilities when he authorized overt attacks on the Catholic Church. His orders to exile priests, close churches, confiscate church property, and desecrate altars, outraged Yucatecans of all social classes and gave planters an issue to use against him.

Alvarado's advocacy of land reform increasingly alarmed planters. The general's program, modeled after the Sonoran experience, favored giving landless Maya small plots of land to farm independently and opposed dismantling the prosperous henequen estates and transforming them into communal units. To force the issue, Alvarado advocated leveling a stiff tax on idle land along the lines suggested by economist Henry George.

Alvarado's model for agrarian reform, in theory at least, would have freed many Maya from their economic dependence on the plantations, without disrupting henequen production and reducing revenues. This comparatively cautious program went too far for President Carranza, however, who would not allow Alvarado to redistribute land. The first chief opposed agrarian reform as an unnecessary disruption of the social and economic order. General Alvarado, by contrast, viewed land reform as a vehicle for social and economic mobility and as a means of forging cross-class coalitions under the patronage of the revolutionary state.

Carranza's veto of Alvarado's agrarian reform also reflected divisions within the hierarchy of the Constitutionalist movement. General Alvarado's impressive record and Sonoran background made him a potential political rival and likely supporter of General Obregón. Nonetheless, as long as henequen revenues kept pouring into Mexico City, President Carranza could not risk removing Alvarado. With the termination of the

First World War, however, commodities prices returned to prewar levels and profits plummeted. During 1919, the price of henequen on the world market dropped from 44 cents to 13.2 cents per kilogram, and the earnings of the Reguladora fell from $91,000,000 to $37,000,000. Yucatán was no longer Carranza's milch cow, and the first chief could risk recalling Alvarado to Mexico City and saddling him with a desk job where he could more easily be watched.

Alvarado's reforms, however, had a lasting impact on the political consciousness of peasants and workers. The Ligas de Resistencia and Alvarado's Socialist Party provided the foundation for a grassroots political movement led by Felipe Carrillo Puerto, an agrarian socialist who defiantly opposed efforts to roll back reforms. Alarmed planters organized the Asociación de Hacendados Henequeneros and launched a propaganda campaign aimed at blaming Yucatán's economic problems on the Reguladora rather than the postwar slump and portraying Carrillo Puerto as a dangerous political extremist. The federal government sold Yucatán's merchant fleet and ordered the army to disband the Ligas. When a defiant Carrillo Puerto backed General Obregón for president in 1920, an outraged Carranza closed down the Socialist Party and forced its leader into exile. The State Congress soon shut down the Reguladora, and planters signed new contracts with U.S. cordage companies that resembled prerevolutionary arrangements.[9]

CARRANZA AND THE PETROLEUM COMPANIES

The petroleum industry, which was directly owned and managed by powerful U.S. and British interests, presented Carranza with complex diplomatic, political, and economic problems that could not be solved through the type of military intervention used in the Yucatán.[10] The big oil companies, enticed and fortified by concessions, tax exemptions, and long-term leases granted during the Porfiriato, had invested millions of dollars in developing wells, storage facilities, pipelines, and transportation networks. The outbreak of the First World War, which dramatically increased demand for petroleum and sent prices skyrocketing, coincided with discoveries of massive reserves that transformed Mexico into the world's second leading oil producer.

Beginning with Francisco Madero, Mexican political leaders increased taxes on petroleum exports, demanded extraordinary contributions from producers, and charged them more for leases. The highly controversial Article 27 of the Constitution of 1917 denied companies ownership of subsoil products, which, if taken to its logical application, would have forced a reconfiguration of the industry at considerable disadvantage to the private sector. The immense amounts of money involved in investments and future profits, as well as the enormous political and economic influence petroleum transnationals commanded during wartime, made implementation of Article 27, as well as the enforcement of higher petroleum taxes, equivalent to pulling wisdom teeth. During Carranza's administration, Gulf Coast strongman Manuel Peláez prevented Constitutionalist forces from consolidating military and political control over the region. He took money from petroleum producers and prevented implementation of government policies that they opposed.

The petroleum industry's defiance of state authority began during Madero's presidency. Oil companies opposed his attempts to increase their taxes in 1911 and 1912 by lobbying Mexican congressmen and publishing pamphlets predicting the demise of the industry. Madero backed down and accepted the transnationals' counteroffer of one-third the proposed tax increase.

General Huerta had enjoyed the support of foreign businessmen, particularly British oil magnate Lord Cowdray, who propped up the dictatorship by underwriting a loan from French banks negotiated by former Díaz treasury minister José Ives Limantour. As Huerta came under intense attack, however, he desperately needed additional revenues to purchase arms and buttress his political support. Huerta levied a $400,000 exaction on Edward Doheny's Huasteca Corporation and issued a 10 percent tax increase on all producers. On the advice of the State Department, Doheny never paid his fine. British and U.S. companies protested the general tax hikes to their governments, which prompted an outraged Huerta to threaten nationalization of the petroleum industry.

The oil companies simultaneously suffered and benefited from Mexico's growing civil conflict. A weakened Huerta could not consistently collect the higher taxes, nor could he follow through with his nationalization threat. By contrast, revolutionaries carrying out military operations near the oil fields rarely missed the opportunity to extort money from petroleum producers. Companies complained bitterly about forced loans, capricious taxation, stolen property, disruption of transportation networks, and the killing of their employees. During the revolution, for instance, 168 Americans died in the Tampico oil district alone. It is unclear, however, if revolutionaries had targeted them as hated representatives of foreign firms, or if, like so many others, they were simply victims of indiscriminate violence.

Carranza raised petroleum taxes and created a petro-bureaucracy to enforce government regulations. The first chief extracted money from the transnationals, and Veracruz's state government annulled land concessions granted to Lord Cowdray in 1906. Nevertheless, Carranza's attempt to hike export taxes by 10 percent failed to stick and the oil companies, through lobbying in Mexico and abroad, succeeded in derailing legislation designed to increase government authority over the industry.

Experienced oilmen such as Doheny and Cowdray pressured their governments to take strong stands against Carranza's policies. Britain protested Carranza's petroleum decrees and refused to recognize his government. The outbreak of World War I diverted British attention away from Mexico and increased the importance of U.S. policy in the region. The Wilson administration also protested new exactions on foreign oil interests, and Republican Senator Albert B. Fall, Dohney's close associate, recommended military intervention. Wilson refused to land the marines to rescue big business, however, which increased the importance of internal Mexican politics.[11]

Carranza's failure to consolidate military and political control over the oil fields decisively limited his ability to enforce his policies. Manuel Peláez, a local hacendado and former Huertista, opposed implementation of Article 27 and successfully fended off several ineffective Constitutionalist generals. According to Jonathan C. Brown, Peláez represents the "serrano" rebel, described by Alan Knight, who took up arms to defend his home ground against outside intruders, in this case the Constitutionalists. Peláez also extorted money from the petroleum companies, which considered him a menace. As a result, he should be viewed neither as their protector nor lackey. Nevertheless, Peláez's actions undermined implementation of Carranza's nationalist policies. This helped the oil companies—the ultimate outsiders—maintain their privileged status and reap record profits. Carranza's 1920 decision to grant the petroleum giants provisional drilling permits represented a victory for the multinationals and underscored the president's financial and political problems.

CARRANZA AND THE COPPER COMPANIES

Powerful overseas corporations also owned and operated Mexico's biggest copper mines and processing facilities, and they resisted enforcement of Constitutionalist decrees that threatened their profits and autonomy. In contrast to the petroleum industry, however, the copper companies did not enjoy the support of a regional strongman. The Constitutionalists' political and military control over Sonora, one of Mexico's primary mining regions, gave them the leverage they needed to enforce revolutionary policies.

The Sonoran revolutionaries, led by future presidents Plutarco Elías Calles and Adolfo de la Huerta, attempted to impose greater government regulation over the regional economy and to bring miners into their political movement. The process required negotiations with entrenched transnationals, militant labor leaders, and progressive municipal officials.

Beginning in March 1915, Carranza issued a series of decrees designed to recast national policy toward foreign capital and mine owners. The first chief increased taxes on mineral exports, raised corporate property taxes, abolished company stores, and established worker tribunals to adjudicate labor disputes. Governor Calles also annulled state and municipal tax exemptions granted to copper companies during the Porfiriato. An intense lobbying campaign against these reforms by Sonora's biggest transnational, the Cananea Consolidated Copper Company, only netted a three-month extension to pay overdue federal taxes.[12]

Copper company executives' unsuccessful attempts to reverse revolutionary policies forced them to turn to Washington for help. They had little confidence, however, that President Wilson would stand up to Carranza on their behalf. In the words of Delbert J. Haff, who represented Cananea and other U.S. corporate interests in Mexico, "You know Mr. Wilson well enough to know, I should think, that we will crawl out some way and that there is no use in our thinking about danger from intervention. He will take anything. He has always done what Carranza told him to do and he will continue to do it."[13] Haff concluded that payment of the new tax schedule would at least buy the company some security against further depredations.[14]

The stakes increased with Carranza's September 1916 decree that threatened to confiscate mines operating at less than full capacity. Representatives from forty-five mining companies operating in Mexico, including Cananea, ASARCO, and Phelps-Dodge, wrote an indictment against Mexico and requested more help from Washington. The companies demanded compensation for illegal taxation, deaths and injuries suffered by employees, loss of equipment and supplies, and reduced profits. Cananea alone claimed payment of $1,621,042.15 in illegal taxes. The companies wanted Wilson's help in securing a return to prerevolutionary tax schedules and compensation for losses. They also sought a diplomatic protest and privately hoped for armed intervention.[15]

Woodrow Wilson, unlike his predecessor William Howard Taft, refused to invade Latin American nations simply to preserve the privileged status of U.S. companies. However, Wilson was not unsympathetic to the plight of U.S. corporations and citizens abroad, and he attempted to link the withdrawal of Pershing's forces to compensation for U.S. firms operating in Mexico. Carranza refused to negotiate on this point and left the mining companies empty-handed.[16]

In addition to their higher taxes, U.S. copper companies complained bitterly about the Constitutionalists' pro-labor policies. Sonoran revolutionaries wanted to incorporate miners into their political movement. Adolfo de la Huerta, as provisional governor, openly courted miners' support. He proclaimed that the "unjust distribution of profits by producing enterprises" had been "one of the principal causes of the revolution," and the government sought the "redemption of the working classes." With the Constitutionalist victory, de la Huerta asserted, workers enjoyed the benevolent protection of the state and should forego strikes that disrupted production and the political order. As de la Huerta put it:

That inasmuch as the triumph of the Social Revolution, headed by Citizen Venustiano Carranza, has brought about the accomplished fact that the proletariat problem has now become one under the State's control, the working man should not, under the present order of things, have recourse any more to the system of strikes, which, since the Constitutionalist Party is the genuine representative of the working men and the supporter of their just demands, becomes unnecessary.[17]

The governor signed a flurry of decrees that seemingly gave substance to his rhetoric. In addition to creating labor councils, the governor decreed an eight-hour workday, a minimum wage, standardized work contracts, restrictions on the use of child labor, and workers' compensation. These reforms and others were subsequently incorporated into the new national constitution.[18]

In May and June 1917 miners at Cananea and El Tigre, emboldened by de la Huerta's policies, struck against the copper companies to force compliance with the new labor laws. Governor de la Huerta and General Calles supported the strikers, but they were unable to force the copper companies to negotiate. Cananea, now owned by industry giant Anaconda Corporation, closed down operations for six months, depriving the government of desperately needed tax revenues and pushing miners and their families to the brink of starvation.

During these conflicts, de la Huerta and Calles exhibited different tolerance levels and negotiating styles. De la Huerta talked with both sides and did not force a settlement. Calles, by contrast, lost patience with strikers at El Tigre and personally negotiated a contract that compromised most of their demands. Calles also deported Industrial Workers of the World (IWW) organizers who were attempting to form a union at Nacozari. The general was also implicated in the assassination of labor activist Lázaro Gutiérrez de Lara. Calles would not tolerate independent labor organizers, particularly those affiliated with international organizations, because they could not be easily incorporated into the Constitutionalist movement. Calles had a similar problem with the Yaqui Indians. Their refusal to submit to the pax revolucionaria resulted in ruthless military campaigns against them in 1916 and 1919.[19]

Homegrown radicals in Sonora's mining towns also fit uncomfortably under the Constitutionalists' unfolding political umbrella. Local unions and progressive municipal politicians clashed with the mining companies, and their confrontational style and rhetoric complicated relations between company managers and Constitutionalist leaders. At Cananea, for example, the Unión Industrial de Trabajadores Asalariados de Cananea wanted miners to "destroy the bourgeoisie . . . , become owners of the integral product of [their] own labor . . . , and achieve the emancipation of the proletariat."[20] Labor leaders emerging from the radical union movement managed to capture Cananea's municipal presidency. The 1919 election of Julián S. González, the Socialist Workers' Party candidate, drew special attention. As editor of the radical newspapers *El Tiempo* and *Revolución,* González had been an outspoken critic of wartime profiteering and an avid union supporter.[21]

Following his election, González supported miners in a major conflict with management over worker dismissals and reassignments in the workplace. At public meetings, labor leaders read aloud from the new constitution, and each reference to workers' newly won rights drew shouts and thunderous applause of approval from the audience. Governor de la Huerta attempted to defuse the situation by personally negotiating behind the scenes with company managers, who still attempted to cling to their traditional control over the workplace and the community. They privately admitted, however, that they no longer had the power to eliminate municipal officials, shut down the press, imprison labor leaders, and run the town.[22] The revolution had changed power relationships and political consciousness, and foreign corporations would have to adjust.

THE 1920 PRESIDENTIAL SUCCESSION CRISIS

The revolution had unleashed a torrent of grievances from workers and peasants, and the new constitution provided a blueprint for redress and reconstruction. Part of the political formula for change reflected concern over the potential for another dictatorship by mandating that an incumbent president could not succeed himself in office. Like many powerful politicians, however, President Venustiano Carranza did not relinquish power easily. The first chief may have quelled rebellious Yucatecans and scored victories over foreign corporations and imperial powers, but he had failed to eliminate powerful rivals within the Constitutionalist movement and to resolve the ideological differences that separated them.

General Alvaro Obregón, whose spectacular victories over Pancho Villa in 1915 secured the Constitutionalist ascendancy, waited in the wings. Signs of Obregón's presidential ambitions had emerged during the Convention of Aguascalientes, and his relationship with Carranza remained somewhat strained throughout the campaign against Villa. Moreover, Obregón's association with the progressives during the constitutional convention widened his breach with the first chief. His resignation as Carranza's secretary of war in 1917 ended their political association.

Obregón broadened his horizons and gained international exposure by traveling to Cuba, Canada, and the United States, where he had an interview with President Wilson. The general also retained his extensive personal and political connections within Mexico and benefited from instant name recognition as the nation's most famous war hero. While Carranza became entangled in the incomplete process of political consolidation, Obregón remained above the infighting and corruption. He announced his presidential candidacy on June 1, 1919.[23]

The presidential race did not hinge on votes but on the support of powerful politicians and generals. President Carranza handpicked Ignacio Bonillas as his candidate. This MIT-educated ambassador to the United States had a close association with the first chief, who believed Bonillas's superior education and pedigree made him presidential material. Bonillas's election, however, depended on Carranza's ability to line up support among the caudillos. In terms of realpolitik, the contest pitted the first chief against Obregón.

Alvaro Obregón amassed political support as if preparing an impregnable defense against an anticipated offensive. Supporters included Luis Morones, the head of the Confederación Regional de Obreros Mexicanos, prominent politician-intellectual José Vasconcelos, and influential politicians and generals who had fallen out with Carranza.

The first chief stubbornly refused to accept Obregón's inevitable victory and attempted to undermine the general's power base in Sonora. He made political overtures to General Calles, sent federal troops into the province, and refused to ratify the peace treaty negotiated by Governor de la Huerta with the Yaquis. These strong-arm tactics failed, however, and the contentious Sonorans issued the Plan de Agua Prieta, calling for the

FIGURE 39: President Carranza's funeral, 1920. Carranza lost out in a power struggle with General Obregón and was assassinated by troops loyal to Félix Díaz while attempting to flee to Veracruz.

Source: Anita Brenner, *The Wind that Swept Mexico: The History of the Mexican Revolution of 1910–1942*, with 184 historical photographs assembled by George R. Leighton (Austin: University of Texas Press, 1971), photograph 117.

nation to rise up and overthrow Carranza. When most governors, caudillos, and generals, including Carranza's longtime associate General Pablo González, joined the Obregonistas, the president fled Mexico City for Veracruz.

Carranza hoped to establish a base camp in the port city and organize a national campaign, just as he had done in 1915. This time, however, he met with disaster. The first chief's train came under continuous attack from adversaries who forced it to stop in the sierra of Puebla. Carranza and a handful of men escaped on horseback into the hills and encamped for the night in the village of Tlaxcalantongo. That evening while he slept, President Carranza, the first chief of the Constitutionalist movement, was assassinated by forces loyal to Félix Díaz.[24]

CHRONOLOGY OF THE MEXICAN REVOLUTION, 1910–1920

1910
  Francisco I. Madero's presidential campaign against Porfirio Díaz
  July: Madero placed under house arrest
  July–November: Antireelectionist junta organized revolution
  November 20: Outbreak of revolution

1911
  May: Battle of Ciudad Juárez
  Rebel occupation of Torreón
  Porfirio Díaz resigns
  Emiliano Zapata's Plan de Ayala

1913
  February: Ten Tragic Days (Decena Trágica)
  Madero assassinated

1913–1914
  Dictatorship of General Victoriano C. Huerta
  Constitutionalist rebellion led by Venustiano Carranza, Alvaro
    Obregón, and Pancho Villa

1914
  U.S. occupation of Veracruz
  Huerta resigns
  Convention of Aguascalientes

1914–1915
   Civil war between Constitutionalists (Carranza and Obregón)
   and Conventionists (Villa and Zapata)

1915
   Obregón defeats Villa at Celaya and León

1916–1920
   Presidency of Venustiano Carranza

1916
   Villa raids Columbus, New Mexico

1916–1917
   Pershing's punitive expedition

1917
   Constitution of 1917

1919
   Zapata assassinated

1920
   Plan of Agua Prieta
   Carranza assassinated

CHAPTER SEVEN

ALVARO OBREGÓN AND THE
RECONSTRUCTION OF MEXICO

General Alvaro Obregón, one of eighteen children raised by proud parents who had fallen on hard times, was educated by his schoolteacher sisters. He displayed enormous energy and intelligence as a young man. After a successful start in commercial agriculture, he joined the revolution in support of Madero and became Mexico's most successful warrior. Although he lost an arm in the battle of León and believed that he was going to die, Obregón survived to vanquish Pancho Villa in 1915, secure the presidency for Venustiano Carranza in 1916, and establish himself as Carranza's inevitable successor. In 1920, at the age of forty, he faced the formidable, some might say impossible, task of rebuilding a war-torn economy and reinventing the Mexican state.[1]

Obregón's upbringing in the secular culture and society of Sonora forged his belief in economic liberalism and modernism. His success as a businessman and revolutionary commander gave him the experience and confidence to find solutions to complex problems. Obregón's approach to social and political reconstruction depended less on ideology than on pragmatism that led to compromises with Porfirian elites, foreign business interests, ruthless caudillos, and land-hungry peasants. The general's

FIGURE 40: General Alvaro Obregón lost an arm in the battle of
León, his decisive victory over Pancho Villa in 1915. Obregón's
victories over Villa secured the presidency for Venustiano Carranza.

Source: Anita Brenner, *The Wind that Swept Mexico: The History of the Mexican
Revolution of 1910–1942,* with 184 historical photographs assembled by
George R. Leighton (Austin: University of Texas Press, 1971), photograph 109.

political alliance with organized labor, a new force in Mexican politics,
helped him stabilize his government.

Solution to Mexico's overwhelming economic difficulties, caused by
loss of life, damage to physical plants, and falling commodities prices,
hinged on increasing petroleum exports and securing a larger share of
profits for the state. Mexico had emerged as the world's second largest
petroleum producer during the First World War, and U.S. and British
producers sought new concessions to exploit proven reserves and increase

production. Obregón's attempts to increase taxes and to exercise more control over the industry met with stern opposition from the U.S. and British governments, however. Both nations withheld diplomatic recognition and demanded that Obregón compromise on Article 27 of the constitution, which had transferred subsoil rights to the state, and that Obregón pay Mexico's substantial foreign debt. Mexico's need for financial solvency and normalization of diplomatic relations resulted in international agreements that simultaneously undermined the constitution and stabilized the revolutionary state.

Social and political peace within Mexico also required decisive measures. Tens of thousands of Mexicans remained under arms, powerful caudillos controlled entire provinces, and thousands of peasants demanded land as their revolutionary inheritance. Obregón confronted each of these challenges with characteristic pragmatism. To recalcitrant generals he offered a "cannon blast of pesos," to powerful political bosses he offered important positions within the government, to agrarian radicals he offered land, and to labor leaders he offered unprecedented political influence. In this fashion, Obregón used money, political patronage, and personalism to create alliances with important individuals and interest groups.

OBREGÓN, DE LA HUERTA, AND MORONES

The Plan de Agua Prieta, organized by General Obregón and his supporters, ousted Carranza and brought to power a succession of revolutionary leaders from Sonora. Adolfo de la Huerta, revolutionary commander and governor of the state, assumed immediate control as interim president until national elections could be arranged to confirm Obregón's ascendancy a few months later. De la Huerta paved the way for a smooth transition when he decreed an unconditional amnesty for all insurgents, including Carranza's closest allies, and convinced Pancho Villa to lay down his arms and accept retirement on the hacienda Canutillo.[2]

President Obregón continued this fence-mending policy with former rivals as well as potential adversaries. He reached an accord with new Zapatista leader Gildardo Magaña and began discussions of a serious land-reform program in Morelos, while simultaneously allowing some Porfirian-era caudillos, such as Luis Terrazas in Chihuahua, to return

FIGURE 41: Pancho Villa in retirement. In a settlement negotiated in 1923,
Villa had agreed to retire from public life on the Hacienda Canutillo in
Chihuahua. Obregón, Calles, and other adversaries viewed him as a continuing
military and political threat, however, and ordered his assassination.

Source: Friedrich Katz, ed. *Imáges de Pancho Villa* (Mexico City:
Instituto Nacional de Antropología e Historia, 1999), p. 60.

from exile and resume business activities. Obregón also secured the
loyalty of high-ranking federal army officers through generous financial
rewards, while simultaneously undermining their ability to develop cadres
of loyal troops by regularly rotating commanders between newly created
administrative military zones.[3]

President Obregón also consolidated his regime by forging political alliances with organized labor. During the revolution Obregón had cultivated labor's support and succeeded in mobilizing worker brigades known as the Red Battalions shortly before his decisive victories over Pancho Villa in 1915. Organized labor's leftward drift, however, alienated the socially conservative President Carranza who suppressed the radical Casa del Obrero Mundial and sponsored a more moderate labor confederation, the Confederación Regional de Obreros Mexicanos (CROM).

In 1919, Obregón signed a secret pact with CROM that secured the labor confederation's backing in exchange for increased political power. CROM subsequently muscled its way into positions of great influence within the government, and Luis Morones, the confederation's powerful leader, emerged as one of Mexico's most influential politicians.

The first years of Obregón's presidency witnessed considerable labor turmoil. The nation's 1.4 million nonagricultural workers suffered inordinately from difficult economic conditions as they faced layoffs and wage stagnation. A tradition of worker militancy dating from the late Porfiriato, coupled with labor's growing political influence and constitutional rights, contributed to an astounding 173 strikes during 1920 and a record 300 conflicts the following year.

President Obregón, seeking labor peace, turned to Morones and CROM for a solution. The confederation's membership had risen from 400,000 to 1,200,000 workers between 1922 and 1924, and it had developed the administrative infrastructure and strong-arm tactics needed to impose its will in the workplace. Strike activity declined in direct proportion to Morones's ascendancy within the administrations of Obregón (1920–1924) and Plutarco Elías Calles (1924–1928). Labor unrest reached its low point during Morones's tenure as Calles's minister of industry, commerce, and labor.

The political and financial gains enjoyed by Morones and his inner circle, however, did not translate into significant benefits for industrial workers. Real wages remained well below the 3-peso minimum daily wage that the national labor commission concluded as necessary for subsistence. CROM's virtual monopoly over organized labor and its cozy relationship with the federal government unraveled at decade's end as the deepening economic crisis, growing worker discontent over low wages, and a presidential succession crisis led to the creation of new unions influenced by anarcho-syndicalism, socialism, and communism.[4]

CAUDILLOS, OLD AND NEW

Obregón's political understanding with organized labor helped stabilize his government, but peace in the countryside required coming to terms with regional elites and interest groups who represented divergent political and economic interests. Agrarian leaders demanded a meaningful land reform, businessmen sought assurances that they would not be heavily taxed, over regulated, or subject to expropriation, and surviving Porfirian elites wanted to retain economic and political influence.

If Obregón's primary concern had been implementation of the new constitution, he would have attempted sweeping reforms less cautiously. The president compromised ideology and revolutionary objectives, however, to achieve political and economic stability. He made deals with the old guard, whose business skills and political resilience he valued, and he limited land reform to areas where agrarians kept up the political pressure.

The political situation in postrevolutionary Chihuahua presented Obregón with serious challenges. The western provinces had produced the revolutionary movements led by Pascual Orozco and Pancho Villa, and fears of a Villista revival preoccupied the victorious Constitutionalists. In 1920, Villa had been asked by Generals Salvador Alvarado and Ramón Denegri to support Obregón in his power struggle with Carranza. Villa refused to take sides, however, on the assumption that the ensuing civil war would weaken both factions and increase his political influence. Obregón's quick victory, however, placed Villa on the defensive. The federal government offered a 100,000-peso reward for Villa's arrest and dispatched troops to Chihuahua. Villa evaded capture by fleeing to Coahuila, where he plundered haciendas and kept the authorities at bay. Interim President Adolfo de la Huerta entered into negotiations with Villa, despite Obregón's reservations, and achieved a settlement. In return for agreeing to retire from public life, Villa received the hacienda Canutillo, formerly occupied by the notorious Tomás Urbina, a personal escort of fifty handpicked men, and land for eight hundred of his soldiers. In the negotiations, Villa never insisted on widespread land reform in

Chihuahua or elsewhere as a condition for his surrender. Villa may have lacked the leverage to make such a demand. However, throughout his revolutionary career Villa's focus had been on rewarding his soldiers with land, rather than advocating a general land redistribution.[5]

Land reform still remained at the heart of social and political conflict in Chihuahua, however. In 1920, Chihuahuans blocked President Carranza's attempt to reinstate Luis Terrazas's haciendas, and in 1923 they thwarted an Obregonista plan to sell U.S. businessman Arthur J. McQuatters a 5,000,000-acre Terrazas estate.[6] The McQuatters deal launched a groundswell of opposition from Chihuahua's popular classes. According to Friedrich Katz, "Long-standing opposition to the Terrazas family and demands for land reform now became linked to revolutionary nationalism. Newly formed peasant unions in Chihuahua, peasant organizations outside the state, and labor unions, as well as many individuals, protested privately and publicly, making their voices heard in the newly elected state assembly."[7] From Canutillo, Villa claimed that the sale represented a plot by American businessmen to overthrow Obregón. Influential Interior Minister Plutarco Elías Calles also opposed the deal. In the end, Obregón bowed to the pressure and reached a compromise settlement. He expropriated the Terrazas estate but compensated the family $5,000,000 and McQuatters $1,000,000.[8]

These incidents and others demonstrated the political necessity of land reform in Chihuahua. Obregón and Governor Ignacio C. Enríquez subsequently distributed 429,317 hectares of land between 1921 and 1924, surpassing all other states except for Yucatán and San Luis Potosí. In many cases, the land went to residents of the same villages where the revolution had originated in 1910 and 1911.[9]

The Porfirian elite in Chihuahua showed political and economic resiliency, however. Elites with diversified holdings had an advantage over those dependent exclusively on the ranching and agricultural economy. The old guard benefited from President Carranza's revolutionary ambivalence. The first chief, eager to strengthen his political base and revive sagging food production, refused to implement an aggressive agrarian reform and invited exiled hacendados back into the country. The more politically astute landlords subsequently formed alliances with revolutionary generals who had become hacendados themselves.[10]

Elites used every means at their disposal to resist implementation of revolutionary policies and to force compromises. According to Mark Wasserman, "Members of the elite employed several strategies, including violence, legal maneuvering, fraud, co-optation, bribery, and exertion of pressure through interest-group associations."[11] For example, to avoid confiscation of their estates, many hacendados subdivided their land among relatives or tenants, who then joined them in opposition to agrarian reform.

No one represented the power and glory of the old regime more than Luis Terrazas and his extended family, and local revolutionaries had targeted the clan for special vengeance. In 1913, Villa expropriated the family's land holdings, banks, mines, and personal property. The Constitutionalists looted other assets through forced loans and confiscations. Nevertheless, during the 1920s and 1930s the family managed to reacquire the best of its prerevolutionary land holdings, about 1.235 million acres of prime land, and the family's extensive urban properties remained untouched by revolutionary governments. The extended family shored up its political influence, moreover, by becoming key members of the most important local interest groups, especially the cattlemen's association, the Rotary Club, the Chamber of Commerce, and the Chamber of Mines. The comeback of the Terrazas clan occurred without opposition from Obregón or his Sonoran successors, who valued their business acumen and financial expertise. In fact, Enrique C. Creel, Luis Terrazas's son-in-law and the former governor of Chihuahua, returned from exile to revitalize the family banking business and become an important advisor to Obregón on monetary policy.

Other Porfirian elites from Chihuahua, such as the Falomirs, Lujáns, and Zuloagas, also returned from exile and rekindled their family fortunes. Success derived from their considerable business skills as well as the cooperation of revolutionary leaders seeking economic stabilization. Revival of economic fortunes, however, did not translate into political power. Revolutionary leaders jealously guarded control over important public office and soon amassed wealth of their own through business deals, graft, and patronage.[12]

THE AGRARIAN IMPULSE

Returning land to Porfirian hacendados while constitutionally guaranteeing the right of peasant villagers to the same land was, according to John
Tutino, "the ultimate contradiction" of revolutionary government.[13]
President Obregón, as a successful agro-businessman himself, believed
that agricultural development depended on investment in infrastructure
and application of modern business practices. He had little faith in the
economic viability of the traditional village economy, nor much concern
for Mexico's downtrodden Indians. To consolidate power, he used land
reform to appease militant agrarian radicals and to recruit them into his
political alliance.

Obregón's agrarian reform law of 1922 defined the limits and possi-
bilities of his guarded commitment. The law prohibited the breakup of
agro-industrial enterprises, such as sugarcane plantations, as well as
smaller properties ranging in size from 150 to 500 hectares that Obregón
believed could develop into productive enterprises. Resident farmhands
on agricultural estates (peones acasillados), who constituted a majority of
Mexico's rural population, were declared ineligible to receive land. They
would remain wage laborers outside of traditional village economies.[14]

Obregón's land reform attempted to appease politically influential
agrarian leaders and their followers. Morelos, the home of Zapatismo,
received special attention.[15] The Zapatistas had enthusiastically
supported Obregón's overthrow of Carranza, whom they considered the
reincarnation of Porfirio Díaz, and Obregón reciprocated by naming
Zapatistas as minister of agriculture, head of the National Agrarian
Commission, and governor of Morelos.

Obregón also distributed large amounts of land to Zapatista villagers,
although not along the lines that they had envisioned. The Zapatistas
could not remain on land occupied during the revolution, nor could they
receive land illegally taken from them by hacendados. Instead, the government created agricultural collectives, the *ejidos*, and selected resident-
owners (*ejidatarios*) to farm the land. The formation of ejidos transferred
land from haciendas to state-owned agricultural enterprises, which also
served the political purpose of weakening the hacendado opposition and
empowering the state. Within ejidos, individuals received specified plots
of land that could remain within families for generations, although not as

their private property. Ejido members planted and harvested their own crops, shared water, woodlands, and pasture, and performed communal tasks such as weeding irrigation canals and building bridges. By 1929, more than 200,000 hectares of land had been distributed to Morelos's peasantry, almost all in the form of ejidos.

Under Obregón, agrarian reform became deeply entwined in political patronage and the federal bureaucracy. Zapatista chiefs within his administration, such as Antonio Díaz Soto y Gama, received the privilege of carrying out land redistributions, which increased their local prestige and ingratiated them to Obregón. Moreover, the agrarian reform process created new political opportunities for ambitious villagers. The government required peasants seeking land to complete a complex application procedure that included completing censuses, questionnaires, reports, and letters, and literate villagers emerged as the indispensable middlemen. In many cases, these individuals had not fought during the revolution but invented fictitious revolutionary careers and assumed positions of political leadership within the villages. In the words of Arturo Warman:

> Soon they took possession even of the defensas sociales, the villages' armed Militias, which had arisen for self-defense when Zapatismo declined. This group, with police functions, exercised real, effective power in the villages. They had become bosses. To legitimize their history, many of the recent arrivals made themselves into old Zapatistas and even veterans. Those who had really fought remember with anger and bitterness how colonels and captains of the Liberating Army of the South who spent the revolution in Atlixco, in Mexico City, or even outside of the country began to appear, with service records issued by mysterious offices using Zapata's name and signed by chiefs whom nobody knew. To top it off, some of these phony veterans with sufficient influence with the government were even given a pension. Bit by bit, even the history of the Zapatista rebellion was changing ownership.[16]

In economic terms the results of the agrarian reform remained mixed. It took villages in the eastern part of the state from five to eight years for their provisional land grants to become definite, and many haciendas remained partially intact. The García Pimentals, for example, had gone into exile during the revolution and rented their land to tenants and rich villagers who planted corn and wheat. The wily hacendados also had instructed trusted managers to dismantle expensive and difficult to replace sugar mills and store them away from the fighting. Such tactics helped local elites survive and hastened the recovery of the sugar industry in Morelos.

Agrarian reform in Morelos, despite its substantial shortcomings, consolidated Zapatista political support for Obregón, who faced similar challenges in other regions. For example, throughout the revolution Saturnino Cedillo in San Luis Potosí had demonstrated a fierce determination to acquire land for villagers and higher wages for hacienda workers. Cedillo had been an early supporter of Zapata's Plan de Ayala, and his consistent advocacy of agrarian issues caused him to break with President Carranza when the first chief failed to enact a meaningful land reform.

In 1920, Cedillo controlled rural San Luis Potosí and expected President Obregón to implement a meaningful agrarian reform. Cedillo believed that every man deserved access to land as well as the opportunity to improve himself through education and social progress. These were things worth fighting for, and Cedillo put it to the government in terms that could not be misunderstood: "I want land. I want ammunition so that I can protect my land after I get it in case somebody tries to take it away from me. And I want plows, and I want schools for my children, and I want teachers, and I want books and pencils and blackboards and roads. And I want moving pictures for my people, too. And I don't want any Church or any saloon."[17]

Cedillo's stress on material progress and social advancement, uncontaminated by Catholicism or alcohol, resonated with General Obregón. Moreover, Cedillo's unmistakable paternalistic ties with Potosinos ("my people," "my children"), coupled with his history of armed rebellion, made him either a dangerous enemy or an useful ally. Obregón responded by authorizing the establishment of military-agrarian colonies carved out of land confiscated from haciendas. Cedillo then distributed the land among his soldiers and peasant followers. These beneficiaries swelled the ranks of Cedillo's private army and allowed him to influence regional politics throughout the remainder of the decade. In return for land reform, President Obregón had gained a valuable political ally.[18]

In other regions, agrarian warlords' attempts at land reform resulted in protracted conflicts with hacendados that defied easy resolution. In Michoacán, for example, agrarian radicals' confiscation and redistribution of hacienda land to poor Indian villagers met with stern resistance by landlords, hacienda workers, and the Catholic Church.

In 1920, General Francisco Múgica became governor of Michoacán. He did so with the support of General Lázaro Cárdenas and agrarian warlords, such as the charismatic Primo Tapia, who organized land-hungry peasants into armed militias. Formed according to extended family units, Tapia's Indian militias sought to recapture land taken from them by hacendados during the Porfiriato.

From 1920 to 1922 the struggle for land pitted agrarian radicals against hacendados and their supporters, including the Catholic Church, which stood to lose revenue and political influence with an agrarian victory. Radical and conservative armies engaged in protracted village-level warfare, with the agrarians managing to grind out some hard-won gains. In those villages controlled by Tapia, priests were driven out and only invited back to officiate at local festivals. Instead of their standard fee of 300 pesos, however, they received only the minimum wage of 3 pesos.

Governor Múgica's inability to bring the internecine conflict to closure, however, resulted in his resignation in 1922. President Obregón replaced him with Emilio Portes Gil, a political moderate now opposed to agrarian reform, with instructions to achieve political stabilization. The agrarian revolution in Michoacán had a momentum of its own, however, and clashes between Indian militias and hacendados' armies continued with villagers gaining little land in exchange for considerable loss of life.[19]

President Obregón's piecemeal agrarian reform partially achieved his objective of political stabilization in the countryside. Hotbeds of peasant unrest such as Morelos, Chihuahua, and San Luis Potosí received some satisfaction while Michoacanos consumed one another. Those landless villagers without strong political representation were ignored by Obregón, who never intended to carry out a national land reform based on economic and social need. In 1923, fewer than 2,700 wealthy families still owned more than one-half of Mexico. Only 114 of these elite families held 25 percent of the land.[20]

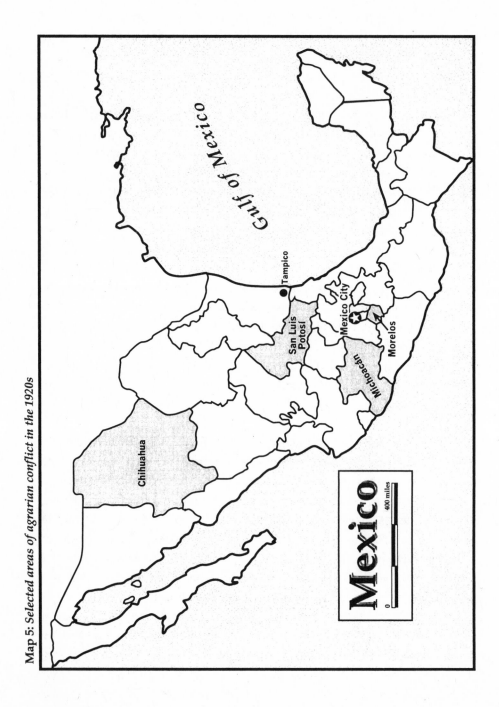

Map 5: Selected areas of agrarian conflict in the 1920s

PETROLEUM AND DEBTS

Defusing the politically volatile countryside through land reform and deal making helped consolidate the Obregón government, but long-term stability also required refinancing Mexico's indebtedness and getting the export economy back on track. The pattern of economic expansion during the Porfiriato, with its heavy dependence on foreign investment and overseas markets, helped create preconditions for revolution and had resulted in Article 27 of the new constitution, which ceded subsoil rights to the nation. Transnationals and their governments, principally the United States and Britain, questioned the legality of Article 27, demanded compensation for losses incurred during the revolution, and insisted on realistic payment schedules for outstanding loans.

From the oil companies' perspective, revolutionary nationalism raised the specter of falling profits and expropriation. They had recently been stung in the oil-rich Baku region of Russia when Standard Oil of New Jersey had gambled and lost that Azerbaijani insurgents would defeat the Bolsheviks, whose subsequent victory led to the nationalization of the petroleum industry in 1920. Worrisome debates over nationalization of foreign oil also occurred in Romania, France, Poland, Colombia, Argentina, El Salvador, and Santo Domingo. U.S. oil companies had the most to lose in Mexico. In 1920, the United States consumed 77 percent of the world's oil and imported more than 100,000,000 barrels of crude, of which 20,000,000 came from Mexico. Mexico's proven reserves, geographic proximity, and low taxes made operations there highly profitable and convenient.

The oil companies, with the help of Gulf Coast strongman Manuel Peláez, had successfully resisted Carranza's attempts to impose higher taxes and greater controls over their industry. Obregón enjoyed Peláez's support, however, which improved his chances of increasing petroleum taxes and enforcing constitutional restrictions on foreign investors. The president recognized that oil represented Mexico's principal hope for repaying its foreign debt and generating the revenues required for repairing infrastructure and underwriting future development. From 1910 to 1916, annual oil production had risen from 3,600,000 barrels to 55,000,000 barrels. Then from 1919 to 1920 production surged again from 90,000,000 to 157,000,000 barrels. By 1920, Mexico was producing 23.78 percent of the world's petroleum and sending 78.08 percent of this production to the United States.[21]

Mexico in return received remarkably little income from oil. It collected a mere 8.9 percent of the value of oil exports in 1920. Obregón levied two new taxes on producers the following year: an *ad valorem* tax of 10 percent earmarked for repayment of Mexico's foreign debt, and an increase in the export tax aimed at slowing the oil depletion rate. In response, some major U.S. producers refused to ship Mexican oil and the five largest companies formed a consortium to pressure Obregón into rescinding the tax increases.

The petroleum companies simultaneously pursued a three-pronged strategy designed to combat erosion of their profit margins and secure adequate supplies. Oil company executives boldly informed Obregón that they wanted firm tax ceilings, freedom to continue wildcat exploration, and an end to "harassing" regulations. At the same time, the more militant captains of industry asked Washington to intervene militarily in Mexico to protect their existing investments and future returns. Republican Senator Albert B. Fall from New Mexico, the industry's principal political supporter, even advocated annexing northern Mexico. As a hedge against hard-line positions, however, major producers also began prospecting for new oil fields in Venezuela.

Disagreements among U.S. and British petroleum companies operating in Mexico further complicated discussions with the Obregón government and created tensions between Washington and London. U.S. oilman Edward Doheny, a pioneer in the Mexican petroleum industry, pressured Washington into withholding diplomatic recognition of Mexico until Obregón compromised on oil policy, while British oil magnate Lord Cowdray favored U.K. recognition of Obregón to foster political stabilization. Although London refused to recognize Obregón, Albert B. Fall, recently appointed secretary of the interior by President Harding, accused Britain of violating a previous agreement with Washington that had pledged cooperation on Mexican petroleum policy, an accusation that London angrily denied.

In the meantime, Lord Cowdray continued to pursue an independent course in Mexico. Cowdray signed a new accord with Obregón that granted his company (El Aguila) drilling rights on coveted federal lands in exchange for higher taxes and tighter government controls. In contrast to Porfirian times, the British company agreed to pay taxes on exports, capital, and production, and to reserve 20 percent of its leased land for government use during the next ten years. The contract incensed U.S. producers, who refused to accept similar terms and increased pressure on Washington to intervene militarily in Mexico.

Instead, timely intervention came from an International Bankers' Committee chaired by Thomas A. Lamont, J. P. Morgan's right-hand man. The bankers, who held most of Mexico's foreign debt, wanted a secure method of payment. Obregón agreed to negotiations and named Treasury Minister Adolfo de la Huerta, a trusted ally and fellow Sonoran, as his chief negotiator. The bankers' extensive experience at negotiating complex international financial accords gave them a critical advantage over de la Huerta who appeared dazzled by his adversaries. Mexico's treasury minister described the American financiers as men of "formidable minds" who "control the world," and referred to Lamont as a "prophet."

From the onset, both sides recognized that Mexico's best hope for paying its foreign debt rested with utilizing petroleum tax revenues, its most secure source of income. De la Huerta proposed that the oil companies pay their export taxes with Mexican bonds at 40 percent par value, which would simultaneously amortize the foreign debt and reduce the export tax by 60 percent. Both Lamont and Obregón rejected this proposal.[22]

Disappointed, de la Huerta soon backpedaled into an agreement that gave the international banking community virtually everything it wanted. Mexico agreed to pay its bonded debt, with the sole exception of bonds issued by General Victoriano Huerta, by diverting tax revenues from both the railroad and petroleum industries. Mexico also pledged to privatize the railroads and to return them to prerevolutionary operating conditions, despite the enormous costs involved. Although Obregón signed the one-sided agreement, de la Huerta's failure to negotiate a better deal angered the president.

Lamont recognized that Mexico's ability to meet its payment schedule hinged on settlement of the oil controversy and U.S. diplomatic recognition. Lamont communicated this to Secretary of State Hughes, whose hard-line position on financial and economic issues had stalled serious talks between Washington and Mexico City over recognition.

Of course the whole situation hangs together as one; that is to say, unless the Mexican government is able to handle itself so as to obtain your recognition the chances are that it will never be able to carry out the agreement with its external creditors. Likewise, unless it adopts a broad and far-sighted policy for oil development by the American companies, the Mexican government will very likely be unable to obtain revenues wherewith it can carry out the agreement with its creditors.[23]

President Obregón believed that Mexico had fulfilled Hughes's key preconditions for recognition by signing the debt agreement and agreeing to adjudicate losses incurred by U.S. citizens in Mexico. Obregón hired former Arizona senator J. L. Schleimer and Governor William Hobby of Texas to advocate his position north of the border. He also arranged for William Randolph Hearst, who owned vast cattle ranches in northern Mexico, to support U.S. recognition in his influential newspapers. By 1923 twenty-three state governments, including Texas, New Mexico, Illinois, Maryland, and Wisconsin, had passed resolutions favoring normalization of relations with Mexico.

While Obregón was gaining support, Secretary Hughes and the petroleum companies lost ground. The *New York World* accused Hughes of receiving funds from the petroleum companies and dubbed him "Secretary of Oil." In addition, the Teapot Dome scandal, which revealed criminal activities by Interior Secretary Albert Fall and oilman Edward Doheny, rocked the Harding administration. The oil companies then broke ranks. Smaller U.S. oil firms that had already accepted Article 27 accused Doheny and others of attempting to monopolize the Mexican oil fields.

President Harding, who had taken a softer position toward Mexican recognition than had Hughes, finally agreed to high-level talks with Mexican representatives. Mexico's minister of foreign relations, Alberto Pani, focused on gaining U.S. diplomatic recognition while preserving the integrity of Article 27 and maintaining the flow of U.S. investment dollars. The negotiations, which took place in the former mansion of Díaz Treasury Minister José Ives Limantour on Bucareli Street, produced a procedure for settling U.S. claims against Mexico as well as a clarification of Article 27. The so-called Bucareli Accords affirmed that petroleum companies would have preferential rights to subsoil development of land that they owned or had "positively" developed prior to promulgation of the 1917 Constitution. The Mexican government, in return, reserved the right to enforce "police regulations, sanitary regulations and measures for public order, and the right . . . to levy general taxes." Within days of the signing of the agreement, the Harding administration recognized the Obregón government.[24]

According to Linda B. Hall, the Bucareli Accords represented an "extraordinary bargain" for Obregón. Mexico had successfully retained ownership over its land and subsoil deposits, established procedures for resolving U.S. claims, and gained diplomatic recognition. Nevertheless, Obregón had forsaken a hard-line nationalist position and still had not achieved diplomatic recognition by Britain. Moreover, petroleum producers feared nationalism under any guise and subsequently scaled back their Mexican operations, which cost Mexico millions of tax dollars. Mexican petroleum exports decreased by 75 percent between 1923 and 1924 as investors turned their attention to Venezuela, where the vast Maracaibo oil fields awaited development under favorable political and economic terms.[25]

THE DE LA HUERTA REVOLT AND THE ASSASSINATION OF PANCHO VILLA

Solving the puzzle of political stability required more than reaching agreements with the United States, the international financial community, and "big oil." Mexico emerged from a decade of revolutionary turmoil with more generals than political vacancies, and the perennial problem of presidential succession still awaited a reliable solution. The continuous meddling of foreign corporations and governments in Mexico's internal affairs also contributed to political instability.

Treasury Minister Adolfo de la Huerta, who negotiated the one-sided debt settlement with bankers, at one time appeared the favorite to succeed Obregón as president. De la Huerta's disappointing performance as treasury minister, however, led the president to support Interior Minister Plutarco Elías Calles.[26] This essentially guaranteed that Calles would become the next president since free elections for Mexico remained a noble concept that political leaders rarely enforced. De la Huerta's considerable support among Mexico's generals and power brokers, however, left him with the political option, so often taken in Mexican history, of launching a rebellion.

De la Huerta apparently assumed, based on his recent negotiations in New York, that he would be supported by the international banking community and the U.S. government. Thomas Lamont and President Calvin Coolidge (Harding's successor) understood, however, that rebellion would disrupt domestic finances and threaten the debt agreement. Coolidge and Secretary of State Hughes, therefore, refused to meet with de la Huerta and eventually sold Obregón $1.28 million worth of weapons. Edward Doheny, who also feared political turmoil, granted Obregón a substantial loan, which the president used to buy military and political support.[27]

On the domestic front, Obregón and Calles feared the political resurgence of Pancho Villa and the likelihood of an alliance with de la Huerta. In 1922, Villa had granted an interview with the Mexico City newspaper *El Universal* and said things that alarmed the president. Villa stated that his pledge to stay out of politics would expire at the end of Obregón's term, and that he was pondering a run for the governorship of Durango. Villa also boasted that he could raise an army of forty thousand men within forty minutes. It was easy to envision Villa supporting de la Huerta. The two had never faced one another on the battlefield, while Villa had suffered his greatest defeats at the hands of Obregón and Calles.

A presidential poll published in *El Universal* on July 10, 1922, further unsettled Obregón and Calles. The poll's results indicated that Villa enjoyed considerable support for president, de la Huerta was more popular than Calles, and that the leading candidate was Senator Carlos B. Zetina, a businessman who had not supported the revolution. A plot unfolded to assassinate Villa. The conspirators included Obregón and Calles, Governor Jesús Agustín Castro of Durango, General Joaquín Amaro, and Deputy Salas Barrazas of Durango. All were Villa's bitter enemies. Salas Barrazas organized the assassination and served as intermediary between government leaders and the assassins. It was known that Villa would be attending a baptism in Río Florido, Chihuahua, and that his route would take him through Parral. On July 20, 1923, Villa, at the wheel of his own car, entered downtown Parral and slowed down to turn a corner. Several men opened fire with rifles. Villa—his body riddled with seventeen bullet wounds—died at the scene.

Villa's elimination cost de la Huerta a likely powerful ally and weakened his impending rebellion. According to Friedrich Katz, Obregón had also viewed Villa's death as a necessary prerequisite to gaining U.S. recognition. Once again, Washington—at least indirectly—had blood on its hands.[28]

When de la Huerta launched his rebellion in December 1923 many Villistas supported his cause. Obregón personally assumed command of government forces, however, and decisively defeated the rebels. The rebellion, as Lamont feared, severely disrupted domestic finances and caused Mexico to default on its foreign-debt payment. In political and military terms, however, Calles benefited from the conflict. De la Huerta fled to Los Angeles and never reemerged as an important force in Mexican politics. Moreover, Obregón's execution of rebellious generals removed dozens of potential political rivals who could have caused problems for the new president.[29]

CONCLUSION

Obregón's administration consolidated the Constitutionalists' ascendancy and established political and ideological guidelines for future administrations. The president managed to pacify, buy off, exile, or execute dangerous rivals and through implementation of new programs created a strong executive branch of government. Obregón's vision for reconstruction borrowed heavily from his experiences as a businessman and farmer in Sonora and from the lessons he had learned about organizing and managing troops while winning a revolution. The Sonoran model favored entrepreneurial initiative and rationalization of production. Productive businessmen—including members of the old regime—benefited from Obregón's blueprint as long as they controlled their political ambitions.

Like most northerners, Obregón viewed Indians as impediments to progress, and he opposed wholesale land redistribution to villagers. Obregón understood, however, the need for a limited agrarian reform to quell hotbeds of rural unrest, and he used the agrarian reform process to gain political allies and to increase the authority of the central government in the countryside.

Obregón also recognized the political utility of forging closer ties with organized labor, and Luis Morones, the powerful leader of CROM, became extremely influential in the Obregón administration.

For Obregón, reconstruction also required resolving Mexico's public indebtedness and gaining political legitimacy in the eyes of the international community. Both solvency and diplomatic recognition involved complex negotiations with the international banking community led by Thomas Lamont and resulted in Mexico agreeing to pay its debts by diverting revenues from the railroad and petroleum industries. Separate negotiations with the U.S. government resulted in an understanding over implementation of Article 27, which affirmed Mexico's ownership of its subsoil rights while allowing U.S. firms to retain special privileges over land developed prior to 1917.

CHAPTER EIGHT

PLUTARCO ELÍAS CALLES AND THE REVOLUTIONARY STATE

A TROUBLED CHILDHOOD forged Sonoran Plutarco Elías Calles's tenacity and secular worldview. Born the illegitimate son of the aristocratic Plutarco Elías, the future president was abandoned by his father and raised by his maternal aunt and her husband, Juan Bautista Calles. The elder Calles was an avowed atheist who instilled in young Plutarco an uncompromising belief in secular education and a fanatical hatred of the Roman Catholic Church. The revolution ended young Plutarco Elías Calles's teaching career and launched one of the most impressive political careers in Mexican history.[1]

Calles joined the Constitutionalist movement following Madero's assassination and received his first revolutionary appointment as police chief of Agua Prieta. Following Huerta's defeat, Calles quickly rose within the Constitutionalist ranks and served as governor and military commander of Sonora during 1916–1917. Calles's progressive beliefs on social issues were tempered by his deadly impatience with those who challenged his authority or threatened to undermine political and economic stability. While governor, Calles ordered the revolutionary army to attack the Yaqui Indians when they refused to surrender ancestral lands, replicating the draconian measures employed a generation earlier by Porfirio Díaz, and forced striking miners back to work at gunpoint, much as General Torres had done at Cananea in 1906.

Calles's authoritarianism while president parallels political and economic policies pursued by other twentieth-century revolutionary leaders seeking to consolidate their authority and create a framework for enforcing state-directed agendas. Calles had the political skill to create a broadly based political party, the Partido Nacional Revolucionario (PNR), as a vehicle for selecting presidents, controlling national politics, and undercutting caudillos' self-destructive tendency to settle political disputes through coups. Calles's pragmatic economic program favored large-scale development projects, such as hydroelectric dams and irrigation projects, and his economic nationalism and toughness allowed him to renegotiate the debt agreement with the United States and receive terms favorable to Mexico.

Calles's social agenda reflected the secular, pro-development convictions characteristic of the Sonoran revolutionary elite. He advocated the expansion of public education to create productive workers and to combat what he saw as the nefarious influence of Catholicism. He supported a limited agrarian reform to maintain political alliances with agrarian leaders. And he fought to keep the Catholic Church out of politics and the union movement and to force its subservience to the state.

Calles's determination to control the Catholic Church provoked a counterrevolution in 1926, known as the Cristero Rebellion, which threatened to destroy the emerging revolutionary state. The rebellion pitted devout Catholics and the church hierarchy against the centralizing regime and the Confederación Regional de Obreros Mexicanos, forces that sought to impose a secular state on Mexicans. The rebellion revealed the difficulty of imposing secularism on traditional peasants whose lives had been significantly shaped by Catholicism. The rebels came primarily from central and western Mexico where the Catholic Church had maintained a strong presence since the sixteenth century. Church leaders mobilized devout villagers to defend the Mexican church, and the revolutionary state mobilized beneficiaries of land reform—who owed the state a favor—to fight the Cristeros. The clash produced thousands of victims and martyrs without either side winning a decisive military victory.

GENERAL ECONOMIC DEVELOPMENTS

Calles, like his fellow Sonoran and patron Obregón, sought to revitalize Mexico's economy through improving economic infrastructure and public finance. Calles's finance ministers, Alberto J. Pani and Luis Montes de Oca, reduced public expenditures by privatizing the railways and eliminating many federal subsidies to private businesses. They also increased government income and improved efficiencies by diversifying revenue sources and by creating a more coherent monetary and credit system through the foundation of Mexico's first central bank, the Banco de Mexico.

Reforms in the national banking system proved crucial in returning the country from the brink of financial disaster. The national bank, based loosely on the U.S. federal reserve model, helped restore stability and confidence in the Mexican peso. The creation of the National Banking Commission gave the government supervisory authority over the banking industry as well as the power to open state banks. These measures eliminated the virtual monopoly that foreign-owned banks had enjoyed over Mexican banking prior to the revolution and gave ordinary Mexicans and entrepreneurs more financial options. The Calles government also opened agricultural credit banks and cooperative agricultural banks to provide credit to impoverished Mexican farmers. These banks suffered from undercapitalization and abuse by powerful politicians such as Obregón who received large loans and then refused to repay them.

Calles's underwriting of huge public works projects facilitated national reconstruction and significantly increased the federal government's role in the national economy. The National Highway Commission fostered economic integration through construction of major arteries linking Mexico City with Pachuca and Puebla and launching the important Acapulco-Veracruz and Panamerican Highways. Financing of highway construction came primarily from a new tax on gasoline consumption. Many contracts went to the construction company owned by the powerful General Juan Andrew Almazán, a well-connected member of Calles's inner circle.

Calles's commitment to agricultural development resulted in the construction of several dams designed to divert rivers into irrigation networks. The newly created National Irrigation Commission collaborated with foreign construction companies on the building of seven dams with the capacity to irrigate nearly a half million acres of formerly unproductive land. Some of these dams, such as the Guatimapé in Durango, suffered from design errors, however, which caused the government to rely less on foreign engineers for future projects.

Calles understood that economic reconstruction required access to overseas financial markets because of large-scale capital flight from Mexico during the revolution. The government's recent default on loan payments under the Bucareli Accords, however, destroyed Mexico's credit rating abroad and made it impossible to negotiate new loans. The accords had required Mexico to pay $700,000,000 to its foreign creditors, an amount that Mexico could not pay because of falling petroleum exports. Thomas Lamont and Mexico's finance minister, Alberto Pani, entered into negotiations in 1925, and Mexico's debt obligation was reduced to $480,000,000 by separating the railroad debt from the overall debt. As a concession to the bankers, Pani agreed to repay Mexico's bonds at their nominal value as opposed to their devalued market rates.

The renegotiated debt agreement bore few positive results. Foreign banks still refused to lend Mexico money, and mounting expenses arising from the Cristero Rebellion caused Mexico to default on its debt payment again in 1928. Economic conditions worsened the following year with the onset of the worldwide Great Depression and the increased political turmoil associated with the presidential elections. In 1930, the international bankers represented by Thomas Lamont once again reduced Mexico's foreign debt. The Lamont-Montes de Oca Treaty reduced Mexico's indebtedness to $267,000,000 by forgiving $211,000,000 in unpaid interest and consolidating general bonded debt with railroad debt. The lingering impact of the Great Depression, however, continued to hinder the government's ability to pay.[2]

The depression undermined overall economic performance and threatened the gains achieved during the first part of Calles's administration. Between 1925 and 1930 Gross National Product declined by one-eighth, and from 1929 to 1932 Gross Agricultural Product fell by one-third.[3] Falling petroleum and mineral prices, in particular, reduced government revenues and resulted in worker layoffs and increased poverty. In addition, xenophobia in the United States resulted in the forced deportation of tens of thousands of Mexican immigrants, including many legal residents and Mexican Americans, who were unfairly accused of taking jobs away from

U.S. citizens. These forcibly repatriated Mexicans swelled the ranks of the impoverished.[4]

AGRARIAN REFORM

Calles never expressed much concern for the plight of Mexico's land-starved rural poor. He did recognize, however, that land redistribution could be used to gain the political support of villagers and powerful agrarian warlords. From 1924 to 1928, Calles distributed 3,045,802 hectares of land to 301,587 peasants, or about 10 hectares per person. Calles's immediate successors later distributed another 3,444,982 hectares of land between 1928 to 1934.[5] The largest redistribution occurred in Morelos (59 percent) and in the Federal District (25.4 percent), two places where Zapatismo had been strongest, and in the Yucatán (30 percent), where land reform undercut the economic power base of the antirevolutionary henequen oligarchy.[6]

Despite these impressive-looking numbers, Mexico's revolutionary presidents from Carranza to Calles had avoided a nationwide land reform aimed at relieving the poverty of land-starved peasants. The northern generals who governed Mexico viewed Indians as crude and uncivilized people capable of fighting and dying in revolutionary armies but incapable of becoming prosperous small farmers and contributing members of society. Since 1917, only 7 percent of Mexico's arable land had been redistributed to villagers. Much of the land granted to villagers was barren, rocky, and unirrigated soil only suitable for dry farming or the grazing of limited numbers of livestock.[7] At the same time, several revolutionary leaders, including Villa, Obregón, and Calles, had acquired lush haciendas through purchase or donation from the state.[8]

Even possession of comparatively fertile land did not necessarily guarantee villagers' prosperity. In Morelos, for example, the pressure of Zapatismo and the loss of 40 percent of the male population during the revolution assured the availability of good land. Peasants still struggled, however, because of credit shortages and the dearth of beasts of burden essential for tilling the soil. Porfirian bankers and merchants had taken their money and fled, and the newly created agricultural banks failed to provide reliable credit. Local moneylenders filled the void but charged peasants 100 percent interest *(la dobla)* for corn and capital. More often than not, these moneylenders were the same interlopers who had gained political office after manufacturing false revolutionary pedigrees. These opportunists also owned most of the oxen that had survived marauding revolutionary armies, and they gave villagers the unenviable choice of pulling their own ploughs or renting animals for outrageous sums.

Corrupt revolutionary generals and politicians were using the new programs to grow rich at the expense of others. Livestock owners appointed to head local agrarian reform commissions distributed the best land to themselves and gave the poorest villagers, who were already indebted to them, the back-breaking tasks of clearing and ploughing their fields. Corruption took on many different forms. Officials in all branches of government demanded bribes *(mordidas)* from citizens who needed their services. Calles authorized highway construction projects that benefited him and his friends. Obregón and other powerful politicians borrowed money from agricultural banks and never paid it back.[9]

The distribution of land to peasants, despite the inefficiencies and corruption of the process, still created a political bond between revolutionary leaders and villagers. Agrarian warlords, such as Saturnino Cedillo in San Luis Potosí, raised large peasant armies and controlled entire provinces, and their political and military support helped Presidents Obregón and Calles survive serious rebellions.

Agrarian leaders, by contrast, could not necessarily count on the political support of the federal government. In the violent and politically precarious process of revolutionary consolidation those agrarian leaders who failed to maintain political stability in their bailiwicks lost the backing of Mexico City. For example, the Sonoran presidents abandoned governors Francisco Múgica in Michoacán and Adalberto Tejeda and Ursulo Galván in Veracruz when their attempts at agrarian reform met with stern resistance from local landlords and the Catholic Church.[10]

THE CRISTERO REBELLION

The centralizing policies of the Calles administration left little leeway for dissent, and those resisting subordination faced suppression regardless of their political ideologies or local power bases.[11] This included traditional sources of institutional and moral authority as much as rival caudillos and noncompliant foreigners. For Plutarco Calles the Roman Catholic Church represented the preeminent obstacle to building a revolutionary state. His determination to enforce the anticlerical provisions of the 1917 Constitution, occasioned by the emerging political rivalry of a revitalized church, plunged the nation into a protracted civil war that threatened to unravel much of the revolutionary agenda.

HISTORICAL BACKGROUND

Reinventing church-state relations had been the principal political objective for Mexico's liberal leadership since independence. Laws stripping the church of land and special courts in the 1850s had plunged the nation into civil war. Although the church's economic strength and judicial independence suffered, most Mexicans remained devout and the church hierarchy's rapprochement with Porfirio Díaz gave it the opportunity to regroup. During the Porfiriato, the church strengthened its political and institutional base by improving its administrative structure, increasing the number of priests and lay workers, opening new seminaries and parochial schools, and advocating labor and agrarian reforms.

A revitalized church viewed the outbreak of the revolution with trepidation, but it also realized that political destabilization created opportunities to reenter the political arena in ways never before envisioned. Clergy believed that Madero's advocacy of democracy assured them a niche in the new political order, and the church took the unprecedented step of founding a new political party, the National Catholic Party (NCP), and announcing slates of candidates for the congressional elections in 1912.

The NCP's electoral success created tensions between the church and Madero and contributed to the destabilization of the first revolutionary government. The NCP's sweep of congressional seats in Jalisco and Zacatecas established it as a major political party, which prompted alarmed Maderistas to annul the electoral results in these states. Such dictatorial tactics, reminiscent of those employed by Díaz, turned the National Catholic Party against Madero.

The Catholic Party's bitter attack on Madero coincided with mounting criticism from populist leaders Pascual Orozco and Emiliano Zapata, whose impatience over the president's failure to carry out agrarian and political reforms soon erupted into outright rebellion. The disintegration of Madero's revolutionary coalition gave counterrevolutionaries the political opening they needed to overthrow the president and place General Victoriano Huerta in power.

Huerta courted the church hierarchy while his populist opponents Zapata and Villa maintained cordial relations with the lower clergy. Huerta's decision to permit the church to consecrate the Mexican nation to Christ the King pleased the bishops but violated the reform laws and convinced Constitutionalist leader Venustiano Carranza that the church had conspired against Madero from the beginning.

Carranza's hostility toward the church, deeply rooted in Mexican liberalism and northern secularism, assured a renewed attack on ecclesiastical rights and privileges following the Constitutionalists' victory. The Constitution of 1917 gave the government sweeping powers over the church, outlawed religiously affiliated political parties and religious orders, and denied clergy the right to own property, teach, and vote.

THE REBELLION

Enforcement of anticlericalism required a strong executive with sufficient political and military support to withstand the predictable backlash. Preoccupation with political consolidation and economic reconstruction prevented presidents Carranza and Obregón from directly confronting the church, but President Calles's determination to subordinate institutions and caudillos to the federal government put him on a collision course with the bishops.

The labor-union movement produced the spark that ignited renewed conflict between church and state. The church hierarchy's decision to found its own labor organization, the Catholic Labor Confederation (CLC), aroused the ire of the Confederación Regional de Obreros Mexicanos (CROM) and its powerful leader Luis Morones. Calles's appointment of Morones as minister of labor consecrated an important political marriage designed to fortify the emerging revolutionary state. Rival labor organizations would not be tolerated. The Catholic Labor Confederation, however, was not easily suppressed. It concentrated its recruiting efforts in rural areas largely ignored by CROM, and through advocacy of land and labor reforms it quickly gained legitimacy among devout peasants. By 1922, CLC membership stood at 80,000, nearly equal to that of the CROM.

Calles and Morones resorted to strong-arm tactics designed to eliminate the competition. Attacks on priests and churches by CROM thugs alarmed devout Catholics, who rallied in support of the church. Organized resistance included formation of the Unión Popular (UP), a grassroots organization composed of workers and peasants, and the National League for the Defense of Religion (LNDR), a confederation of Catholic trade-union and lay organizations. Voices of moderation existed within both the Calles government and the church hierarchy, but defiant statements by Archbishop José Mora y del Rio provoked a violent reaction by the president.

In February 1926, newspapers quoted the archbishop as reaffirming the church's opposition to the anticlerical provisions of the constitution. The archbishop's statement did not represent new church policy, but the timing of his public reaffirmation of church rights enraged Calles, who reacted by closing Catholic schools and convents, deporting foreign priests, and allowing governors to limit the number of clergy in their jurisdictions. Outraged bishops demanded reformation of the constitution as a solution to the crisis. Calles rejected this as a direct attack on the revolution itself.

Calles's refusal to compromise gave church leaders little choice between caving in to state control of religion or mounting a full-scale resistance to preserve ecclesiastical autonomy. On July 31, 1926, the Mexican Episcopate took the radical step of suspending public worship with the clear intention of arousing popular support for the church against Calles and Morones. The denial of religious services created a profound crisis among devout Catholics whose lives revolved around the church and its representatives.

Throughout Mexico the church failed to provide its followers with clear political direction. Most priests in rural areas fled to the comparative security of cities and attended to the spiritual needs of wealthy Catholics, frequently residing in their homes. Others simply left the country. According to Jean A. Meyer, 3,390 of the 3,600 priests residing in

Mexico abandoned the villages, and only forty clerics openly supported the Cristeros.

Direction of the popular rebellion against the government, therefore, fell to the National League in Defense of Religion and to local leaders. The league's leadership, composed of middle-class urban professionals, proved incapable of coordinating a political and military offensive against the Calles regime. Rebel commanders commissioned by the league from among friends and associates with little or no military experience proved inept as field commanders. In addition, the league's sponsorship of a national boycott against manufactured goods failed to destabilize the government because most Cristeros had little money to withhold.

Devoid of national direction, the rebellion emerged as a series of unco-ordinated local protests against the revolutionary state. Within months, villages across Michoacán, Jalisco, the Bajío region of Guanajuato, south-ern Coahuila, and Colima—areas where the church had maintained an ingrained presence since the sixteenth century—were in open revolt against Calles. Rebel anger in these regions, moreover, did not emanate exclusively from opposition to the government's anticlericalism. Many villagers in central and western regions also resented the growing intrusion of the government in their lives, particularly midsized ranchers and farmers who violently opposed an agrarian reform predicated on the confiscation of private property and the formation of collective farms (the ejidos).

In southern and northern Mexico, by contrast, Calles's policies provoked little reaction because of the comparative weakness of the church. As Dudley Ankerson explains:

> In Oaxaca and Chiapas, where the church still competed with a strong indigenous cultural tradition and the institutions of government had less impact upon most people's daily lives, Calles's religious policies pro-voked little opposition. There was also less unrest in areas where land reform resulted from a popular movement under local leadership, such as in eastern San Luis Potosí or in districts where ejidos had been intro-duced to meet popular needs without prejudice to local hacienda peons.[12]

In Veracruz, Yucatán, and Tabasco rabidly anticlerical governors applauded Calles's crackdown on the church and authorized attacks on clergy and desecration of churches. In Tabasco, Governor Tomás Garrido took the extreme steps of destroying churches, burning religious statues and icons, expelling priests, and renaming villages and towns that had been named after saints. Garrido's enthusiastic promotion of socialist education included supporting atheist clubs throughout the state.[13]

Resistance to anticlericalism was weak in Tabasco and other historically liberal regions where the church had failed to establish a strong institutional presence. In parts of western and central Mexico, however, Catholicism was embedded into the lives of villagers, and they defended the church. The community of San José de Gracia, Michoacán, studied by the Mexican historian Luis González, provides insights into the unfolding of the Cristero Rebellion at the village level.[14] Within the community's collective memory, the church had always provided spiritual sustenance, moral guidance, and political direction. The local seminary was the only source of formal education, and news of the outside world was filtered through church publications and Sunday sermons. Madero's revolution had received tentative endorsement from San Joseans, but subsequent revolutionary governments seemed alien and disconnected with their world. They knew nothing of Calles's success at national reconstruction. They knew only of his inexplicable and blasphemous attacks on the Mother Church.

The village priest, Padre Federico, was the most important voice within the community. Federico came from a prominent local family, which allowed him to serve as intermediary between hacendados and farmers. For example, Federico convinced the owner of the largest hacienda to partition his estate into small plots and sell them to land-hungry peasants at reasonable prices, thereby forestalling an agrarian reform at the hands of outsiders.

The Cristero Rebellion in San José started when the local civil defense commander from a neighboring town attempted to arrest Father Federico. When the priest managed to escape, the military chief turned his anger on the town and looted homes and stores. This turned the entire community against the government. Padre Federico consulted with the local bishop, the Unión Popular, and neighboring clergy, and then urged San Joseans to rebel.

The community solidly supported the church, and a modest army of forty men volunteered to fight. About half of the recruits received rifles; the rest armed themselves with machetes, knives, clubs, or farm implements. In the words of Luis González:

> Some of these men had come out of the Zamora seminary only the year before; some were small landowners and cattlemen (or their sons); and the rest were corn farmers or ordinary ranch hands. A third of them were married men with children. Their ages ranged from eighteen to forty; they knew something about firearms and horses, but they had no military training.[15]

The National League for the Defense of Religion appointed military commanders to lead Cristero villagers, but they proved useless and local caudillos soon took charge. These local leaders led contingents of ten to twenty rebels throughout the countryside, periodically raiding federal outputs, assassinating government supporters, and then escaping into the hills. The Cristeros' lack of arms and military training prevented them from overrunning and controlling cities, but their guerrilla-style tactics frustrated federal forces, whose practice of looting Cristero villages and hanging anyone who looked suspicious only stiffened rebel resolve.[16]

The national army's inability to defeat the Cristeros forced Calles to mobilize grassroots peasant armies of his own. The president turned to agrarian warlords, such as Saturnino Cedillo, and asked them to raise agrarista battalions to crush the Cristeros. Agraristas, who had already clashed with Cristeros over land in west-central Mexico, were now forced to fight again as further payment for their land. Cedillo's men succeeded in defeating the Cristeros in Guanajuato and San Luis Potosí, and the military tide turned in the government's favor.[17]

In July 1927, the National League for the Defense for Religion, desperately seeking clear military direction, appointed former Porfirian general Enrique Gorostieta to command rebel forces in Jalisco. Gorostieta succeeded in expelling the federal army from the state, and in October 1928 he was appointed supreme military commander of rebel forces. Gorostieta's fifteen-point manifesto articulated the Cristeros' political objectives.

Recognition of the Constitution of 1857 *without the reform laws;* refusal to recognize the authorities; adoption of laws based on the peoples' wishes and on tradition; votes for women; syndicalism; agreements between holders of ejido lands and property owners for the payment of indemnities; distribution of rural properties in a just and equitable way after indemnification; plans to make land available to the greatest number; baptism of the Cristero army as the "National Guard"; and adoption of the motto "God, Country, and Liberty."[18]

Gorostieta's manifesto provides a summary of the conservative reaction to revolutionary change since the 1850s. The Cristero leader demanded equitable land reform with indemnification for hacendados as well as revocation of the reform laws that had stripped the church of its special courts and haciendas. He questioned the legitimacy of revolutionary legislation since the 1850s and advocated a Cristero "National Guard" that would presumably protect the church and its hacendado allies from future reforms. Gorostieta's advocacy of syndicalism and voting rights for women also reflected progressive stances on some social issues adopted by liberal clergy and lay workers since the Porfiriato. In effect, Mexico's conservative leadership supported limited social and political liberalization under the watchful eye of church-sponsored political parties and unions. It rejected anticlericalism and state-directed land reform.

"EL MAXIMATO" AND THE END TO THE CRISTERO REBELLION

Gorostieta's success on the battlefield forced Calles to reconsider his options, which became disturbingly narrow as the presidential election of 1928 approached.[19] Plutarco Elías Calles had been a strong president, but the most popular man in Mexico remained General Alvaro Obregón, whose supporters pushed through Congress a new election law that allowed former presidents to run for a second term. During the campaign, Obregón visited communities throughout the nation and reminded Mexicans of his military triumphs and political accomplishments. Behind closed doors he shored up his support among influential generals and caudillos. On election day General Obregón won as expected, but before he could take office he fell victim to an assassin's bullet. A religious fanatic named José de León Toral murdered Mexico's greatest living general. While Obregón's assassination was mourned by revolutionaries, Cristeros and their allies celebrated his death.[20]

The 1928 election underscored Mexico's inability to escape revolutionary bloodshed and to establish a peaceful method of presidential succession. In addition to lingering church-state conflict, ambitious generals who felt unrewarded for their heroic deeds, whether real or imagined, resorted to violence when their financial and political goals went unfulfilled. During the 1928 electoral campaign, for example, Generals Arnulfo R. Gómez and Francisco R. Serrano concluded that Obregón's election was a forgone conclusion and, under the banner of a resurrected Anti-Reelectionist Party, attempted to seize power before Obregón could take office. The rebellion failed and Gómez, Serrano, and dozens of their supporters were arrested and executed.

The Gómez-Serrano affair and Obregón's assassination generated serious attempts at resolution to the crisis of presidential succession. During the mid-1920s, an important venue of political discourse emerged at the National University in Mexico City. It revolved around the imposing figure of José Vasconcelos, former minister of education and rector of the National University. Vasconcelos inspired a generation of student activists who subsequently sought a voice in the political process and helped form two political parties, the right-wing Partido Acción Nacional (PAN) and the progressive Partido Popular (later the Partido Popular Socialista). Mainstream revolutionary leaders also recognized the existence of a reservoir of political talent at the National University and recruited student leaders into their expanding political family.

Calles's solution to the problem of presidential succession and militarism rested on the creation of a political party large enough to accommodate Mexico's diverse assortment of revolutionary caudillos. The Partido Nacional Revolucionario (PNR), forerunner of the present-day Partido Revolucionario Institucional (PRI), became the primary vehicle for selecting Mexico's presidents as well as popularizing and implementing their programs. The party would work hand and glove with the government to maintain a political elite in power through patronage and corruption, downsizing the military, and controlling political opponents through electoral fraud, violence, and manipulation of the judiciary.

With the creation of the PNR in 1929 and the removal of important rivals, Calles could now dominate Mexican politics for the foreseeable future. He sought compliant successors who would not challenge his status as Mexico's most powerful caudillo, the *jefe máximo* (hence "el Maximato"), and who would allow him to rule from behind the scenes. At Calles's request, Congress named General Emilio Portes Gil to serve out the first two years of Obregón's term. The PNR subsequently nominated General Pascual Ortiz Rubio as its presidential candidate in 1929.

The 1929 presidential election proved more contentious than Calles had envisioned. Ortiz Rubio was challenged by the popular José Vasconcelos who enjoyed widespread support among university students as well as the Cristeros. Moreover, disgruntled Obregonista generals who had hoped to profit from a second Obregón administration now attempted to seize control of the government. Led by General Gonzalo Escobar, this conflict forced Calles to divert troops and resources away from fighting the Cristeros, and the government lost 40,000,000 pesos and 2,000 troops before Escobar could be defeated.

Ortiz Rubio's subsequent election to the presidency initiated a cycle of presidential contests won by the emerging official party. Nevertheless, violence remained ingrained within the Mexican political system. Shortly after Ortiz Rubio's inauguration, a gunman fired six shots into the president's car. One bullet passed through his wife's ear and another shattered Ortiz Rubio's jaw, while flying glass lacerated the president's niece. The triggerman, Daniel Flores, was identified under torture as a Vasconcelos supporter. The regional military commander, General Eulogio Ortiz, decided to avenge the president by arresting, torturing, and executing dozens of Vasconcelos's supporters. The discovery of the remains of sixty victims at Topilejo, along the highway connecting Mexico City with Cuernavaca, caused a public scandal that remained in the headlines until the government silenced the press. The use of assassination, torture, and execution by hitmen and security forces would continue to characterize modern Mexican politics.[21]

The Escobar revolt and Vasconcelos's challenge, although successfully blunted, still diverted government efforts away from crushing the Cristeros. Millions of pesos and hundreds of troops were expended to assure Portes Gil's ascension to the presidency, and the likelihood of a military victory by either side now appeared dim. Portes Gil lost little time in negotiating with the church. The groundwork for a peace treaty had been already laid by Obregón during 1927 in talks with church representatives, and Calles cooperated by releasing imprisoned LNDR leaders and instructing his minister of foreign affairs, Aaron Sáenz, to participate in the negotiations.

Dwight Morrow's timely appointment as U.S. ambassador to Mexico also contributed to an eventual agreement between the Mexican government and the Catholic Church. Morrow approached his new assignment with enthusiasm and intelligence. He and his wife, both wealthy New York socialites, studied Spanish and developed a personal rapport with Calles and other government elites. This personal relationship helped Morrow reach a quick settlement on the petroleum crisis. The ambassador also scored points with the Mexican public by arranging for visits by the renown humorist Will Rogers and the famous aviator Charles Lindberg, who later married Morrow's daughter following a whirlwind romance in Mexico City.

Morrow's active involvement in negotiations between the government and the Cristeros began in January 1928 in Havana, Cuba. There he met with representatives from the Vatican and the Mexican church. He later produced an outline for a final settlement that was endorsed by Calles, President Portes Gil, the Vatican, and the Mexican bishops. The settlement announced in June 1929 declared the status quo ante bellum: the anticlerical laws remained unchanged, but the government would not enforce them in a manner hostile to the church. The civil war, which seemingly changed little in political terms, had cost the lives of ninety thousand combatants and tens of thousands of civilians. The compromise settlement reflected the inability of either side to win on the battlefield and postponed a political solution. In the years ahead, the growing power of the federal government and the official party would assure state supremacy over the church. Mexico's peasantry and clergy, however, stubbornly resisted renewed attempts by Mexico City and radical state governors in the 1930s to enforce educational and religious reforms.[22]

President Ortiz Rubio, embarrassed and angered by Calles's heavy-handed manipulation of his presidency, stepped down in 1932. Calles's handpicked choice to serve out the term was General Abelardo Rodríguez, the former governor of Baja California, who had made a fortune promoting gambling and prostitution. Calles and Rodríguez faced an economic depression that had virtually paralyzed Mexico's principal export industries and caused widespread hardship in rural areas. They rejected government financed programs to save the economy in favor of scaling back on agrarian reform and consolidating their political authority through downsizing and professionalizing the military. They reduced the number of officers and enlisted men and created the Superior War College in 1932. Rodríguez also promoted economic integration through the construction of a major highway linking Mexico City with Nuevo Laredo on the Texas border, and he displayed nationalist credentials by writing proposals to place key industries, such as mining, oil, and electricity, under Mexican control.

CONCLUSION

Despite the unsettled social and economic conditions in rural regions, Calles remained in power for ten years by ruling through puppet presidents and creating the PNR to alleviate the crisis of presidential succession. Calles's clash with the Catholic Church, evidence of grassroots resistance to liberal and revolutionary secularism, ended in a bloody stalemate and left unresolved the cultural differences between traditional and revolutionary Mexicans. U.S. Ambassador Dwight Morrow's positive role in negotiating a settlement to the Cristero Rebellion signaled improving relations with the United States, which also led to renegotiation of Mexico's international debt.

Plutarco Calles's success in laying the foundation for a corporate state controlled by revolutionary generals and their civilian allies inaugurated a new political era. The PNR managed the selection of presidents, essentially by rubber-stamping the outgoing president's choice, and helped keep the revolutionary elite in power by promoting and implementing government programs. The creation of a political party, however, did not end violence as a method of resolving political disputes. Assassination and political arrests remained commonplace, and revolutionary leaders did not hesitate to mobilize agraristas and other allies to fight their opponents.

Calles's vision for Mexico also included economic integration through large-scale construction projects and improved management of government finances. Like most of his Constitutionalist brethren, Calles had little interest in alleviating the plight of Mexico's impoverished villagers through land reform and other social programs. He and his puppet successors left unresolved the crisis of rural poverty and other underlining causes of the revolution, notably the predominance of foreign capital in the national economy, which remained issues to be addressed by others.[23]

POLITICAL CHRONOLOGY, 1917–1934

1917–1920, Presidency of Venustiano Carranza
    Emiliano Zapata assassinated, 1919
    Pancho Villa retires, 1919
    Venustiano Carranza assassinated, 1920

1920–1924, Presidency of Alvaro Obregón
    Bucareli Agreements, 1923
    De la Huerta revolt, 1923
    Pancho Villa assassinated, 1923

1924–1928, Presidency of Plutarco Elías Calles
    Cristero Rebellion, 1926–1929
    Obregón reelected and assassinated, 1928

1928–1934, El Maximato of Plutarco Elías Calles
    Partido Nacional Revolucionario (PNR) founded, 1929
    Interim presidency of Emilio Portes Gil, 1928–1930
    Presidency of Pascual Ortiz Rubio, 1930–1932
    Interim presidency of Abelardo L. Rodríguez, 1932–1934

CHAPTER NINE

LÁZARO CÁRDENAS AND THE SEARCH FOR THE REVOLUTIONARY UTOPIA, 1934–1940

THE FOOT SOLDIERS OF THE REVOLUTION and their radical allies, largely bypassed by the programs of the triumphant Sonorans, awaited their savior. His coming appeared unlikely, however, because of Calles's control over the presidential selection process and the economic and political rewards caudillos received for remaining loyal to the regime. Moreover, conservative forces outside of the PNR, such as the Cristeros, businessmen, and hacendados, opposed social programs beneficial to workers and landless peasants. Given the strength of the opposition, grassroots radical movements appeared unlikely to force a significant shift in government policy. Redirection would require a political insider with the skill to outmaneuver Calles from within the PNR as well as the ability to reunite Mexico's peasants and workers under his political leadership.

Lázaro Cárdenas, the son of a grocer in Jiquilpan, Michoacán, rose rapidly through the revolutionary ranks to overtake Calles and become the champion of the popular classes. Cárdenas's remarkable political journey began in the army where he had formed a close relationship with General Calles. Calles served as his political mentor and benefactor during and after the revolution. By 1934, Cárdenas had served in a variety of important

FIGURE 42: Lázaro Cárdenas joined the Revolution at age fifteen.
He rose quickly through the ranks and became president in 1934.

Source: Anita Brenner, *The Wind that Swept Mexico: The History of the Mexican Revolution of 1910–1942*, with 184 historical photographs assembled by George R. Leighton (Austin: University of Texas Press, 1971), photograph 96.

political positions and had earned the right to be named PNR candidate for president. Unwilling to serve as Calles's puppet, however, Cárdenas formed his own coalition of military, agrarian, and labor supporters, wrestled control over the government from the jefe máximo, and succeeded in implementing a progressive agenda that favored agrarian reform, socialistic education, and economic nationalism.

Cárdenas's efforts on behalf of workers and peasants transformed him into an icon of the Mexican left. His luster, however, outlasted many of his programs. Succeeding presidents paid homage to the historical Cárdenas, but they did not consistently adhere to his policies and ideals. Already by 1940, his conservative opponents and a flagging economy compelled Cárdenas to select a moderate successor, General Manuel Avila Camacho, whose policies favored economic development and political stability over the interests of peasants and workers. Cardenismo's most enduring legacies rested on the revitalization of Mexican nationalism—achieved in the oil expropriation of 1938—and in the commitment to public education and social opportunity. Despite valiant efforts at land reform, communal farming faced widespread opposition from large landowners, the church, and rancheros who favored capitalistic systems of production. Moreover, Cárdenas's reorganization of the Partido Nacional Revolucionario (PNR) into the Partido de la Revolución Mexicana (PRM), which was intended to benefit the popular classes and consolidate their gains, resulted in centralized authority without assuring long-term social and material benefits for the common citizen.

THE EDUCATION OF A REVOLUTIONARY

Cárdenas's rapid advance through the military ranks during the revolution reflected his political skills as well as the opportunities for mobility created by the volatile environment. Cárdenas's excellent penmanship, unusual in an overwhelmingly illiterate army, caught the eye of his commanding officer who promoted him to lieutenant in charge of correspondence at age nineteen. He soon came to the attention of General Calles, the master politician and former schoolteacher, who took a personal liking to the young officer and nicknamed him "the kid." Calles carefully observed Cárdenas's leadership and military skills and entrusted him with the first line of defense at the battle of Agua Prieta, an important Constitutionalist victory over Pancho Villa. Cárdenas's continued military accomplishments won him promotion to colonel by 1918, and his support of Obregón's overthrow of Carranza in 1920 assured him further military and political advancement.[1]

The Obregonistas represented the progressive wing of the Constitutionalist movement, and the coup had the support of Zapatistas, labor leaders, and small businessmen. Obregón implemented a strategic land reform designed to reward political supporters and to undermine political opponents, and he appointed key progressives to positions of authority. Powerful regional caudillos who had supported the coup, such as General Saturnino Cedillo in San Luis Potosí and General Francisco Múgica in Michoacán, also used their grassroots political organizations to claim political office.

In Michoacán, Governor Múgica—Cárdenas's close friend—attempted to enforce land reform and socialist education within an unsafe political environment. Múgica's mobilization of agraristas led to land seizures and internecine conflict, and his attacks on the Catholic Church sparked counteroffenses against the government by conservatives. In February 1922, the opposition had succeeded in ousting the controversial Múgica, and Obregón stood aside and let it happen. The following year Obregón, upset over Múgica's continuing association with agrarian radicals, ordered his assassination and gave the assignment to Michoacán's military commander, Brigadier General Lázaro Cárdenas. Cárdenas refused to acknowledge receiving the order to execute his friend, however, and skillfully managed to avoid political repercussions during the remaining months of Obregón's presidency.[2]

General Múgica's survival allowed him to exert an important influence on Cárdenas's political formation. Múgica's radicalism at the constitutional convention in 1916 contributed significantly to articles mandating land reform, anticlericalism, and state ownership of subsoil rights, and he remained committed to these and other progressive viewpoints. Anticlericalism and public education were also favored by Cárdenas's political mentor General Calles, who succeeded Obregón as president in 1924.[3]

President Calles's appointment of Cárdenas to important military and political posts assured him influence within the revolutionary inner circle. From 1925 to 1928, General Cárdenas served as military commander of the Huasteca, the region that produced the bulk of the nation's petroleum and tax revenues. Ongoing discussions with the foreign petroleum companies over enforcement of Article 27 of the constitution, as well as the potential for labor unrest, made this a particularly sensitive assignment. Reflecting on his tenure in the region, Cárdenas recalled that the foreign oil companies viewed the Huasteca as "conquered territory," cheated the government of tax revenues, fouled the environment, and refused to build schools, hospitals, or recreational facilities for Mexican workers and their families. Cárdenas was also outraged when, a few days after his arrival, the petroleum company managers offered him a bribe of $50,000 dollars and a new Packard automobile delivered to his door. The oil executives mistakenly assumed that these gifts would cause the proud general to ignore their violations of the law.[4]

In 1928, President Calles appointed Cárdenas governor of his home state of Michoacán. The Cristero Rebellion had torn apart the region, and following the negotiated peace in 1929 the new governor attempted to enforce a controversial social agenda. Cárdenas's commitment to land reform, nationalism, and secularization was reminiscent of Múgica's agenda and stemmed from their faith in socialistic solutions and the revolutionary process.

Cárdenas organized local political supporters into a new organization, the Michoacán Revolutionary Confederation of Labor. The eclectic confederation included Primo Tapia's disbanded Agrarian League, teachers dedicated to secular education and socialism, and Communist Party members. Within four years, the confederation boasted 4,000 agrarian committees and 100,000 members, making it Mexico's first mass organization created by and linked to the government. Cárdenas used the confederation to agitate for his policies, particularly land reform and secular education.[5]

Teachers became the shock troops of cultural revolution. They ventured into Cristero strongholds to teach reading, writing, and technical skills and to preach against clerical influence and traditional vices such as alcoholism. Assuming the role of latter-day secular missionaries, they taught peasants practical skills, such as soap making and fruit preservation, that improved their health and economic self-sufficiency. They also preached the benefits of labor unions and cooperative farming. Teachers had to overcome cultural barriers as well as violent resistance. They often carried firearms when entering haciendas and other conservative strongholds. Cárdenas sometimes prevented conflict by asking his close friend Luis María Martínez, the bishop of Morelia, to reassign those priests who preached armed resistance to the secular word. In the end, the Cardenistas succeeded in improving literacy rates and technical skills, but they found it impossible to undermine Catholic traditions instilled in peasant culture for more than three hundred years. Cárdenas would persist with his cultural agenda while president and would achieve similarly mixed results on the national level.[6]

Lázaro Cárdenas's solution to alleviating peasant's poverty was in the formation of communal farms (ejidos) on an unprecedented scale.[7] From September 1928 to September 1932, Cárdenas distributed 141,663 hectares among 181 villages in Michoacán, as compared to the 131,283 hectares given to 124 pueblos by his predecessors from 1917 to 1928. While president, Cárdenas created ejidos on an unprecedented scale and introduced collective farming based on the Soviet kolkhoz, which involved profit-sharing and self-management.[8]

Cárdenas's faith in the ejido stemmed from his assumptions about the viability of communal farming in colonial times as well as his belief in socialistic solutions to economic underdevelopment. He hoped that the ejido would liberate peasants from the clutches of hacendados, reduce the need for wage labor, increase agricultural output, and feed the nation. The ejido, however, had its critics. Most hacendados, rancheros, and conservatives opposed state-imposed land reform under any format, while liberals (including some clergy) favored granting land to villagers as private property and encouraging investment in technical improvements. President Calles favored this format as a means of increasing rural income and agricultural production.[9]

Cárdenas's communication and personal skills helped him build a popular base and increase his influence within the Partido Nacional Revolucionario. As governor he traveled to remote Indian villages to promote secular education and campaign against alcoholism. He spoke in nonthreatening terms, met with villagers individually, and actively cultivated paternalistic relationships with impoverished natives. He sometimes directed bilingual associates to deliver speeches in Indian languages, which clarified programs and demonstrated respect for indigenous culture. For example, when villagers protested the installation of a cultural center in Carapan, Cárdenas went to the pueblo accompanied by a political aide, Victoriano Anguiano, who addressed the assembled residents in their native tongue. He relates the impact of his speech on the audience:

The Governor ordered me to explain to them that they had been deceived by those who had said those missionaries of culture were going to deprive them of the Catholic religion . . . that the education to be given to adults and children was so that they might live better, in less unhealthy and impoverished conditions. I began my address in Spanish, but soon realized that it was like pouring water in the ocean. Then I began to explain things to them in our sweet and melodious Purépechan language and the effect was magical. Their faces were transformed by expressions of confidence, looks of comprehension and smiles of recognition for a fellow Indian. And of course they understood and accepted my explanations; their reserve, their doubt, their distrust—with which people descended from pre-Columbian culture always view the mestizos—changed to ingenuous joy and complete confidence.[10]

Even assuming some self-serving embellishment, Anguiano's account demonstrates the impact of Cárdenas's journeys to remote places. His populist message resonated among Mexico's poorest citizens, and many of them came to view him as a father figure, especially after he became president.

The governor's deft political skills also surfaced in gatherings of high-ranking party officials, and in November 1930 they picked him to serve as president of the Partido Nacional Revolucionario. During his nine-month tenure, Cárdenas attempted to increase popular support for the PNR by reorganizing the party newspaper *(El Nacional)*, founding the National Sports Confederation, campaigning against alcoholism, and traveling to Oaxaca to personally dispense government aid to earthquake victims. In the power struggle between Calles and President Ortiz Rubio, Cárdenas tilted toward the president but avoided quarreling with the jefe máximo. Partly because of the feud, however, Cárdenas resigned his position and, after a two-month tenure as minister of the interior, left Mexico City.[11]

Cárdenas's resignation removed him from the political crossfire that ended with Ortiz Rubio's ouster and the appointment of Callista loyalist Abelardo Rodríguez as president. Cárdenas then briefly served as military commander of Puebla before returning to the cabinet as Rodríguez's minister of war and the navy. As this president's truncated term drew to a close, however, party leaders faced the difficult decision of selecting the next chief of state. Calles wanted to remain the power behind the scenes but needed a figurehead with the skill and experience to manage an increasingly complex country.

Lázaro Cárdenas was an inspired but politically risky choice. Cárdenas had been a loyal Callista since the revolution, and his extensive administrative experience as governor, party leader, and cabinet member had given him intimate knowledge of the Mexican political system. Calles also reportedly loved Cárdenas like a son. However, there were signs that Cárdenas could not be easily controlled. As governor of Michoacán, he had pursued progressive programs that demonstrated ideological differences with Calles, Rodríguez, and other party leaders. Cárdenas's ability to communicate with workers and peasants also gave him the potential for marshaling substantial popular support and forming an independent political base.[12]

POWER STRUGGLE

Cárdenas's nomination as the PNR candidate for president assured his election either by popular vote or fraud. Still, he launched the most impressive cross-country campaign in Mexican history in order to mobilize popular support for his candidacy and develop an independent political base. He attracted workers and peasants by advocating labor rights and land reform and met with regional caudillos including those who had opposed the Sonorans in 1927 and 1929. In the Yucatán, he told peasants toiling on the henequen plantations that the land should be returned to them; in Veracruz he promised to dedicate himself to reuniting divided workers; and in Coahuila he lamented the terrible social conditions of the Tarahumara Indians and migrant workers.

With electoral formalities completed, Cárdenas made important symbolic gestures designed to establish ties with peasants and workers. He moved his official residence from the sumptuous Chapultepec Castle to the more modest Los Pinos, installed a direct telegraph line to hear the complaints of all Mexicans, and opened the doors of the National Palace to Mexico's poorest citizens.[13]

During the first two years of his presidency, Cárdenas worked to fashion a governing coalition that would allow him to steer an independent political course. Contemporaries remembered Cárdenas as an usually skilled politician who carefully plotted an end game without revealing his hand. For example, Gonzalo N. Santos, a veteran caudillo from San Luis Potosí, observed, "Professional Cardenistas paint Cárdenas as a Saint Francis of Assisi, but that's the last thing he was. I have known no other politician who was better at hiding his intentions and feelings than General Cárdenas . . . he was a fox."[14] Narciso Bassols, former minister of education, remembered Cárdenas as neither exceptionally intelligent nor cultured. But he "had something much more valuable. He had political instinct at the tip of his fingers."[15]

Cárdenas used these skills to forge alliances with those willing to challenge Callista hegemony. He cut deals with regional bosses of varying ideological persuasions and historical loyalties, gained greater control over congress and the judiciary, made key alliances with leftist labor unions discontented with CROM, solidified his support among the peasantry, and reorganized and strengthened the national party. His political muscle allowed him to implement a reform agenda that focused on land redistribution, public education, expropriating the foreign-controlled petroleum industry, and defending national sovereignty.[16]

Cárdenas's quest to seize control of the presidency—to cut the puppeteer's strings—required taking steps that increased presidential authority and the strength of the national party. These centralizing political maneuvers allowed Cárdenas to achieve independence from Calles and to carry out reforms mandated by the constitution. Cárdenas's success at revamping the PNR made possible the emergence of a powerful, inclusive, national party that could serve as a vehicle for enforcing reforms. Unfortunately, the strengthened national party under different presidential leadership would also have the potential to block implementation of reforms or to enforce antireform measures.

Making bargains with regional caudillos, who ran the ideological gauntlet from conservative to radical, gave Cárdenas clout at a crucial juncture. These headstrong revolutionary veterans, however, also retained important decision-making authority and patronage networks in their provinces. The endurance of caudillismo worked as a brake against the creation of an all-powerful presidency, and it raises interesting questions for future research on the character of the revolutionary state.[17]

As a revolutionary general who became president, Cárdenas understood the enduring importance of senior military personnel in national and regional politics. As a result, he promoted Callista generals into positions of political insignificance in the provinces. He offered others early retirement with generous pensions, replacing them with generals loyal to him. These new appointees included former Zapatistas, Carrancistas, and Villistas who had been passed over by Obregón and Calles.

Cárdenas also undercut his opponents in the judiciary and Congress. He lobbied for new legislation that eliminated lifetime appointments for judges and reduced judicial terms to six years. Cárdenas also arranged the resignation of several Callista senators and deputies who had vocally opposed his labor policies.[18]

Cárdenas's alliances with emergent, leftist labor organizations buttressed his political independence, but also created tensions with Calles. Cárdenas recognized the political utility of labor's support, favored unions over business, and supported the right to strike and workers' participation in managerial decision-making (including, in extreme cases, worker control of industries and agricultural cooperatives). Calles, by contrast, favored business over labor, had a cozy relationship with Morones and CROM, and had shown impatience with striking workers.[19]

Workers' growing displeasure over the ineffectiveness and corruption of CROM caused them to join alternative unions. Vicente Lombardo Toledano, Mexico's preeminent Marxist intellectual and labor activist, played a pivotal role in organizing the anti-CROM labor movement through the National Committee for the Defense of the Proletariat. Officially recorded strikes increased from a mere 13 in 1933 to a disturbing 202 in 1934, and then escalated dramatically to 642 in 1935. CROM suffered a telling blow when five union leaders in Mexico City—the famous "five little wolves" (the nickname referred to their short stature)—defected and sided with Lombardo. The charismatic Marxist then assembled numerous unions recently involved in militant strikes, including railroad hands, miners, petroleum workers, tram-workers, electricians, and printers, into the Confederación de Trabajadores Mexicanos (CTM). The CTM, which stood squarely on the left and included many communist workers, claimed 3,594 affiliates and 946,000 members, which made it Mexico's largest labor confederation and limited CROM's influence primarily to company unions and the textile industry. CTM hegemony stopped at the city's edge, however, as Mexico's vast peasantry remained outside of its control.[20]

Rising labor unrest, some of it encouraged by the government, greatly disturbed Plutarco Elías Calles. The jefe máximo of the revolution issued public statements blasting labor radicalism and hinted at removing Cárdenas. Calles's condemnations, which were widely publicized in the Callista press, criticized the regime's "communist" tendencies and compared it unfavorably with European fascist governments. Such disturbing statements helped mobilize organized labor and public opinion against Calles, and influential party insiders such as Governor Adalberto Tejeda in Veracruz and General Juan Andrew Almazán urged Cárdenas to take action against the jefe máximo.

Calles, however, represented a formidable opponent. His supporters included cabinet ministers, army generals, congressmen, CROM leaders, and members of the business community and urban middle class. Influential Callista Juan de Dios Bojórquez, the secretary of government, feared the outbreak of a full-scale civil war and urged Calles and Cárdenas to reach a political compromise.

Cárdenas chose to take the offensive. After securing the support of key political figures such as Saturnino Cedillo, General Almazán, and former president Emilio Portes Gil, Cárdenas boldly removed Callistas from his cabinet and replaced them with Cardenistas. There then followed a purge of Callista congressmen, PNR officials, governors (including the rabidly anticlerical Garrido Canabal in Tabasco), and various regional caudillos. Cárdenas also removed Callista generals and police commanders from important positions and replaced them with loyalists. By 1938, 91 generals had been removed, or nearly one-quarter of the 350 on duty in 1934.[21]

The final confrontation between Calles and Cárdenas came in April 1936. Buttressed by the support of thousands of militant workers who poured into the streets of Mexico City and demanded Calles's removal, President Cárdenas ordered the exile of the former jefe máximo to the United States. Calles had lost the political battle between revolutionary titans. Cárdenas quickly took steps to heal the political wounds created by twenty-five years of revolution by pardoning ten thousand political prisoners and inviting back to Mexico prominent exiles, including former President Adolfo de la Huerta and the son of Porfirio Díaz. These measures helped create the political climate Cárdenas required to carry out his ambitious reforms.[22]

AGRARIAN REFORM

Although the revolution had been largely fought over ownership of land, revolutionary governments from Carranza to Rodríguez had viewed agrarian reform primarily as a means of gaining the support of local agrarista leaders and punishing conservative hacendados. In most regions, haciendas still occupied the best land, controlled water resources, and produced the bulk of agricultural products. Moreover, many ejido members (or ejidatarios) in Morelos and elsewhere received inferior land and suffered from lack of capital. The neglect of the peasantry reflected the attitude of presidents who questioned the viability of the ejido, favored government-assisted capitalist development, and had little sympathy for Indian villagers.

Lázaro Cárdenas hailed from Michoacán where the struggle over land had shaped his revolutionary consciousness. Cárdenas represented the leftist faction within the revolutionary leadership, a faction favoring an agrarian reform aimed at destroying the hacienda and improving peasants' standard of living. By 1940, Cárdenas had redistributed land to more people than all of his predecessors combined, created an agricultural credit bank, and undermined the traditional latifundium.

Land reform, however, remained a contentious and incomplete process. Opposition from hacendados, rancheros, and the church blocked its full implementation in many regions, and corrupt federal and local officials undermined the economic viability of the ejido elsewhere. Agricultural production declined and the deepening global depression reduced prices of agricultural products and dried up capital resources. In the end, there was no obvious solution to Mexico's rural poverty. Beginning in the 1940s, thousands of villagers would seek economic salvation through migrating to urban areas, especially Mexico City, and crossing the border into the United States—either legally or illegally—in search of a living wage.

Cárdenas's agrarian reform provoked varied responses depending upon local economic, political, and cultural histories.[23] The president's home province of Michoacán provides a good example. Not surprisingly, Indian communities that had lost land to hacendados and rancheros during the Porfiriato, such as the Zacapu region studied by Paul Friedrich, produced grassroots agrarian movements.[24] Conversely, native villages and ranchero communities that had retained their land resisted land reforms as outrageous government intrusions in community life.[25] Rancheros also believed that land should be acquired only through purchase or inheritance and they opposed forced redistributions as a violation of private property rights.[26]

The community of San José de Gracia, Michoacán, inhabited primarily by mestizo rancheros, offers insights into the difficulties faced by the Cardenista agrarian reform. The community had formed a united front against anticlericalism in the 1920s, and the church and landowners also opposed agrarian reform. With the onset of the Great Depression, however, many landless villagers welcomed land distribution as a means of surviving.

Governor Gildardo Magaña, the veteran Zapatista and former governor of Baja California, created a local agrarian party and instructed it to mobilize political support for land reform. The party attracted some local villagers, but its most ardent supporters were outsiders imported by the governor. Conservatives countered by organizing their own political organization, the "Law and Order" party, which included rancheros, businessmen, small farmers, and individuals who anticipated inheriting property.[27]

State-imposed agrarian reform revealed previously masked class divisions that were sometimes expressed in self-righteous terms. Landowners called agraristas "heretics, blasphemers, atheists, thieves, and desecrators" and referred to themselves as "more intelligent, industrious, and cultured than their workers." Agraristas characterized themselves as "virtuous and poor" and believed that "agrarianism had no quarrel with God and his priests." They also rejected the insult that they were "dumb, lazy, or ignorant." In fact, they believed that "educated people were inept when it came to raising crops and handling cattle."[28] Among the agraristas, ingrained hatred of the government was now directed toward "rich people." Landowners directed their hatred at the agraristas, land commissioners, and Mexico City.[29]

In 1934, the Consolidated Agrarian Commission's study of San José concluded that local haciendas should be divided among 610 working-age males. Landowners blocked agrarian commissioners' attempts at land redistribution, however, by employing a variety of illegal tactics. For example, hacendados bribed government surveyors to falsify boundaries, offered ejidatarios land that they did not own, and used their private armies to intimidate, injure, and murder peasants.

As a result of these illegal and violent tactics, land redistribution proved entirely inadequate. Only two of five haciendas lost land to villagers, and the two hundred beneficiaries of this redistribution received small plots inadequate for either stock raising or dry farming. This led inevitably to frequent conflicts among farmers. Land disputes deteriorated into fistfights and shootouts, and many unhappy villagers resorted to working part-time on neighboring haciendas or migrating to the United States.

Political opposition to agrarian reform intensified, thus weakening Cardenismo locally. Father Federico González Cárdenas, who had led San José's Cristeros, publicly criticized the ejido for decreasing production and sowing social dissension, and he soon organized an opposition political party. In 1940 San Josean Gildardo González founded the pro-clerical, antirevolutionary Sinarquista Party, whose many followers in the central-west and northern regions denounced Cardenismo.

In the end, San José proved to be infertile ground for revolutionary change. The town's ranchero community had escaped serious land consolidation during the Porfiriato, had avoided fighting in the revolution, and had successfully resisted Calles's anticlerical reforms. The agrarian reform faced stiff opposition from landowners and clergy and revealed class conflicts that tore apart the community. Nonetheless, President Cárdenas himself, who hailed from a nearby village, was largely disassociated from the conflict provoked by his policies. He was instead viewed as a local hero and father figure, and his visit to the village in 1940 evoked an outpouring of affection. One villager remarked, "He did not kill; he was merciful; he held back religious persecution; he brought peace."[30]

John Gledhill's study of Guaracha, which bordered Cárdenas's birthplace of Jiquilpan, chronicles another difficult transition from hacienda to ejido. In 1933, local agraristas occupied 300 hectares of the sugar plantation that had dominated the local economy. Three years later the president transformed it into the ejido "Emiliano Zapata." The planter Manuel Moreno retained ownership of the mill, however, and worked diligently to undermine the ejido's success.

Despite the formation of the revolutionary state, local notables in Guaracha and elsewhere retained coercive power that blunted the effectiveness of presidential policies. Violence clearly played a role in slowing social change. Hacendados organized private police forces, sometimes including ex-Cristero pistoleros, to terrorize ejidatarios. Priests also used the confessional to gather information that they shared with conservative allies, and they denounced agraristas from the pulpit as communists headed for eternal damnation.

Guaracha's ejido also suffered from structural deficiencies. Sugar production declined from lack of capital resources and organizational problems. The falling market price of sugar drove even efficient producers out of business. Moreover, the ejido provided fewer job opportunities for seasonal employment than had the former plantation. This undermined the reform's creditability among villagers. Local agrarian authorities and labor leaders also used their influence to line their pockets, and labor disputes in the mill disrupted production. Support for the agrarian reform remained strongest among midsized farmers and returning migrants, whose experience in the United States and elsewhere had widened their economic and ideological horizons. Nevertheless, Guaracha's ejido failed, and in January 1940 the land was divided into individual parcels and the sugar mill was closed down.[31]

Structural and administrative problems also undermined the ejido in Morelos, the home of Zapatismo. By the 1930s, revolutionary governments had already divided many haciendas into ejidos in the state, but corruption and lack of capital undermined their efficiency. In 1936, President Cárdenas attempted to alleviate credit shortages by creating the National Bank for Ejidal Credit and capitalizing it at 51,000,000 pesos for that year. Loan requests far exceeded this amount, however, and the bank favored ejidos whose success would reap the greatest political and economic return for the state. For example, ejidos in the cotton-rich La Laguna region, whose creation involved the Confederación de Trabajadores Mexicanos and the Mexican Communist Party, received two-thirds of the total budget in 1936.

Population increases also aggravated economic conditions in Morelos. During the 1930s, the number of inhabitants rose from 132,700 to 182,700. This figure included 10,000 migrants who assumed that the extensive redistribution of land had created new economic opportunities. Instead, the population influx put tremendous pressure on land and water resources, created surplus labor pools, and forced many peasants to sell their labor or move into the cities.[32]

Perhaps the most dramatic agrarian reform occurred in La Laguna, the region where Durango and Coahuila intersect. A large-scale strike by cotton workers in 1935–1936 gained national attention. The regional cotton economy had declined dramatically in the 1920s because of falling cotton prices, pest infestation, and drought. Massive layoffs of workers and labor unrest resulted. The worldwide depression threw the regional economy into renewed chaos. Labor conflict now unfolded within a political climate more receptive to popular interests. Strikers received strong support from unions in nearby Torreón and Gómez Palacio, the Mexican Communist Party, the Confederación de Trabajadores Mexicanos (CTM), and President Cárdenas. Newly formed unions presented demands that included higher wages and improved working conditions and referred to themselves as organizations of "workers and peasants," which accurately captured their transitional social status.

During a year of labor unrest most cotton estates had become unionized. A general strike in August 1936 halted production. By that point, Vicente Lombardo Toledano, president of the CTM, openly advocated expropriation of the haciendas. In response, Cárdenas soon informed strike committees that, if they would end the strike, he would turn the estates into ejidos.

The dramatic transformation of capitalist enterprises into collective ejidos ended in failure. Cotton planters, aided by army and paramilitary units, undermined the transition by decapitalizing estates, selling farm machinery, wasting irrigation water, and harassing peones. The number of peones seeking ejido membership also overwhelmed the government. The initial decision to restrict membership to resident peones was reversed when seasonal workers protested their exclusion. As a result, ejidos envisioned to accommodate 16,000 resident peones now had to find land and water resources for an additional 25,000 seasonal laborers. The Mexican

Communist Party's commitment to the ejidos, while instrumental in their formation, subsequently aroused opposition to the project among mainstream politicians in the 1940s.[33]

In summary, Cárdenas's sweeping land reform, which earned him recognition as the agrarian president, attempted to improve the lives of Mexico's peasantry and to undermine the economic base of his political enemies, the hacendados. The ejido—like other twentieth-century experiments in collective agriculture—failed to generate sufficient wealth to sustain Mexico's growing rural population. The hacendado class, by contrast, mostly passed from the scene to be replaced by a retinue of agrarian reform officials, union leaders, local political officers, and middlemen, through whose hands—and sticky fingers—federally funded programs passed. The tenacity of traditional forces of conservatism also undermined Cardenismo in some regions. For example, in Michoacán the clergy used their political influence to oppose agrarian reform. In Chihuahua descendants of the Porfirian elite became industrialists, cattle ranchers, and bankers, joining forces with the revolutionary nouveau riche to oppose Cárdenas's revolutionary reforms.[34]

The balance sheet for the agrarian reform yielded mixed returns. More peasants had access to land and water resources, and the poverty index declined by 8 percent from 1930 to 1940. In addition, through collectivization and grassroots electioneering villagers were brought into national politics and given a voice. Nevertheless, the persistence of rural poverty underscores the gravity of the problem Cárdenas faced. In 1940, 26.6 percent of the total population was too poor to afford shoes, and in regions with large Indian populations, such as Chiapas and Tabasco, this number soared to 75 percent. Outside of Mexico City, 80 percent of the population had no indoor plumbing or sewage disposal, and in some states, such as Guerrero, Oaxaca, and Zacatecas, only 2 to 3 percent of households had such modern facilities.[35]

Beyond land reform, Cárdenas pursued the transition from an agrarian to an industrial economy in the midst of a global depression. This had nothing to do with theoretical assumptions about opportunities created in dependent economies when capitalist centers decline. Rather, it hinged on the common belief that industrialization would create wealth, full employment, and social advancement. With the collapse of global industrial and financial centers, however, it became virtually impossible to raise capital abroad and government resources were insufficient to underwrite the transition. As a result, pressure was placed on the peasantry, who constituted two-thirds of the population, to generate surplus capital by producing agricultural products at low prices and to consume domestically produced manufactured goods at higher prices. As a result, even those peasants who received land via the agrarian reform faced economic difficulties.[36]

For peasants, migration into the cities and across the border into the United States became an increasingly common response to rural poverty. Beginning in 1942, the Bracero Program sent hundreds of thousands of Mexicans across the border to offset wartime labor shortages in the United States, and millions of illegal migrants would follow in their paths. The rapid infusion of rural migrants into Mexico City would inexorably transform the capital into one the world's largest cities, creating both a surplus labor market and a host of intractable social problems associated with rapid urbanization.

Mexico's overall economic performance gradually improved on the strength of silver and petroleum exports, which benefited from comparatively inelastic demand, and a doubling of manufacturing production between 1933 and 1940. The 23.2 percent increase in Gross Domestic Product between 1930 and 1940 also reflected Cárdenas's prudent fiscal and monetary policies, and the successful generation of capital from domestic sources.[37]

Table 7

Percent of Economically Active Population Employed in Agriculture

YEAR	PERCENT
1910	68.3
1921	68.8
1930	67.7
1940	63.4

James W. Wilkie, *The Mexican Revolution: Federal Expenditure and Social Change Since 1910* (Berkeley and Los Angeles: University of California Press, 1967), table 8–6, 193, (adapted).

Table 8

Recipients of Land by Presidential Term, 1920–1940

YEAR TERM ENDS	PRESIDENT	NUMBER OF RECIPIENTS	AVERAGE HECTARES
1920	Carranza	46,398	3.6
1920	De la Huerta	6,330	5.3
1924	Obregón	128,468	8.6
1928	Calles	297,428	10.6
1930	Portes Gil	171,577	10.0
1932	Ortiz Rubio	64,573	14.6
1934	Rodríguez	68,556	11.5
1940	Cárdenas	811,157	22.1

James W. Wilkie, *The Mexican Revolution: Federal Expenditure and Social Change Since 1910* (Berkeley and Los Angeles: University of California Press, 1967), table 8–7, 194, (adapted).

THE SECULAR REVOLUTION: EDUCATIONAL AND RELIGIOUS REFORMS

In Cárdenas's mind, economic reforms alone would not free villagers from the clutches of hacendados and priests. Their emancipation required a modern education that would dispel their antiquated reliance on the spiritual to order their lives and explain the universe. Reborn Mexicans would become responsible citizens capable of making rational decisions under the guidance of party officials, who would safeguard their interests as well as the endurance of the revolutionary state.

The ideological origins of the government's secular mission emanated from the Enlightenment and the French Revolution. Both sought to forge societies based on civil religion of humanity. Other philosophical sources were nineteenth-century liberalism, scientific positivism, Marxism, and Protestantism. The secularization process was necessarily accelerated by revolutionary movements determined to uproot traditional belief systems and sources of authority.[38]

According to socialist reformers, the clergy purposely kept villagers in a state of ignorance about scientific and historical truth in order to exploit them. Peasants' material progress required stripping away the aura and power of religion, Marx's "opium of the masses," and replacing it with a newly defined patriotism and cultural nationalism. In the words of Celso Flores Zamora, head of the Department of Rural Education, "In the modern capitalist nations the foundation of religion is primarily social. Modern religion is firmly rooted in the social oppression of the working classes."[39] According to these critics, only through studying the natural and physical sciences could peasants acquire the knowledge they needed to reject superstitious beliefs and accurately comprehend the world around them. Minister of Education Ignacio García Téllez explained:

[T]he lack of confidence in human resourcefulness leads the oppressed masses to expect everything from a supra terrestrial being. Their state of ignorance keeps them from understanding the physical or chemical processes that determine the formation of the earth, the manifestations of flora and fauna, the natural phenomena and social processes. . . . They don't find any logical explanations because they ignore scientific truths, as these have never been taught to them. They attribute occurrences to the mysterious faculties of material or animated objects that they comprehend, thus falling into primitive states of idolatrous superstition.[40]

The state's project involved nothing short of an attempted revamping of Indian culture as the Ministry of Education's social architects imperfectly understood it. Central to their mission was the eradication of the church's suffocating influence and allegiance to the revolutionary state. Instruction in health care, sex education, and the marketplace would also help natives to achieve economic self-sufficiency through family planning and increased productivity. From indigenous culture, urban educators only sought to retain traditional skills, which they considered artistically and historically interesting. In the hands of revolutionary artists like muralist Diego Rivera, indigenous representations and themes also served to illustrate natives' natural beauty and grace as well as to portray their exploitation by Europeans from the conquistadors to contemporary hacendados and industrialists.[41]

Rural education with a Marxist tinge began in the 1920s under the direction of education ministers Narciso Bassols and Moisés Sáenz. Cárdenas modified the process by using the classroom as a means of popular mobilization and inclusion in the revolutionary state. In the words of historian Mary Kay Vaughan:

> Teachers were to join forces with peasants to ensure land reform, higher wages, loans, and fair prices. Action education became a vehicle for the policies of oppressed groups. Projects were to aim at increased production and a redistribution of wealth. The teacher was to explain local and national structures of property and power. Arithmetic problems calculated the excess profits of factory owners. Geography teaching explained ownership and use of regional resources and elucidated the impact of imperialist exploitation of Mexico's natural wealth.[42]

Marxist historian Luis Chávez Orozco and others produced new textbooks that portrayed Mexican history as a constant struggle of the oppressed masses against the capitalist classes, imperialist interlopers, and the Roman Catholic Church. Teachers also received compulsory training in a variety of practical skills at specially designed institutes, such as the one described by Vaughan in Hermosillo, Sonora:

> They received instruction in small industries (tanning, embroidery, furniture making) from teachers at the Cruz Gálvez trade school and in the care of pigs, chickens, and seedlings from an agronomist at the Escuela Rural Normal at Ures. Federal health agents lectured them on smallpox. The Michoacán inspectors drilled them in Mexican sociology. The inspectors stressed unionization and cooperation and taught the teachers revolutionary and folk music, theater, and dance. At the institute's conclusion, teachers formed the Federación de Agrupaciones de Maestros Socialistas de Sonora.[43]

The church understood that socialist education would unravel its spiritual monopoly and erode its material base. Although the twentieth-century Mexican church did not consistently conform to the government's facile and dated stereotyping, its worldview clashed with Cardenismo's political and economic paradigms. Further, it opposed sex education, birth control, and equal status for women. Conservative villagers looked to priests for guidance whenever controversy arose, and the clergy responded by portraying teachers as sexual predators and satanic atheists. Verbal conflicts and violent confrontations greeted the introduction of socialist ideas in conservative villages, and teachers sometimes lost their lives to lynch mobs. In other places, however, the clash of ideas produced compromises that brought lasting educational benefits. These negotiated settlements between teachers and peasants produced a cultural revolution in some regions.[44]

Although anticlericalism represented federal policy, it burned deepest in those states with radical governors and a comparatively weak ecclesiastical presence. In Sonora, Sinaloa, Chiapas, and Tabasco, for instance, governors confiscated churches and turned them into community centers, cultural centers, or union headquarters. They also prohibited pilgrimages, religious processions, bell ringing, and offerings to the dead. By 1935, radical governors had expelled priests from seventeen states, mostly in the North and Southeast, and only 305 legally registered clerics remained in Mexico. The church remained strongest in Jalisco, San Luis Potosí, and Morelos, regions where it had maintained a continuous presence since the sixteenth century.

Destruction of religious documents and saints' images, reminiscent of the church's own attempts to eradicate pagan idolatry among Indian peoples following the Spanish Conquest, was encouraged by radical governors and the federal government. "Saint burners" *(quemasantos)* broke into churches, convents, seminaries, Catholic schools, and private homes and destroyed images of Christ, the Virgin Mary, and saints. Postal officials also randomly censored religious material sent through the mail, and librarians removed devotional publications from public libraries. Such heavy-handed tactics incensed the devout who, like their pagan ancestors centuries earlier, managed to acquire new religious statues, trinkets, and icons.[45]

Apart from iconoclasm and book burning, the government's de-fanaticization campaign hinged on reeducating Mexico's rural masses. The battle over Mexicans' minds occurred in public spaces and classrooms throughout the country. For example, the regime attempted to fashion secular associations by naming streets, plazas and towns for revolutionary heroes, by creating new national holidays that commemorated secular occasions (such as Cinco de mayo and "Revolution Day"), by hanging pictures of political leaders in classrooms and public buildings, and by sponsoring anticlerical plays, murals, posters, poetry, and songs (*corridos*). This addition to the Mexican pledge of allegiance encapsulated the regime's socialist message: "I will fight the three powerful enemies of our Fatherland . . . the Clergy, Ignorance, and Capital."[46]

The secular missionaries of the revolutionary state had their greatest impact in states already controlled by radical governors sympathetic to Cárdenas's policies. Even in these areas, however, limitations were imposed by the meager material resources placed at their disposal by the state, the uneven quality of individual teachers, and the reluctance of Indians—based on well-founded mistrust—to accept state-imposed change.[47]

In those states with conservative or moderate leadership, such as Puebla, teachers learned to tread carefully or to face dire consequences. In some villages, introduction of the new curriculum provoked a mass exodus of children from the classroom. Resourceful teachers then dropped daily instruction in favor of using carefully scripted public festivals that promoted new civic traditions, such as celebration of Cinco de mayo, glorification of revolutionary heroes like Zapata, and loyalty to the state, as the most practical means of instruction. Residents accepted these types of activities and their persistence signaled a negotiated understanding between teachers and community members regarding secular education that fostered the formation of a modern citizenry.[48]

In villages with strong pro-clerical traditions, however, socialist education faced sterner resistance. For example, priests and Catholic lay groups in Michoacán falsely accused teachers of having sex with children and burning religious icons and urged parents to boycott the schools. In 1935, the municipal president of Zamora lamented that only 391 of 5,000 children remained in school, and teachers were compelled to abandon anticlericalism.[49] In Puebla priests reputedly led an organized campaign against the schools by spreading outrageous rumors labeling federal education as the "Devil's work."

One teacher was reported to seduce men's wives while they were off tending their animals—a politically convenient story concocted to alarm indigenous men. In the federal schools, girls and boys were said to undress in front of one another to demonstrate the teachings of sexual education. The government was kidnapping children. They were being sent to the United States and turned into oil for airplanes. In a region where forced military recruitment had perennially terrorized communities and [Indians believed that] the Devil turned men into animals or elements, such stories struck like lightning. In 1935, federal schools emptied.[50]

Elsewhere, clerical campaigns against socialist education produced tragic results. In Michoacán, historian Marjorie Becker uncovered forty-two lynchings of Cardenista teachers at the hands of villagers.[51] Simón Villanueva Villanueva, a schoolteacher from Durango, recalled the fate of a husband and wife who attempted to teach children that God did not exist.

The female teacher asked the children to say "There is no God" when they greeted her, and she would answer "Nor was there ever one." The male teacher would ask the children "Where is God?" and the students would answer "In heaven, on earth, and in all places"; then the teacher told them "Well, then I urinate on God, because he doesn't leave me any space to urinate."

The lesson, however, ended badly:

Some time later, they were found dead, the woman teacher naked, raped, and with her breasts cut off, the male teacher castrated, with his penis cut off, and on one of those little wooden shingles that they use for roofing houses and with a piece of pinewood charcoal they wrote some awkwardly spelled words that said "So you don't go around peeing on God."[52]

Popular resistance to anticlericalism and mounting opposition from social conservatives pressured Cárdenas to reign in attacks on the church. Organized political campaigns by Catholic lay organizations and the bishops against socialist education were especially fierce. Church leaders organized public protests, priests attacked radical teachings from the pulpit, and bishops lobbied conservatives within the PNR. The maintenance of peace with the church served as a powerful political incentive to abandon radical anticlericalism in the public schools.[53]

In a March 1936 speech in Guadalajara, Cárdenas evoked the bitter memory of the religious wars of the 1920s: "The government will not make the error committed by previous administrations of considering the religious problem as a prime problem to which all other aspects of the program of the revolution must be subordinated. It is not the government's business to promote antireligious campaigns."[54] Bewildered teachers received instructions from the Ministry of Education to limit de-Christianization to "careful" and "intelligent" discussion based on scientific persuasion.[55]

The church had won another political compromise and rural Mexico remained more Christian than secular. But the growing power of the federal government and national party, both products of the revolutionary process, increased the political authority of the state at the expense of the church. Apart from its vitriolic anticlericalism, the revolutionary government's commitment to public education put more children into the classroom and increased opportunities for social mobility and material progress. Between 1910 and 1940 school attendance for youngsters between the ages of six and ten increased from 30 to 70 percent. This must be considered one of the revolution's greatest achievements.[56]

NATIONALISM ASCENDING: CÁRDENAS'S EXPROPRIATION OF THE FOREIGN-OWNED PETROLEUM COMPANIES

By 1938, Cárdenas's most radical social programs in education, religion, and agrarian reform had been derailed or modified, and their long-term impact remained uncertain. Under increasing pressure from conservatives from inside and outside of the revolutionary hierarchy to moderate policies, Cárdenas was on the defensive when a strike by petroleum workers, recently affiliated with the Confederación de Trabajadores Mexicanos, paralyzed Mexico's preeminent industry and fired revolutionary nationalism.

Since 1915, labor conflict had afflicted Mexico's oil fields and refineries as Mexican workers had struck for higher wages, an end to the dual wage scale that favored foreigners, and improved job security. Competition among rival unions for control over the workplace, however, weakened the movement and permitted the powerful petroleum companies to employ divide and conquer tactics. Worse yet, during the 1920s, development of new petroleum fields outside of Mexico increased worldwide supplies, lowered prices, and resulted in massive layoffs of Mexican oil workers from 50,000 in 1920 to 15,000 in 1935.[57]

Two corporate giants dominated the Mexican petroleum industry: the British-owned Royal Dutch Shell, which had purchased El Aguila in 1919, and Standard Oil of New Jersey (now Exxon), which had acquired Huasteca in 1932. Their profits rose during the mid-1930s as layoffs reduced costs and domestic industrial growth increased demand and pushed prices upward. Petroleum workers saw improved market conditions as an opportunity to reassert their long-festering grievances, and they insisted on higher wages and job security.[58]

The rise of Cardenismo radicalized and consolidated the labor movement and provided it with decisive political support from Mexico City. In 1935, the nineteen separate petroleum workers' unions merged to form the Sindicato de Trabajadores Petroleros de la República Mexicana and became affiliated with Vicente Lombardo Toledano's CTM.[59] Constitutional mandates endorsing workers' rights and state ownership of subsoil resources came together in dramatic political fashion. In 1933, the petroleum industry had received special attention in the Partido Nacional Revolucionario's Six-Year Plan. Party elders favored higher wages, increased export taxes, and the eventual nationalization of the industry. Cárdenas campaigned on these issues in 1934 with a conviction fortified by his bitter memories of oil company corruption during his tenure as military commander in the Gulf region.[60]

On November 3, 1936, the Mexican Oil Workers Syndicate demanded a wage increase of 26.4 million pesos and unprecedented control over the workplace. Labor and management both refused to compromise and an industry-wide strike seemed inevitable. Such a stoppage would have paralyzed industrial production, urban transit, power generation, and agricultural harvests throughout Mexico. Therefore, President Cárdenas intervened and invoked his legal right to impose state mediation. The timely intervention failed to produce a contract, however, and talks collapsed in May 1937.

Cárdenas intervened a second time to keep the oil flowing. Under the authority of the 1931 Labor Law, he constituted a three-man commission to determine if the union's demands could be met. The commissioners, led by Professor Jesús Silva Herzog of the National University, analyzed data on taxes, profits, expenses, and wages and made a recommendation to the Federal Board of Conciliation and Arbitration. The board deliberated for several months before endorsing the union's demand for a $26.4 million peso pay increase and more control over the workplace.[61]

The oil companies stalled compliance by filing an injunction with Mexico's Supreme Court and stepping up their lobbying efforts in Washington, London, and Mexico City. When the court upheld the board's decision on March 2, 1938, oil executives simply ignored the court's ruling. This created a dangerous political impasse. The oil companies' attempts to stand above the law transformed a labor conflict into a struggle over national sovereignty. Cárdenas could not tolerate foreign firms' arrogant defiance and expect his government and the constitution to survive.

Petroleum company executives misread both the domestic and international political situations. They may have believed that Cárdenas, weakened by opposition to his radical reforms and resurgent conservatism, could not withstand their determined lobbying efforts. Foreign firms' open defiance of Mexican law, however, fired Mexican nationalism and gave Cárdenas unprecedented political support. Oil executives also smugly believed that Mexico's lack of qualified technical personnel rendered expropriation untenable. Since the revolution, however, unions had forced petroleum companies to train increasing numbers of Mexican technicians.

On the international front, oil executives apparently discounted or misunderstood President Franklin D. Roosevelt's Good Neighbor Policy. In 1933 and 1936, the Roosevelt administration, concerned over rising anti-Americanism in Latin America, had renounced unilateral military intervention in the region. Washington's concern over hemispheric solidarity further increased with the spread of European fascism and

Japanese militarism and the possibility of renewed global war. Mexico's leaders and diplomats understood the implication of these developments for their national interests, and Cárdenas steadfastly opposed fascism at home and abroad as antithetical to the Mexican Revolution and international socialism.

Since the outbreak of the revolution, the United States had attempted to influence the course of events in Mexico without much success. Woodrow Wilson's occupation of Veracruz in 1914 helped to tumble Victoriano Huerta, but his clumsy efforts to capture Pancho Villa and to intimidate Venustiano Carranza failed. Republican Presidents Warren G. Harding, Calvin Coolidge, and Herbert Hoover concentrated on extracting compensation from Mexico for losses incurred by U.S. investors during the revolution and on protecting the oil companies. These efforts had not been entirely successful.

By the late 1920s, the United States showed its concern with improving diplomatic relations with Mexico by appointing better qualified ambassadors. Ambassador Dwight Morrow enjoyed an excellent rapport with President Calles and helped to negotiate an end to the Cristero Rebellion. President Franklin D. Roosevelt's choice of Josephus Daniels, a personal associate and committed New Dealer, signaled continuing commitment to improved relations. F. D. R. and Daniels had served together in the War Department during the Wilson administration, and in 1914 Daniels had been secretary of the navy and Roosevelt his undersecretary when Woodrow Wilson had ordered the marines to occupy Veracruz. Both Daniels and Roosevelt had forgotten this by the 1930s, but Mexicans with longer memories protested Daniels's appointment. The protests faded, however, when Daniels's liberal views became known.

In 1938, the oil crisis had put Mexico on the front page of U.S. newspapers, and Roosevelt and Daniels sought a peaceful exit. Daniels viewed the crisis in historical and legal terms, and he recommended that producers pay the 26.4-million peso pay increase as ordered by the Mexican Supreme Court. "The only recourse open to the oil companies is by appeal to the Mexican courts. We have no more right to demand any specific decrees by the courts for our nationals than Mexicans in the United States would be justified in asking the State Department to request the Supreme Court to render a certain decision."[62]

Daniels also argued that the petroleum companies owed something to Mexico. He was particularly troubled by the manner in which the multinationals had hoodwinked ordinary Mexicans into leasing them immensely valuable property for next to nothing. For example, the ambassador noted that the Huasteca Petroleum Company paid an Indian women 1,000 pesos annually for a lot that produced 100,000,000 barrels of oil; that another transnational compensated a poor farmer in Veracruz 150 pesos per year for land that yielded 75,000,000 barrels; that Amatlán Oil paid 10 pesos for land that produced 7,000,000 barrels; and that Huasteca spent 200,000 pesos for the famous Cerro Azul property that produced 181,870,538 barrels. Within this context, the large wage increase now demanded by petroleum workers seemed reasonable.[63]

Oil company executives, not surprisingly, did not share Daniels's viewpoint. Instead, they forged ahead with schemes aimed at pressuring Cárdenas and undermining his government. Harold P. Walker, vice president of Huasteca, arranged for J. Rueben Clark, a highly regarded former diplomat, to meet with Plutarco E. Calles, Cárdenas's old political adversary. Walker hoped that Clark could convince Calles that the union's demands violated the petroleum agreement signed with the multinationals during his administration. The State Department rejected Walker's request to sanction the mission as an official visit, and the talks failed to shake the government.

Although the Clark mission had floundered, oil executives remained confident that Cárdenas would not expropriate. Jack Armstrong, secretary of the Association of Petroleum Producers in Mexico, told Ambassador Daniels that Mexico lacked the technicians to run a petroleum industry, that no one would buy expropriated oil, and that shipping companies would refuse to transport tainted crude.[64]

Despite the bravado, the oil companies were worried. When the Special Commission had recommended for the union, they had agreed to pay 20 million pesos in wage increases. However, their refusal to concede the remaining 6 million and grant workers more autonomy fueled the crisis. Washington's reluctance to pressure Cárdenas by withholding silver purchases, which would have devastated the Mexican economy, told the petroleum producers that they were largely on their own.[65]

Cárdenas viewed the conflict as an historic opportunity for Mexico to defend its national sovereignty. He wrote in his diary: "I believe that there are few opportunities so special as this for Mexico to achieve independence from imperialist capital, and because of this my government will comply with the responsibility conferred by the revolution." He added that "countries have lost their liberty through the indecision and timidity of their leaders."[66] The international context, particularly the Allied defense of self-determination against Nazi Germany, also worked in Mexico's favor.

> Various administrations since the revolution have attempted to do something about the subsoil concessions being enjoyed by foreign firms, but up until now domestic problems and international pressure have mitigated against this effort. Today, however, the circumstances are different: there are no internal struggles going on, and a new world war is about to begin. It is a good time to see if England and the United States, which talk so much about democracy and respect for the sovereignty of other countries, will in fact stand up to their spoken convictions when Mexico exercises its rights. The government over which I preside, knowing that it has the support of the people, will carry out the responsibility that is incumbent upon it in this hour.[67]

During the oil crisis, Cárdenas conferred with Vicente Lombardo Toledano, head of the CTM, and with his close friend and advisor General Francisco Múgica, one of the architects of the 1917 Constitution. Cárdenas told Daniels as little as possible and largely ignored the British, whose problems in Europe and elsewhere made them appear less threatening. Indeed, Cárdenas's secretary of foreign relations, after studying the nationalization of British oil interests in Persia, concluded that the British Empire "is sick and with a weak soul."[68] Prime Minister Neville Chamberlain's acquiescence to Hitler at Munich also seemed to confirm this assessment and lessen the likelihood of British intervention in Mexico.

As the oil crisis lingered, Cárdenas's unflinching resolve unnerved the petroleum companies, and they hastily offered to pay the full 26.4 million peso pay increase. They refused to grant the union's demand for greater control over the workplace, however, and Cárdenas would not compromise. At 10:00 P.M. on March 18, 1938, the president of Mexico went on radio and told the nation that he had ordered expropriation with compensation of the foreign-owned petroleum companies. The shocking announcement caught the press corps, diplomatic community, and oil executives completely by surprise.

Daniels, awakened by an aide to hear Cárdenas's speech, attempted damage control. He knew that the petroleum companies had violated the law and could not appeal to courts outside of Mexico. If Cárdenas fairly compensated U.S. firms for their losses, Daniels argued, then the United States should not take action against Mexico. Cárdenas intended to compensate the oil companies, but he had no intention of offering them the enormous sums they would demand. Moreover, financial exigencies prevented him from making an immediate payment, as required by international law. The conflict over compensation gave the petroleum companies political and legal leverage in their home countries.[69]

The oil industry mobilized against Cárdenas and Mexico. Executives of Royal Dutch Shell convinced London to protest vigorously against the expropriation, which led an offended Cárdenas to recall Mexico's ambassador to Britain. Worse yet, Standard Oil and Royal Dutch Shell also organized a global boycott of Mexican petroleum and continued meddling in Mexican politics. The oil companies closed down overseas markets to Mexican oil, refused to sell Mexico specialized equipment, and kept oil tankers away from Mexican harbors. Mexican petroleum exports fell from 24,960,335 barrels in 1937 to 14,562,250 the following year, and the number of wells in production decreased from 981 to 756. With the outbreak of the Second World War, Mexico also eventually lost the German and Italian markets.

U.S. oil companies also increased their political pressure on Cárdenas. They established a special office in Rockefeller Center in New York City to generate anti-Mexican propaganda, including the vitriolic biweekly *Looking at Mexico,* and to coordinate lobbying efforts. The *New York Times,* the *Wall Street Journal,* the *Washington Post,* and the Hearst newspaper chain all editorialized against the Cárdenas administration, and congressmen and senators publicly condemned Cárdenas and Ambassador Daniels. These attacks helped turn public opinion in the United States against Mexico and contributed to a one-third decline in the tourist trade, thereby damaging another important sector of the Mexican economy.

The Roosevelt administration, while rejecting unilateral military intervention in Mexico, lobbied Latin American nations to boycott Mexican oil and stopped buying Mexican silver. The latter measure dealt a severe blow to the Mexican economy. The United States had been the leading purchaser of Mexican silver, Mexico's biggest export earner. Mexico's silver exports declined by 50 percent during 1938, fell further in 1939, and plummeted another 25 percent in 1940. Cárdenas responded by dramatically increasing federal taxes on silver mines, which were largely U.S.-owned, and by hinting at the possibility of expropriation.

The petroleum transnationals also resorted to political skullduggery within Mexico. In April 1938, petroleum executives told Ambassador Daniels that an armed revolt against Cárdenas would occur within thirty days, a prediction that suspiciously coincided with the actual rebellion of Saturnino Cedillo. The disenchanted agrarian leader from San Luis Potosí, who had served as Cárdenas's minister of agriculture, had become increasingly marginalized within the administration and broke with the president over agrarian policies. Although Cedillo may have received support from the petroleum companies, his revolt quickly floundered.[70]

Indeed, the expropriation increased Cárdenas's popularity at home and minimized the likelihood of a coup. Even the hierarchy of the Catholic Church, which had opposed the president's agrarian and educational reforms, supported expropriation and hoisted the Mexican flag above the national cathedral during a Cardenista rally. Ordinary Mexicans also voiced their support by contributing money to a special fund established to compensate the oil companies for expropriated property. Donations sometimes occurred within the context of mass pro-Cardenista demonstrations. Ambassador Daniels witnessed a remarkable gathering of thousands of women in the capital's central plaza, the Zócalo: "They took off wedding rings, bracelets, earrings, and put them, as it seemed to them, on a national altar. All day long, until the receptacles were full and running over, these Mexican women gave and gave. When night came crowds still waited to deposit their offerings, which comprised everything from gold and silver to animals and corn."[71]

More firsthand testimony comes from British novelist Graham Greene who, traveling in the remotest regions of backwater Chiapas, reported that villagers knew about the expropriation and spoke hardly of anything else.[72] It appears that Cárdenas's bold defense of the national sovereignty had galvanized Mexican nationalism across class lines and geographical locations.

The lifting of the U.S. boycott of Mexico's silver and petroleum industries required resolution of the compensation crisis. The oil companies were unlikely to budge, but the Roosevelt administration felt a sense of urgency with the outbreak of the Second World War. Latin American solidarity against Hitler's Germany and Imperial Japan took precedence over compensation for the oil companies.

In the struggle against fascism, moreover, the ideological similarities underpinning Cárdenas's Mexican-style socialism and Roosevelt's New Deal acquired greater significance. Cárdenas's fight against fascism at home and abroad underscored this kinship. He supported the Spanish Republicans against General Francisco Franco and admitted thousands of Spanish exiles into Mexico, including prominent intellectuals who founded the Casa España (which later became El Colegio de México). On the domestic front, Cárdenas also faced challenges from Mexico's formidable right-wing Sinarquista Movement, composed of Cristeros, hacendados, and businessmen, as well as from the fascistic General Juan Andrew Almazán, who had grown rich from government construction contracts and shady deals and who now threatened to muscle his way into power. Almazán enjoyed the backing of wealthy norteño businessmen, including anti-Cardenista Monterrey industrialists, who had formed the conservative Partido Acción Nacional (PAN) party in 1939.[73]

In 1940, Almazán's presidential candidacy under the aegis of the PAN increased pressure on Cárdenas to select a PNR candidate who could overcome the right-wing threat. The leading contenders occupied different ideological niches. General Francisco Múgica, the president's close friend and advisor, would provide programmatic continuity. However, Múgica's governorship in Michoacán had witnessed internecine conflict with the forces of conservatism, and his presidency might be littered with similar disputes. In contrast to Múgica, General Manuel Avila Camacho belonged to the moderate wing of the PNR. He had earned his political stripes as boss of Puebla before becoming a highly effective member of Cárdenas's cabinet. An Avila Camacho administration would likely pursue less aggressive policies on social issues of great importance to the president, such as agrarian reform, but would appeal to the business community at home and abroad and likely blunt the right-wing threat. Cárdenas's selection of Avila Camacho over his longtime friend Múgica was a painful choice made in the interest of political peace and stability.

Manuel Avila Camacho won a bitterly disputed election over General Almazán, whose supporters launched an ill-conceived rebellion that was quickly suppressed. Avila Camacho was a competent moderate who made peace with the church and favored business over labor. From the perspective of the United States, this augured well for a settlement of the long-festering petroleum crisis. Allied setbacks in 1940–1941 underscored the urgency to secure Latin American loyalty and natural resources for the United States. The State Department proved more anxious to negotiate than the oil companies, however, which stubbornly refused to accept Mexico's terms for negotiations. Washington proceeded to talk with Mexico City anyway, while keeping the petroleum firms appraised of the discussions.

During the summer of 1941 the negotiating teams agreed that Mexico should compensate U.S. petroleum companies $24 million for their losses. The major U.S. firms rejected the settlement as a violation of their property and civil rights and accused the Roosevelt administration of mirroring Axis policies. The bombing of Pearl Harbor took precedence over these objections, however, and in April 1942 Washington and Mexico City signed an agreement. Although Mexico did not explicitly agree to compensate the oil companies for the value of subsoil deposits, the payout included compensation for untapped petroleum reserves. In other words, Mexico upheld the principle of subsoil ownership, but the oil companies got their cash. Although the oil executives could not be forced to sign the agreement, Secretary of State Cordell Hull warned them that noncompliance would cost them government support in future negotiations. There followed several months of additional haggling before a modified version of the settlement was accepted by all parties. In October 1943, the Mexican government agreed to compensate the firms $30 million in annual installments over a four-year period.[74]

Negotiations between Mexico and Britain over compensation proved equally difficult. Acrimony over expropriation of El Aguila, owned by Royal Dutch Shell, as well as British aversion to the Mexican Revolution, had resulted in the rupturing of diplomatic relations. Although the two nations exchanged ambassadors again in October 1941, lingering bitterness and Mexico's economic woes delayed negotiations until well after the termination of the Second World War. Only in August 1947, after Mexico had made its final installment to the U.S. oil companies, did the avowedly pro-business President Miguel Alemán sign a compensation agreement with Britain. Mexico agreed to pay Royal Dutch Shell's shareholders $81,250,000—plus 3 percent interest retroactive to 1938—during a fifteen-year period beginning in 1948.[75]

ASSESSING THE IMPACT OF EXPROPRIATION

Following his expropriation of the oil companies, Cárdenas had created Petroleos Mexicanos (PEMEX) to manage Mexico's newly acquired petroleum industry. PEMEX survived the economic warfare waged against it by the transnationals largely because increased domestic demand for petroleum products offset the loss of overseas markets. The oil companies survived the loss of their Mexican reserves through development of newly discovered oil deposits in Venezuela and elsewhere. Compensation from Mexico provided them with some of the capital they required to bring new discoveries into operation.

Expropriation fueled revolutionary nationalism, reduced Mexico's dependence on foreign corporations, and helped mold the image of Lázaro Cárdenas as icon of the Mexican left. The struggle with the transnationals and their governments during the middle of the Great Depression, however, also left economic and political scars that stalled progressive policies. The petroleum crisis resulted in short-term losses in oil and silver sales, decreasing foreign investment, and devaluation of the peso by 39 percent from 3.6 to 5.0 pesos to the dollar. These setbacks wounded an economy already suffering from crop failures, floundering agrarian reform, and skyrocketing unemployment. In political terms, this weakened Cárdenas and the left-wing of the PNR and compelled the president to reassure businessmen and foreign investors by slowing progressive reforms after 1938 and choosing Avila Camacho as his successor.[76]

THE CORPORATE STATE AND CAUDILLISMO: THE MEXICAN REVOLUTIONARY PARTY AND LOCAL POWER BROKERS

Three weeks following his expropriation of the oil companies, Cárdenas announced his intention of reorganizing the Partido Nacional Revolucionario (PNR) to incorporate carefully defined sectors—workers, peasants, government employees, and the military—into the governing party. It was a bold political move designed to empower those groups most supportive of his progressive programs. He succeeded in creating a broadly based political party, renamed the Partido de la Revolución Mexicana (PRM), capable of dominating national politics for the reminder of the century.[77]

Specialized political organizations assumed responsibility for mobilizing and controlling each sector. The Confederación Nacional Campesina (CNC) represented the peasantry (ejidatarios and villagers), the Confederación de Trabajadores Mexicanos enjoyed unparalleled influence among organized labor, the Federación de Sindicatos de Trabajadores en el Servicio del Estado represented state employees (who owed their jobs to government patronage), and the Secretariato de la Defensa Nacional represented the military.

Selection of military personnel was carefully scripted. The secretariat selected forty representatives, one from each of the thirty-three military zones, one from each of the two naval districts, three from the department level at the secretariat, and two named by the president.[78] Although it may seem curious that Cárdenas would include the military in his realignment, the president came from a military background and recognized the political utility of having the support of the armed forces. As Roderic Ai Camp explains, "Cárdenas created the military sector to bring the officers into the open and force them to channel their political activities through the party, where they could be kept in check by other sectors."[79] Moreover, Cárdenas himself observed, "[W]e are not involving the army in politics, it is already involved. In fact, it has dominated the situation, and we are reducing its influence to one out of four votes."[80] In other words, the military's inclusion was a political maneuver designed to limit its ability to undermine the system. By 1943, President Avila Camacho and party leaders, presumably convinced that the military leadership had been sufficiently incorporated into party patronage networks, formally rescinded the military's special status within the PRM.[81]

Despite the creation of the PRM, a seemingly monolithic political apparatus, peasants, workers, government employees, and soldiers did not necessarily receive corresponding material benefits. The empowerment of organizations designed to represent these sectors created new government-sanctioned bosses who embarked on their own particularistic political careers sometimes without regard for the interests of their constituencies. For example, Arturo Warman laments the plight of postrevolutionary Morelean peasants whose access to land and credit was limited by the corrupt leadership of the CNC.[82] In other words, despite the best intentions of Cárdenas, the financial and political opportunities created by the formation of new bureaucracies, and the strengthening of existing organizations such as the CTM, proved too tempting for ambitious and corrupt officials.

The creation of the PRM, moreover, did not assure that presidents or party kingpins could uniformly impose their will on provincial political bosses who remained entrenched in hamlets, towns, and cities throughout the country. These caudillos were the political descendants of revolutionary-era bosses who controlled local patronage networks and party machinery, and whose power gave them a voice in shaping or defying government and party policy. These kingpins remained secure in their bailiwicks, forcing presidents and the party to filter programs through them before they reached the people.

The persistence of local bossism, despite postrevolutionary political consolidation, is also tied to the divisiveness of Cardenismo. Cárdenas's power struggle with Calles during 1934–1936 forced him into alliances with strange political bedfellows, including moderates such as the Avila Camacho brothers in Puebla, who supported his presidency but opposed his radical social and agrarian policies. The popular and political resistance to these policies created additional fissures in the presidential edifice. Finally, the oil crisis, while firing Mexican nationalism, weakened the economy, alienated big business, and forced Cárdenas into naming Manuel Avila Camacho as his successor.[83]

CONCLUSION

Although he did not achieve all of his objectives, Lázaro Cárdenas remains Mexico's most appealing twentieth-century president. He tried to make the revolution work through implementation of the most vital tenets of the 1917 Constitution: agrarian reform, ownership over subsoil rights, state supremacy over the church, labor reform, and socialist education. Cardenista ideologues, such as Francisco Múgica, hoped that the Mexican Revolution would serve as a model for socialist revolution around the globe. They envisioned the revolution's principal supporters would be the youth of the 1930s and 1940s whose disenchantment with communism would lead them to embrace Mexican-style revolutionary nationalism.[84] The vision did not become reality, although Cardenismo would continue to inspire Mexican leftists throughout the twentieth century.

The oil expropriation was Cárdenas's greatest achievement, despite short-term economic damage and serious political fallout. According to Adolfo Gilly, it signifies historic retribution against U.S. imperialism: "The oil expropriation remained fixed like a magic moment in national life. In the collective imagination it was revenge for the war over Texas and for the Treaty of Guadalupe-Hidalgo. (It meant) the return of the subsoil from the hands of those who, less than a century earlier, had taken half of the land inherited from New Spain."[85] Cárdenas's victory over the multinationals and their governments required political resilience, the ability to mobilize the masses, and impressive diplomatic skills. The president and the Mexican people withstood the economic and political pressures directed at them by powerful nations and corporations.

Cárdenas's vast cultural project promoted socialist education and new civic traditions. From intense and tumultuous interactions between radical teachers and traditional communities emerged a reconstituted Mexican nationalism centered on secular saints and holidays as well as a negotiated curriculum for public schools. Although Cárdenas's de-Christianization campaign ultimately failed, enrollments in primary schools dramatically increased and opportunities for social mobility improved.

Peasants' hunger for land had driven them to rebellion, and Cárdenas distributed more land to villagers than all previous revolutionary presidents combined. Land reform faced stern political opposition from hacendados,

FIGURE 43: President Lázaro Cárdenas (left) traveled to remote villages where
he listened to peasants' concerns and promoted his radical reforms.

Source: Anita Brenner, *The Wind that Swept Mexico: The H;istory of the Mexican
Revolution of 1910–1942*, with 184 historical photographs assembled by
George R. Leighton (Austin: University of Texas Press, 1971), photograph 148.

rancheros, and the church, however, and the ejido suffered from bureaucratic malfeasance and credit shortages. Neither communal farming nor
capitalist enterprise provided solutions to rural poverty, and millions
migrated into the cities or to the United States in search of a living wage.

Lázaro Cárdenas, born of modest means in Jiquilpan, Michoacán,
worked hard to form a personal bond with common Mexicans. Toward
the end of his term, the magazine *Hoy* reported, "In the five-year period
from December 1, 1934, to December 1, 1939 (1,825 days) President
Cárdenas was absent from the capital for one year, four months, and four
days—or 489 days and nights—while visiting a total of 1,028 towns in
every state of the republic."[86] Even in those villages that had opposed his
agrarian and educational reforms, like San José de Gracia, Cárdenas was
revered. Throughout his life, he remained the hero of the Mexican left, the
general who stood up to the imperialists, the Catholic Church, and the
hacendados. Lázaro Cárdenas was the president who truly cared about
the poverty of the foot soldiers of the revolution.

FIGURE 44: President Cárdenas opened the doors of the presidential residence to poor Indians, the foot soldiers of the Revolution.

Source: Anita Brenner, *The Wind that Swept Mexico: The History of the Mexican Revolution of 1910–1942,* with 184 historical photographs assembled by George R. Leighton (Austin: University of Texas Press, 1971), photograph 147.

CONCLUSION

O<small>N</small> J<small>ULY</small> 2, 2000, Vicente Fox Quesada, the candidate of the centrist-right Partido Acción Nacional (PAN) won the Mexican presidency over Francisco Labastida Ochoa, the standard bearer of the Partido Revolucionario Institucional (PRI). When Fox assumed office in November 2000, he ended seventy-one years of rule by the official political party created by Plutarco Elías Calles to govern revolutionary Mexico. This shocking turn of events brought to an end a regime that had remained in power longer than the Soviet Communists or the Democratic Party machine in Chicago. The outcome reflects public discontent over decades of government corruption, scandal, economic mismanagement, and neglect of revolutionary principles.

Political bloodshed and economic woes since the 1970s reached a crescendo in 1994. In that year, the assassinations of PRI presidential candidate Luis Donaldo Colosio and PRI Secretary-General José Francisco Ruíz Massieu, President Carlos Salinas's former brother-in-law, shocked the nation. Raúl Salinas, the president's brother, was later arrested and convicted of planning the assassination, and President Salinas, his term completed, went into exile. That same year, a rebel movement in Chiapas, calling itself the Zapatistas, demanded political autonomy, native rights, increased government spending on health and education, and redistribution of agricultural lands. The movement garnered widespread sympathy from the middle classes. The rebellion also coincided, not coincidentally, with the signing of the North American Free Trade Agreement (NAFTA). This pact created a free-trade zone for the continent that required amending the constitution to rescind Mexican sovereignty over its subsoil rights. Even more unsettling for the regime in political terms was the extraordinary run on the peso in late 1994, shortly after President Ernesto Zedillo took office. This led to capital flight, financial crisis, and joint intervention by the World Bank and the United States to stabilize the Mexican currency. Suddenly, once-proud Mexico seemed like just another Third World country.

Since the presidency of General Lázaro Cárdenas, Mexico's political bosses had gradually set aside original revolutionary objectives, as articulated in the Plan de Ayala and the Constitution of 1917, in favor of maintaining political control and overseeing economic development. They stayed in power through electoral fraud and patronage and by fostering economic prosperity for the upper and middle classes. They largely ignored struggling workers and starving peasants. For the most part, the revolution was reduced to monuments, holidays, heroes, and collective memory.

What revolutionary covenants did Mexico's official party leaders and their supporters violate? The answer lies in the revolutionary process and the reasons why Mexicans revolted against Porfirio Díaz in the first place. In 1910, Mexicans rebelled, above all, to get land—in many cases, the same land that had been taken from them by hacendados during their lifetimes. Land loss threatened their traditional livelihoods, undermined their sense of community, and forced them into becoming full- or part-time wage laborers with declining standards of living.

Mexicans also rebelled over the centralizing political policies of the Díaz regime, which angered people from all social groups and made possible the forging of cross-class revolutionary coalitions. Many Mexicans, particularly provincial elites and workers, also resented the special treatment afforded foreign companies and foreign workers by the government. The outburst of revolutionary nationalism, especially important to the Carrancistas, encompassed a vision of state building that empowered the government to manage the economy, control foreign investment, and subordinate the church to the state.

The revolutionary leaders who ran Mexico after 1916 also had an important cultural agenda for their countrymen. They continued reforms of secular origin to control drunkenness, gambling, prostitution, and blood sports that had begun during the Porfiriato, and they imposed reforms of socialistic origin such as public education (which empowered the masses and undercut the church) and the development of a civic culture based on postrevolutionary image making. Mexico's leaders wanted to refashion Mexican nationalism in a way that empowered the national party through belief in a molded institutionalized revolution.

AGRARIAN REFORM

Although Mexicans had fought over land since colonial times, during the Porfiriato the unprecedented convergence of land consolidation, population growth, and inflation in food prices resulted in a groundswell of protest that resulted in revolution. Morelos and Chihuahua, the birthplaces of Zapatismo and Villismo respectively, became the principal focal points of agrarian protest. In Morelos, the unprecedented expansion of sugarcane plantations cost natives land, water, and control over their livelihoods. The Zapatistas' Plan de Ayala linked villagers' demand for recovery of ancestral lands with issues of liberty and justice. The Zapatistas' single-minded campaign for land reform kept other revolutionary factions focused on this issue and helped assure that the Constitution of 1917 would authorize the government to confiscate and redistribute land.

If Emiliano Zapata represented the soul of the land reform movement, Pancho Villa represented the muscle. During the eighteenth century, many of Chihuahua's villages had been founded as military colonies to secure the silver-rich region for Spain against the ferocious challenge of the Apaches. The struggle between villagers and Indians continued into the Porfiriato. The final victory over the Apaches coincided with railroad construction and rising land values, and the local elite, led by Luis Terrazas and Enrique Creel, shepherded through new legislation that facilitated confiscation and sale of village land. Western Chihuahua gave birth to revolutionary movements led by Pascual Orozco, who helped Francisco Madero overthrow Porfirio Díaz, and by the legendary Villa. Villa formed Mexico's largest revolutionary army composed of angry villagers and ranchers. He paid them by maintaining Chihuahua's vast cattle estates and selling livestock across the border in the United States.

Villa's decision to postpone land reform until military victory had been achieved, however, cost him the type of die-hard loyalty that bound Zapatistas together even in defeat.

The Constitutionalist military victory over Villa and Zapata in 1915 represented a setback for those committed to agrarian reform. The movement's leadership hailed from the northern states of Coahuila and Sonora where pressures for land redistribution paled in comparison with Chihuahua, Morelos, and elsewhere. Moreover, Constitutionalist first chief Venustiano Carranza owned haciendas and favored capitalist development over formation of communal ejidos. Generals Alvaro Obregón and Plutarco Elías Calles, who followed Carranza in the presidency, promoted rationalization of production through direct investment, large-scale irrigation projects, and protection of highly capitalized agro-businesses such as sugarcane plantations. They authorized politically strategic land redistributions in some regions, such as Morelos, Chihuahua, and San Luis Potosí, where grassroots pressure from agraristas forced their hand.

Radical General Lázaro Cárdenas succeeded the Callistas in power in 1934 and instituted Mexico's most comprehensive land reform. Cárdenas sought to destroy the traditional hacienda, provide villagers with economic independence, feed the nation, and create strong paternal ties with grateful peasants. His attempts met with mixed success. The traditional estate gradually passed from the countryside, and Cárdenas became a revered father figure. Imposition of the ill-conceived ejido, however, faced stern opposition from hacendados, rancheros, Catholic clergy and laymen, and villagers who retained ample land. Moreover, corrupt agrarian reform administrators undermined the program by pocketing public funds, demanding bribes, and working hand and glove with local elites. Population increases, credit shortages, and a sagging economy squeezed the peasantry, and steady streams of impoverished villagers migrated into urban areas and the United States in search of work.

POLITICAL REFORM

Rebellious Mexicans frequently linked economic security with the ideology of self-determination, and the desire to control local government motivated many to take up arms. Mexicans from all social classes protested against the centralizing policies of the Díaz dictatorship. Provincial elites articulated their anger in terms of a yearning for democracy, which for many meant "no reelection" for Díaz and his allies and greater access to political office for themselves. Disgruntled gentry, some of whom were wealthy hacendado-businessmen, also resented Díaz's policy of lavishing tax breaks on foreign investors while denying them the same concessions. In 1910, many elite outsiders supported the vice-presidential candidacy of General Bernardo Reyes, the pro-business governor of Nuevo León, whom they viewed as a likely successor to Díaz. When Reyes withdrew from the race at the dictator's insistence, many Reyistas threw their support to maverick presidential candidate Francisco I. Madero.

Madero's campaign garnered support from provincial elites, village notables, landless peasants, workers, and artisans. All harbored political grievances against the regime. Miners and textile workers, whose numbers had grown in the wake of industrial expansion, wanted unions, higher wages, improved working conditions, and political voice. They had experienced layoffs and hard times following the economic downturn of 1906–1907, and their attempts at unionization had been crushed by the regime. Workers supported Maderismo and the progressive Partido Liberal Mexicano.

The centralizing policies of the regime also outraged village leaders accustomed to running local government and patronage networks. Stripped of their traditional authority through the creation of new political posts by the Porfirians, they mobilized supporters from among villagers angered over the imposition of officials disconnected and uninterested in them and their communities. The outburst of village-level revolution, particularly prominent in northern and isolated regions, has been termed the "serrano rebellion" by Alan Knight.

Madero's victory in 1911 produced a short-lived euphoria. The president's failure to enforce comprehensive agrarian and labor reforms cost him peasant and worker support, and his annulment of Catholic Party electoral wins in 1912 tarnished his democratic credentials. Desperate to shore up his government, Madero embraced the federal army and Porfirian politicians, who soon left him to back counterrevolutionary General Victoriano Huerta.

Huerta's overthrow and execution of Madero outraged revolutionary

Mexicans who joined together under the Constitutionalist banner to over-throw the dictator. U.S. President Woodrow Wilson, seeking to promote democracy and increase U.S. influence in the region, invaded Veracruz and helped drive Huerta out. Among the victorious revolutionaries, Zapata and Villa represented agrarian, populist movements devoid of compre-hensive political programs, while Carranza and Obregón forged cross-class coalitions by articulating broad reform agendas and winning battles.

Obregón's military victories over Villa in 1915 secured the presidency for Carranza. Despite assurances of free elections, the former Porfirian politician and hacendado pursued political consolidation with little regard for the full implementation of participatory democracy. Bloodshed continued among surviving revolutionary generals. Carranza arranged for Zapata's assassination in 1919; Carranza fell victim to followers of Félix Díaz the following year; Villa died in a hail of bullets in 1923; and Obregón was killed in 1928. Violence also characterized political life at the regional and local levels.

Something innovative was required to rescue the victorious revolu-tionaries from themselves. In 1929, Plutarco Elías Calles, having recently completed a term as president, sought to eliminate the bloodshed and remain the power behind the scenes. He created the Partido Nacional Revolucionario as an umbrella political organization for surviving revo-lutionaries and their political families (camarillas). Lázaro Cárdenas, seeking to empower his political constituencies, reorganized the party as the Partido Revolucionario Mexicano in 1938. The PRM provided formal representation for peasants, workers, government employees, and the military. In practice, this gave greater influence to these sectors' represen-tative organizations and their leaders, such as the Confederación de Trabajadores Mexicanos and Vicente Lombardo Toledano, without providing lasting political and material rewards for members. The PRM then evolved into the hegemonic Partido Revolucionario Institucional (PRI), which worked hand in glove with government to run Mexico.

ECONOMIC NATIONALISM

Mexico's rapid economic expansion during the Porfiriato hinged on the infusion of overseas capital from the United States and Western Europe.

Díaz and the Científicos attracted investment by providing overseas firms with tax exemptions and other incentives that gave them a competitive edge over Mexican producers. Within a few decades, U.S. companies controlled major railroads, silver and copper mines, and petroleum operations. British firms had substantial investments in mining and oil, and the French in textiles and banking. By the early twentieth century, political pressure began to build, even from within the regime, to curtail the predominance of foreign capital in the national economy. Clashes between foreign managers and Mexican workers at Cananea and Rio Blanco, and the complicity of government in suppressing strikers, also raised public concern over foreign autonomy.

Carranza, in particular, insisted on increasing government control over foreign companies, and Obregón, de la Huerta, and others favored granting Mexican workers equal pay for equal work. The Constitution of 1917 granted Mexico control over its subsoil properties and authorized dramatic labor reforms. Petroleum companies and their governments, however, successfully opposed attempts by revolutionary governments to increase taxes and limit operations. The Bucareli Accords signed by the Obregón administration and the United States in 1923 acknowledged the legitimacy of the Article 27, but left untouched petroleum fields developed before 1917.

In 1938, Cárdenas's expropriation of foreign-owned petroleum companies, following a crippling strike by CTM-led oil workers, represented a major victory for revolutionary policy. Cárdenas withstood the economic and political pressures from the multinationals and their governments, and Petroleos Mexicanos (PEMEX), created as a government-run industry, served the growing domestic market. Mexico paid a heavy price, however, for implementation of revolutionary nationalism. The Roosevelt administration's decision to withhold silver purchases severely reduced export earnings, weakened the leftist faction within the ruling party, and contributed to Cárdenas's decision to select moderate General Manuel Avila Camacho as his successor.

CHURCH-STATE RELATIONS

Since the overthrow of imperial Spain in 1821, liberal attempts to erode the traditional privileges and wealth of the Mexican church had ignited bloody revolutions that had undermined political and economic stability. General Porfirio Díaz, riding the crest of liberal victory over the church and the French at midcentury, mended political fences with the bishops without returning to them their confiscated haciendas or rescinded judicial privileges. Anticlericalism ran deep among Mexican liberals, and those revolutionaries with political roots in the Porfiriato, such as Carranza, joined forces with northern rebels with strong secular convictions, such as Obregón and Calles, in attacking the church.

Agrarian leaders and their followers, by contrast, did not share the Constitutionalists' anticlericalism. The Zapatistas hailed from villages with strong Catholic traditions, and they protected clergy and rebuilt torched churches. The Villistas represented a more eclectic movement, and Villa personally disliked priests. Villistas, however, did not persecute clergy or insist on new anticlerical laws.

The Constitutionalists' victory assured that the new constitution would include an array of anticlerical provisions. Although delegates were deeply divided over the need to impose extreme measures, progressive floor leaders hostile to the church, such as General Francisco Múgica, won the debate. Their vision of a revolutionary state, influenced by liberalism, contemporary Mexican history, and socialism, required a church boxed-in by government controls, incapable of mounting a political challenge to revolutionary authority, and unable to retard Mexico's entry into the modern world.

Subordinating the church to the state, however, required political stabilization and political courage. Keeping the church underfoot could risk endangering revolutionary gains, and neither Carranza nor Obregón would take this gamble. Carranza struggled to pick up the pieces from seven years of constant warfare, and Obregón focused on securing the presidency, negotiating the Bucareli Accords, and gaining U.S. diplomatic recognition. Calles inherited a comparatively more stable country, however, and he correctly viewed the church as an obstacle to political centralization. As an avowed atheist and anticleric, Calles's hatred of the church was unmatched among revolutionary presidents. The successful organization of workers and farmhands into church-affiliated unions undercut Calles's plan to consolidate organized labor under the authority of CROM kingpin and Labor Minister Luis Morones. CROM responded by authorizing bombings of churches and assassinations of priests. This led Mexican bishops to close down houses of worship.

The Cristero Rebellion pitted the centralizing forces of the revolutionary state, as represented by the federal government, CROM, and the Callista camarilla, against devout Mexicans and the church. Cristeros generally hailed from conservative regions outside of the revolutionary vortex. Villagers in Jalisco, Michoacán, and elsewhere in the center-west region of Mexico valued the spiritual and political guidance of the church over the ideology and programs of revolutionary government. They rushed to the aid of persecuted priests. Grassroots militia units battled the government to a virtual military stalemate without much useful guidance from the Cristero leadership, which included Porfirian-era generals, clerics, and die-hard conservatives. In 1929, the leadership settled for a return to the status-quo ante bellum: the anticlerical laws remained on the books, but would not be enforced by the federal government.

In the provinces, however, church-hating governors in Tabasco, Veracruz, and elsewhere enacted anticlerical laws and sanctioned attacks on the church. In political terms, the institutional church was no match for the burgeoning state. The federal government collected the taxes, made the laws, created the bureaucracies, and bullied the opposition. As the revolutionary state grew stronger, the political and economic power of the church faded. A different outcome would have been bizarre in the modern world.

THE CULTURAL REVOLUTION

The revolutionary state also viewed its political struggle with the church in cultural terms. Beginning in the 1920s, Mexican governments attempted to reinvent Mexican popular culture and nationalism by eroding folk Catholicism and creating secular saints and holidays. The objective was the creation of a modern, secular citizenry devoid of traditional loyalties to clergy, purged of religious superstitions, and wedded to the revolutionary state. New ideas and attitudes would be imparted by legions of schoolteachers, the shock troops of the cultural revolution.

Stamping out three hundred years of popular culture rooted in Catholic ritual, observance, faith, and celebration proved daunting.

Ham-fisted attempts to enforce political centralization and suppress local religious cults during the Porfiriato provoked violent resistance. These violations of sacred space, tradition, and political autonomy unsettled society on the eve of the revolution and foretold of the difficulties that revolutionaries would face in the 1920s and 1930s.

Public schools took root in urban areas and in rural zones with secular traditions, particularly in the North. Elsewhere, teachers and government officials clashed with clergy and villagers over curriculum, religion, and ideology. Socialist teachers who preached atheism were killed; others perished because priests characterized them as the devil's agents. More typically, however, teachers and villagers avoided violence by negotiating school plans that included recognition of important secular events (Cinco de mayo), political heroes (Emiliano Zapata), and the like. Villagers continued to attend religious services and to celebrate traditional festivals, but they also developed secular visions of themselves and their past that gradually altered their national identity.

Revolutionary governments invested hundreds of millions of pesos in education, with corresponding increases in literacy and growth of the middle class. The poorest regions, however, lagged behind, prisoners of the past and government neglect. The standard of living for small farmers and day workers remained dismal and migration into cities or across the border into the United States appeared the only escape from grinding poverty. Official government propaganda that praised Zapata's struggle for land and liberty and castigated Díaz's abuse of the rural poor became hollow over time.

INTRODUCTION

1. Paul Friedrich, *Agrarian Revolt in a Mexican Village,* 2d ed. (Chicago: University of Chicago Press, 1977), chap. 3.
2. Alan Knight, *The Mexican Revolution, 1910–1920,* 2 vols. (Cambridge: Cambridge University Press, 1986).

CHAPTER ONE

1. Colin M. MacLachlan and William H. Beezley, *El Gran Pueblo: A History of Greater Mexico* (Englewood Cliffs, N.J.: Prentice Hall, 1994), 193.
2. William Randolph Hearst to his mother (no day or month given), 1886, Hearst Family Papers, file 82168c, folder 10, Bancroft Library, University of California, Berkeley. Quoted by permission of the Bancroft Library.
3. Friedrich Katz, *The Secret War in Mexico: Europe, the United States, and the Mexican Revolution* (Chicago: University of Chicago Press, 1981), chap. 1.
4. Robert Holden, *Mexico and the Survey of Public Lands* (DeKalb: Northern Illinois University Press, 1994). See section on agriculture in this chapter for information on tariff and labor policies.
5. Laurens Ballard Perry, *Juárez and Díaz: Machine Politics in Mexico* (DeKalb: Northern Illinois University Press, 1978).
6. Ibid., 168–76.
7. Ibid., 179–200.
8. MacLachlan and Beezley, *El Gran Pueblo,* 79.
9. Friedrich Katz, "Mexico: Restored Republic and Porfiriato, 1867–1910," in *The Cambridge History of Latin America,* vol. 5, 1870 to 1930, ed. Leslie Bethell (Cambridge: Cambridge University Press, 1986), 21.

10. Alan Knight, *The Mexican Revolution, 1910–1920,* 2 vols. (Cambridge: Cambridge University Press, 1986), 1:15. On the Terrazas family during this period, see Mark Wasserman, *Capitalists, Caciques, and Revolution: The Native Elite and Foreign Enterprise in Chihuahua, Mexico, 1821–1911* (Chapel Hill: University of North Carolina Press, 1984).

11. Knight, *The Mexican Revolution,* 1:17.

12. MacLachlan and Beezley, *El Gran Pueblo,* 153–55.

13. Knight, *The Mexican Revolution,* 1:25–30; MacLachlan and Beezley, *El Gran Pueblo,* 155–56.

14. Oscar Lewis, *Pedro Martínez: A Mexican Peasant and His Family* (New York: Vintage Books, 1964), 75.

15. MacLachlan and Beezley, *El Gran Pueblo,* 149, 155.

16. Ibid.

17. Ibid.

18. Ibid., 87–90; Katz, "Restored Republic," 25–27.

19. Paul J. Vanderwood, *Disorder and Progress: Bandits, Police, and Mexican Development,* rev. and enlarged ed. (Wilmington, Del.: Scholarly Resources, 1992).

20. Knight, *The Mexican Revolution,* 1:17–18.

21. Jean A. Meyer, *The Cristero Rebellion: The Mexican People Between Church and State, 1926–29,* trans. Richard Southern (Cambridge: Cambridge University Press, 1976), chap. 1; Knight, *The Mexican Revolution,* 1:19.

22. MacLachlan and Beezley, *El Gran Pueblo,* 163–65.

23. Ibid.

24. Ibid.; Deborah J. Baldwin, *Protestants and the Mexican Revolution: Missionaries, Ministers, and Social Change* (Urbana: University of Illinois Press, 1990).

25. Polk's well-known quote is noted in K. Jack Bauer, *The Mexican War 1846–1848* (Lincoln: University of Nebraska Press, 1992), 67–68.

26. Katz, "Restored Republic"; MacLachlan and Beezley, *El Gran Pueblo,* 97–98.

27. John H. Coatsworth, "Obstacles to Economic Growth in Nineteenth-Century Mexico," *American Historical Review* (Feb.–Dec. 1978): 80–100.

28. Ibid.

29. John Mason Hart, *Revolutionary Mexico: The Coming and Process of the Mexican Revolution* (Berkeley and Los Angeles: University of California Press, 1987), 131–39.

30. Ibid.

31. Coatsworth, "Obstacles to Economic Growth," 91.

32. Ibid. See below for details on the development of commercial agriculture and mining.

33. Ibid.; and Michael J. Gonzales, "United States Copper Companies, the State, and Labour Conflict in Mexico, 1900–1910," *Journal of Latin American Studies* 26 (Oct. 1994): 653–54; Marvin Bernstein, *The Mexican Mining Industry, 1890–1950* (Albany: State University of New York Press, 1964), 28.

34. MacLachlan and Beezley, *El Gran Pueblo,* 89.

35. Juan Manuel Romero Gil, *El Boleo: Santa Rosalia, Baja California, 1885–1954* (Hermosillo: Universidad de Sonora, 1991), 13–84.

36. General Superintendent to Dr. L. D. Ricketts, 10 Apr. 1920, Cananea to Warren, Arizona, Cananea Company Archive (CCA), 1920 Documental 0063; W. C. Greene to A. S. Dwight, 15 Feb. 1904, New York to Cananea, Arizona Historical Society (AHS), Cananea, Box 1, MS 1032; Document dated 23 Mar. 1904, CCA, 1904, Documental 0043.

37. Holden, *Mexico and the Survey of Public Lands,* for a detailed analysis of the question. Meyers writes about the disproportionate percentage of part-time wage earners *(eventuales)* in revolutionary armies in the La Laguna region. William K. Meyers, *Forge of Progress, Crucible of Revolt: The Origins of the Mexican Revolution in La Comarca Lagunera, 1880–1911* (Albuquerque: University of New Mexico Press, 1994), 128.

38. John Tutino, *From Insurrection to Revolution in Mexico: Social Bases of Agrarian Violence, 1750–1940* (Princeton, N.J.: Princeton University Press, 1986), chaps. 7–8.

39. Katz, "Restored Republic," 28.

40. Friedrich Katz, "Labor Conditions on Haciendas in Porfirian Mexico: Some Trends and Tendencies," *Hispanic American Historical Review* 54, no. 1 (Feb. 1974): 15, 18.

41. François-Xavier Guerra, *México: Del Antiguo Régimen a la Revolución,* trans. Sergio Fernández Bravo, 2 vols. (Mexico City: Fondo de Cultura Económico, 1988), 2:58.

42. Katz, "Labor Conditions," 1–47.

43. Gilbert M. Joseph, *Revolution from Without: Yucatán, Mexico, and the United States, 1880–1924* (Cambridge: Cambridge University Press, 1982), chap. 1. Also see Nelson Reed, *The Caste War of Yucatán* (Stanford, Calif.: Stanford University Press, 1964); and Moisés González Navarro, *Raza y tierra* (Mexico City: El Colegio de México, 1970); and Terry Rugeley, *Yucatan's Maya Peasantry & the Origins of the Caste War* (Austin: University of Texas Press, 1996).

44. Joseph, *Revolution from Without,* 20–30.

45. Tutino, *From Insurrection to Revolution,* 294–95.

46. Evelyn Hu-DeHart, *Missionaries, Miners and Indians: Spanish Contact with the Yaqui Nation of Northwestern New Spain, 1633–1820* (Tucson: University of Arizona Press, 1981); Evelyn Hu-DeHart, *Yaqui Resistance and Survival: The Struggle for Land and Autonomy, 1821–1910* (Madison: University of Wisconsin Press, 1984); Joseph, *Revolution from Without,* 66, 78.

47. Joseph, *Revolution from Without,* 72. We know comparatively more about the history of Chinese plantation workers in Peru. See Michael J. Gonzales, "Chinese Plantation Workers and Social Conflict in Peru in the Late Nineteenth Century," *Journal of Latin American Studies* (Oct. 1989): 385–424.

48. Although it would be difficult to envision a significant revision of the accepted interpretation of labor contracting (or *enganche*) in the Yucatán, virtually no archival research has been done on the topic. Again, we know comparatively more about Peru, where recruits were not mere pawns in the historical process but often found ways of resisting total domination through running away, accepting loans under false names, and resorting to violence. Admittedly, these forms of protest would have been more difficult for Mexicans living and working greater distances from their homes. See Michael J. Gonzales, *Plantation Agriculture and Social Control in Northern Peru, 1875–1933* (Austin: Latin American Monographs, No. 62, Institute of Latin American Studies, University

of Texas, 1985), chap. 7; and Michael J. Gonzales, "Capitalist Agriculture and Labour Contracting in Northern Peru, 1880–1905," *Journal of Latin American Studies* (Oct. 1980): 291–315.

49. Joseph, *Revolution from Without,* 37–65, quotes from 47 and 49, respectively.

50. Ibid., 36–65.

51. Ibid.

52. On this latter point, see ibid., 49–50.

53. See below for further details.

54. Joseph, *Revolution from Without,* 54.

55. Thomas Benjamin, *A Rich Land, A Poor People: Politics and Society in Modern Chiapas* (Albuquerque: University of New Mexico Press, 1989), pt. I.

56. Katz, "Labor Conditions," 19–20, based on the observations of German agronomist Karl Kaerger, *Landwirtschaft und Kolonisation im Spanischen Sudamerika,* 2 vols. (Leipzig: Verlag von Duncker & Humboldt, 1901–1902), 2:543–47.

57. Ricardo Pozas, *Juan, The Chamula,* trans. Lysander Kemp (Berkeley and Los Angeles: University of California Press, 1959).

58. Ibid.

59. Tutino, *From Insurrection to Revolution,* 292–97.

60. Ward Barrett, *The Sugar Hacienda of the Marqueses del Valle* (Minneapolis: University of Minnesota Press, 1970); Cheryl English Martin, *Rural Society in Colonial Morelos* (Albuquerque: University of New Mexico Press, 1985).

61. Arturo Warman, *"We Come to Object": The Peasants of Morelos and the National State,* trans. Stephen K. Ault (Baltimore, Md.: Johns Hopkins University Press, 1980), chap. 2.

62. Ibid.

63. Ibid. This can be contrasted with the experience of Peruvian sugarcane planters: labor shortages compelled planters to provide workers with a daily ration of rice and beef. See Gonzales, *Plantation Agriculture,* chap. 7.

64. Warman, "We Come to Object," chap. 2.

65. MacLachlan and Beezley, *El Gran Pueblo,* 100.

66. Warman, "We Come to Object," 47.

67. John Womack Jr., *Zapata and the Mexican Revolution* (New York: Vintage, 1968), 49.

68. For example, Warman retells the story of García Pimental's son who invited a famous bullfighter to the plantation to engage in the slaughter of dozens of prize bulls. This at a time when laborers were struggling to find the price of corn. See Warman, "We Come to Object," 54.

69. Womack, *Zapata,* chap. 1.

70. Tutino, *From Insurrection to Revolution,* 324.

71. Womack, *Zapata,* 62–65.

72. See Meyers, *Forge of Progress, Crucible of Revolt.* The following discussion of the La Laguna is based on Meyers.

73. MacLachlan and Beezley, *El Gran Pueblo,* 154.

74. Bernstein, *The Mexican Mining Industry,* chaps. 1–21; Jesús Gómez Serrano, *Aguascalientes: Imperio de los Guggenheim* (Mexico City: Fondo de Cultura

Económico, 1982); Isaac F. Marcosson, *Metal Magic: The Story of the American Smelting and Refining Company* (New York: Farrar, Straus and Company, 1949); Hart, *Revolutionary Mexico,* 142.

75. Meyers, *Forge of Progress, Crucible of Revolt.*
76. Katz, "Labor Conditions," 31–37; Wasserman, *Capitalists,* 104–16.
77. Friedrich Katz, *The Life and Times of Pancho Villa* (Stanford, Calif.: Stanford University Press, 1998), 18–29; Tutino, *From Insurrection to Revolution,* 297–301.
78. Tutino, *From Insurrection to Revolution,* 297–301, quote from 300.
79. Ibid.
80. Paul Vanderwood, *The Power of God Against the Guns of Government: Religious Upheaval in Mexico at the Turn of the Nineteenth Century* (Stanford, Calif.: Stanford University Press, 1998), 131.
81. Hu-DeHart, *Yaqui Resistance and Survival;* Ramón Eduardo Ruíz, *The People of Sonora and Yankee Capitalists* (Tucson: University of Arizona Press, 1988), 148–52.
82. Peter J. Bakewell, *Silver Mining and Society in Colonial Mexico: Zacatecas, 1546–1700* (Cambridge: Cambridge University Press, 1971); David A. Brading, *Miners and Merchants in Bourbon Mexico, 1763–1810* (Cambridge: Cambridge University Press, 1971); Robert W. Randall, *Real del Monte: A British Mining Venture in Mexico* (Austin: University of Texas Press, 1972).
83. Bernstein, *The Mexican Mining Industry,* 28; Juan José Gracida Romo, "Génesis y Consolidación del Porfiriato en Sonora (1885–1895)," in *Historia General de Sonora,* vol. 4 *Sonora Moderno: 1880–1929,* ed. Cynthia Radding Murrieta (Hermosillo: Universidad de Sonora, 1985), 22–23.
84. Gonzales, "United States Copper Companies," 654.
85. Ibid., 653–54; George H. Hildebrand and Garth L. Mangum, *Capital and Labor in American Copper, 1845–1990* (Cambridge, Mass.: Harvard University Press, 1992), 94–95. Demand for copper increased following Faraday's discovery of electromagnetism and the practical application of electricity by Edison and others. Copper proved ideal for use in motors, generators, wiring, cable, and switch gear, particularly in the communication and transportation industries.
86. Romero Gil, *El Boleo,* 13–84.
87. W. C. Greene to C. E. Taylor, 8 Apr. 1900, Hermosillo to Bisbee, CCA, 1900 Documental 0020; S. M. Aguirre to W. C. Greene, 19 Apr. 1900 (telegram), Bisbee to Cananea, CCA, 1900 Documental 0020; W. C. Greene to George Mitchell, 26 July 1901, New York to Cananea, AHS, Box 1, MS 1032; W. C. Greene to George Mitchell, 12 Aug. 1901, New York to Cananea, AHS, Box 1, MS 1032; General Superintendent to Dr. L. D. Ricketts, 10 Apr. 1920, Cananea to Warren, Arizona, CCA, 1920 Documental 0063; W. C. Greene to A. S. Dwight, 15 Feb. 1904, New York to Cananea, AHS, Cananea, Box 1, MS 1032; Document dated 23 Mar. 1904, CCA, 1904 Documental 0043; George Young, Secretary, to T. Evans, General Superintendent, 29 Apr. 1921, CCA, 1921 Documental 0089; letter dated 25 Apr. 1908, CCA, 1908 Documental 0001; General Manager to Tomás Macmanus, 21 June 1909, Cananea to Mexico City, CCA, 1909 Documental 0042; J. W. Rennie to George Mitchell, 25 Aug. 1901, Cananea to New York, Centro Regional de Sonora (CRS),

Cananea, Microfilm #72/150, Reel 1; General Manager, Cananea Copper Co. to Señor Coronel Juan Fenochio, 28 June 1902, Cananea to Hermosillo, CRS, Cananea, Microfilm #72/150, Reel 1. Also see Jason H. Kirk, Manager, Mining Division, to W. C. Greene, 1 Aug. 1902, Cananea to New York, Cananea Consolidated Copper Co. Records, 1898–1969 (separate collection donated by former company employee Robert F. Torrance), AHS, MS 1033, Box 1.

88. Hart, *Revolutionary Mexico,* 141–45.

89. Ibid.

90. Marcosson, *Metal Magic.*

91. Political significance of strikes is discussed in the following chapter.

92. Bakewell, *Silver Mining and Society,* for early migration to mines.

93. Gonzales, "United States Copper Companies," 658.

94. Ruíz, *People of Sonora,* 110–13; Aviso, 1903, AHS, Cananea, MS 1032, Box 1; A. S. Dwight, Gerente General, to Don Pablo Rubio, Comisario, Ronquillo, 30 Jan. 1905, AHS, MS 1032, Box 3; Romero Gil, *El Boleo,* 113–38, for El Boleo.

95. Romero Gil, *El Boleo,* 113–38, tab. 22, 136, and 205–8; Gonzales, "United States Copper Companies," 658–59.

96. Romero Gil, *El Boleo,* 136.

97. Gonzales, "United States Copper Companies," 659–60; Juan Luis Sariego, *Enclaves y minerales en el norte de México: historia social de los mineros de Cananea y Nueva Rosita, 1900–1970* (Mexico City: CIESAS, 1988), 119–22; Jonathan C. Brown, "Foreign and Native-Born Workers in Porfirian Mexico," *American Historical Review* 98, no. 3 (June 1993): 786–818.

98. Employees by nationality, 30 July 1902, CRS, Cananea, Microfilm # 72/150, Reel 4.

99. Employees by nationality, 30 July 1902, CRS, Cananea, Microfilm # 72/150, Reel 4; General Timekeeper to A. S. Dwight, General Manager, 8 June 1906, CRS, Cananea, Microfilm # 72/150, Reel 1.

100. Hart, *Revolutionary Mexico,* 63.

101. Gonzales, "United States Copper Companies," 658–81, and below.

102. The following discussion of the petroleum industry is based on Jonathan C. Brown, *Oil and Revolution in Mexico* (Berkeley and Los Angeles: University of California Press, 1993).

103. Unless otherwise noted, this section is based on Stephen H. Haber, *Industry and Underdevelopment: The Industrialization of Mexico, 1890–1940* (Stanford, Calif.: Stanford University Press, 1989).

104. Alex M. Saragoza, *The Monterrey Elite and the Mexican State, 1880–1940* (Austin: University of Texas Press, 1988), chaps. 1–2.

CHAPTER 2

1. See Alan Knight, *The Mexican Revolution, 1910–1920,* 2 vols. (Cambridge: Cambridge University Press, 1986), vol. 1.

2. Rodney Anderson, *Outcasts in Their Own Land: Mexican Industrial Workers, 1906–1911* (DeKalb: Northern Illinois University Press, 1976); Jonathan C. Brown, "Foreign and Native-Born Workers in Porfirian Mexico," *American*

Historical Review 98, no. 3 (June 1993): 786–818; and Michael J. Gonzales, "United States Copper Companies, the State, and Labour Conflict in Mexico, 1900–1910," *Journal of Latin American Studies* 26 (Oct. 1994): 651–81.

3. John Tutino, *From Insurrection to Revolution in Mexico: Social Bases of Agrarian Violence, 1750–1940* (Princeton, N.J.: Princeton University Press, 1986), esp. chap. 8.

4. William K. Meyers, *Forge of Progress, Crucible of Revolt: The Origins of the Mexican Revolution in La Comarca Lagunera, 1880–1911* (Albuquerque: University of New Mexico Press, 1994); John Womack Jr., *Zapata and the Mexican Revolution* (New York: Vintage Books, 1968).

5. John Mason Hart, *Revolutionary Mexico: The Coming and Process of the Mexican Revolution* (Berkeley and Los Angeles: University of California Press, 1987), 171–73.

6. Colin M. MacLachlan and William H. Beezley, *El Gran Pueblo: A History of Greater Mexico* (Englewood Cliffs, N.J.: Prentice Hall, 1994), 174–75.

7. Anderson, *Outcasts in Their Own Land,* 100–184. Quote from Díaz in Friedrich Katz, "Mexico: Restored Republic and Porfiriato, 1867–1910," in *The Cambridge History of Latin America,* vol. 5, 1870 to 1930, ed. Leslie Bethell (Cambridge: Cambridge University Press, 1986), 66.

8. Anderson, *Outcasts in Their Own Land,* 190–224.

9. Ibid., 184–90.

10. Knight, *The Mexican Revolution,* 1:44–45; MacLachlan and Beezley, *El Gran Pueblo,* 188–89.

11. Héctor Aguilar Camín, *La frontera nómada: Sonora y la Revolución Mexicana* (Mexico City: Siglo Veintiuno, 1985), 115–19.

12. Gonzales, "United States Copper Companies," 663–68.

13. Strike leaders to the President of the C.C.C. Co., S.A., June 1906, AHS, Cananea, MS 1032, Box 1; W. C. Greene to Colonel Myron M. Parker, 11 June 1906, Cananea to Washington, D.C., CCA, 1906 Documental 0050.

14. W. C. Greene to Colonel Myron M. Parker, 11 June 1906, Cananea to Washington, D.C., CCA, 1906 Documental 0050.

15. Ibid.; Statement by Arthur S. Dwight, 6 June 1906, CRS, Cananea, Microfilm #72/150, Reel 4; George Young, "Summary of Labor Conflicts at Cananea, 1906–1913," CCA, 1916 Documental 0032.

16. W. C. Greene to Colonel Myron C. Parker, 11 June 1906, Cananea to Washington, D.C., CCA, 1906 Documental 0050; George Young, "Summary of Labor Conflicts at Cananea, 1906–1913," 1 Feb. 1913, CCA, 1916 Documental 0032; Aguilar Camín, *La frontera nómada,* 120; C. L. Sonnichsen, *Colonel Greene and the Copper Skyrocket* (Tucson: University of Arizona Press, 1974), 188–207. Sonnichsen's lively account contains useful information, but tends to romanticize Greene outside the context of Mexican history.

17. W. C. Greene to Don Enrique C. Creel, Governor of Chihuahua, 10 June 1906, CCA, 1906 Documental 0046.

18. W. C. Greene to Don Enrique C. Creel, Governor of Chihuahua, 10 June 1906, CCA, 1906 Documental 0046; W. E. D. Stokes to W. C. Greene, 21 June 1906, CCA, 1906 Documental 0086. To replace the vice-consul, Greene's attorney had spoken with both Secretary of State Root and President Roosevelt.

19. *Mexican Herald,* 24 June 1906, 1–2.

20. Anderson, *Outcasts in Their Own Land,* 112–13.

21. Aguilar Camín, *La frontera nómada,* 95.

22. Knight, *The Mexican Revolution,* 1:148. For a more detailed discussion of the 1906 strike, see Gonzales, "U.S. Copper Companies."

23. Marvin Bernstein, *The Mexican Mining Industry, 1890–1950* (Albany: State University of New York Press, 1964), 78–83.

24. Ibid.; MacLachlan and Beezley, *El Gran Pueblo,* 99.

25. Charles A. Hale, *The Transformation of Liberalism in Late Nineteenth-Century Mexico* (Princeton, N.J.: Princeton University Press, 1989), chap. 4.

26. Ibid.

27. Knight, *The Mexican Revolution,* 1:55–76; MacLachlan and Beezley, *El Gran Pueblo,* 186–87.

28. Stanley Ross, *Francisco I. Madero, Apostle of Mexican Democracy* (New York: Columbia University Press, 1955).

29. Quoted in Ramón Eduardo Ruíz, *The Great Rebellion: Mexico, 1905–1924* (New York: W. W. Norton, 1980), 140.

30. Womack, *Zapata,* 57.

31. David G. LaFrance, *The Mexican Revolution in Puebla, 1908–1913* (Wilmington, Del.: Scholarly Resources, 1989), 3–47.

32. Ross, *Francisco I. Madero,* 123–29.

33. Knight, *The Mexican Revolution,* 1:179–80, 196–97.

34. James D. Cockcroft, *Intellectual Precursors of the Mexican Revolution, 1900–1913,* 2d ed. (Austin: University of Texas Press, 1976), 176–83.

35. Michael J. Gonzales, "U.S. Cooper Companies, the Mine Workers' Movement, and the Mexican Revolution, 1910–1920," *Hispanic American Historical Review* 76, no. 3 (Aug. 1996): 503–35.

36. Cockcroft, *Intellectual Precursors,* 182; Ross, *Francisco I. Madero,* 145.

37. Ross, *Francisco I. Madero,* 135–41; Colin M. MacLachlan, *Anarchism and the Mexican Revolution* (Berkeley and Los Angeles: University of California Press, 1991), for the persecution of Flores Magón in the United States.

38. Womack, *Zapata,* 60–68; Samuel Brunk, *Emiliano Zapata! Revolution and Betrayal in Mexico* (Lincoln: University of Nebraska Press, 1995), chaps. 1–2.

39. Brunk, *Emiliano Zapata,* chap. 2; Ian Jacobs, *Ranchero Revolt: The Mexican Revolution in Guerrero* (Austin: University of Texas Press, 1982), chaps. 1–2.

40. Michael C. Meyer, *Mexican Rebel: Pascual Orozco and the Mexican Revolution, 1910–1915* (Lincoln: University of Nebraska Press, 1967), chaps. 1–2; William H. Beezley, *Insurgent Governor: Abraham González and the Mexican Revolution in Chihuahua* (Lincoln: University of Nebraska Press, 1973).

41. M. Meyer, *Mexican Rebel,* 27–38.

42. Friedrich Katz, *The Life and Times of Pancho Villa* (Stanford, Calif.: Stanford University Press, 1998), 47–48, 88–98.

43. Ross, *Francisco I. Madero,* 155–66; M. Meyer, *Mexican Rebel,* chap. 2.

44. Quoted in Arturo Warman, *"We Come to Object": The Peasants of Morelos and the National State,* trans. Stephen K. Ault (Baltimore, Md.: Johns Hopkins

University Press, 1980), 125. This taunt is also attributed to Orozco by Juan G. Amaya. Quoted in M. Meyer, *Mexican Rebel*, 24.

45. Knight, *The Mexican Revolution*, 1:204–9, compares the Juárez Treaty with Munich ("It seemed a good idea at the time"); Ross, *Francisco I. Madero*, 172–78.

46. Ibid.

47. Ross, *Francisco I. Madero*, 166–71.

48. Quoted in Knight, *The Mexican Revolution*, 1:218.

49. Ibid., 1:247; Ross, *Francisco I. Madero*, 171–75.

50. Knight, *The Mexican Revolution*, 1:208–17. The Chinese community in Lima and Cañete suffered similar fates at the hands of mobs during the War of the Pacific. See Michael J. Gonzales, "Chinese Plantation Workers and Social Conflict in Peru in the Late Nineteenth Century," *Journal of Latin American Studies* (Oct. 1989): 385–424.

51. François-Xavier Guerra, "La Révolution Mexicaine: d'abord une révolution minière?" *Annales E.S.C.* 36 (1981): 785–814; Gonzales, "United States Copper Companies."

52. Gonzales, "Mine Workers' Movement."

53. Ibid., 508–10. See below, chapter 4, for a fuller discussion of strike activity at Cananea and its relationship with provincial and national political developments.

54. Knight, *The Mexican Revolution*, 1:232–35.

55. Brunk, *Emiliano Zapata*, 41–42.

56. Ibid., 43–50.

57. Ibid., 51–60.

58. Ross, *Francisco I. Madero*, 200–230; Knight, *The Mexican Revolution*, 1:248–53.

59. Ibid.; Jean A. Meyer, *The Cristero Rebellion: The Mexican People Between Church and State 1926–1929*, trans. Richard Southern (Cambridge: Cambridge University Press, 1976), 10–11, claims that the Catholic Party lost seats through fraud, which is difficult to prove but probably true.

60. Ross, *Francisco I. Madero*, 220–21.

61. Knight, *The Mexican Revolution*, 1:230–65.

62. Brunk, *Emiliano Zapata*, 65–70.

63. Ibid., 70–78.

64. Knight, *The Mexican Revolution*, 1:291–300. Knight minimizes PLM and nationalist influences on the Orozquista movement. Mark Wasserman accepts the view of the U.S. consul in Chihuahua that the Terrazas family "organized, directed, and financed" the Orozco rebellion. See Mark Wasserman, *Persistent Oligarchs: Elites and Politics in Chihuahua, Mexico 1910–1940* (Durham, N.C.: Duke University Press, 1993), 26. Katz also argues convincingly that Orozco worked hand and glove with the Chihuahuan elite and should not be viewed as a social revolutionary (Katz, *Pancho Villa*, 140–46).

65. M. Meyer, *Mexican Rebel*, 67–85.

CHAPTER 3

1. Alan Knight, *The Mexican Revolution, 1910–1920,* 2 vols. (Cambridge: Cambridge University Press, 1986), 1:253–55.

2. Peter V. N. Henderson, *Félix Díaz, the Porfirians, and the Mexican Revolution* (Lincoln: University of Nebraska Press, 1981), 52–65.

3. The best account is Knight, *The Mexican Revolution,* 1:482–90. Also see Michael C. Meyer, *Huerta: A Political Portrait* (Lincoln: University of Nebraska Press, 1972), 47–62; Henderson, *Félix Díaz,* chap. 5; and Stanley Ross, *Francisco I. Madero, Apostle of Mexican Democracy* (New York: Columbia University Press, 1955), 276–92. Revealing of Wilson's character and his involvement is his memoirs, Henry Lane Wilson, *Diplomatic Episodes in Mexico, Belgium and Chile* (New York: Doubleday, 1927), 252–89.

4. Meyer, *Huerta,* 67–69. Meyer, who views Huerta as a reformer frustrated by events beyond his control, puts a more positive spin on these events.

5. Knight, *The Mexican Revolution,* 2:62–65.

6. Meyer, *Huerta,* 86; Knight, *The Mexican Revolution,* 2:15–17.

7. Meyer, *Huerta,* 86–87.

8. Knight, *The Mexican Revolution,* 2:77–80.

9. Meyer, *Huerta,* 168–69; Knight, *The Mexican Revolution,* 2:64.

10. Friedrich Katz, *The Secret War in Mexico: Europe, the United States, and the Mexican Revolution* (Chicago: University of Chicago Press, 1981), chap. 5; Knight, *The Mexican Revolution,* 2:68–70.

11. Katz, *The Secret War,* chaps. 5–6; Meyer, *Huerta,* chap. 6; Knight, *The Mexican Revolution,* 2:139–40.

12. This summary is based primarily on Knight, *The Mexican Revolution,* 2:69–75. Knight argues that Wilson's break with Huerta did not occur until the Domínguez affair (see below for a discussion of this event). However, Lind's proposal, as Knight notes, clearly stated that the U.S. would not accept Huerta as a presidential candidate.

13. Meyer, *Huerta,* 136–50.

14. Ibid., 150–55.

15. Knight, *The Mexican Revolution,* 2:77.

16. Katz, *The Secret War,* 173–95.

17. See the following chapter for more information on Carranza and the Constitutionalist movement.

18. Katz, *The Secret War,* chap. 5. On the stockpiling of arms, see John Mason Hart, *Revolutionary Mexico: The Coming and Process of the Mexican Revolution* (Berkeley and Los Angeles: University of California Press, 1987), 290–92, 312.

19. Katz, *The Secret War,* chap. 5.

20. Hart, *Revolutionary Mexico,* 290–92, 312.

CHAPTER 4

1. Douglas W. Richmond, *Venustiano Carranza's Nationalist Struggle, 1893–1920* (Lincoln: University of Nebraska Press, 1983), chap. 1; Ramón Eduardo Ruíz, *The Great Rebellion: Mexico, 1905–1924* (New York: W. W. Norton, 1982), 152–55.

2. Richmond, *Venustiano Carranza's Nationalist Struggle,* chap. 2; Ruíz, *The Great Rebellion,* 155. Richmond considers Carranza's policies innovative, but there is an undeniable Porfirian strain to them. Concerns over public morality, cleanliness, and education are documented in William E. French, *A Peaceful and Working People: Manners, Morals, and Class Formation in Mexico* (Albuquerque: University of New Mexico Press, 1996). On public education, see Charles A. Hale, *The Transformation of Liberalism in Late Nineteenth-Century Mexico* (Princeton, N.J.: Princeton University Press, 1989).

3. Richmond, *Venustiano Carranza's Nationalist Struggle,* chap. 2.

4. Alan Knight, *The Mexican Revolution, 1910–1920,* 2 vols. (Cambridge: Cambridge University Press, 1986), 2:11–23.

5. Richmond, *Venustiano Carranza's Nationalist Struggle,* 45.

6. Friedrich Katz, *The Secret War in Mexico: Europe, the United States, and the Mexican Revolution* (Chicago: University of Chicago Press, 1981), 130–32.

7. Ramón Eduardo Ruíz, *The People of Sonora and Yankee Capitalists* (Tucson: University of Arizona Press, 1988).

8. Héctor Aguilar Camín, *La frontera nómada: Sonora y la Revolución Mexicana* (Mexico City: Siglo Veintiuno, 1977), 85; Susan M. Deeds, "José Maria Maytorena and the Mexican Revolution in Sonora," part 1, *Arizona and the West* 18, no. 1 (spring 1976): 24.

9. Deeds, "José Maria Maytorena," 24; Héctor Aguilar Camín, "The Relevant Tradition," in *Caudillo and Peasant in the Mexican Revolution,* ed. David Brading (Cambridge: Cambridge University Press, 1971), 119. In 1914, Maytorena, then embroiled in an intense struggle for political control over Sonora, supported Cananea's striking miners in an attempt to weaken his rival Calles. This was the only occasion when he openly backed labor over capital. See Michael J. Gonzales, "U.S. Copper Companies, the Mine Workers' Movement, and the Mexican Revolution, 1910–1920," *Hispanic American Historical Review* 76, no. 3 (Aug. 1996): 514–15.

10. Aguilar Camín, "Relevant Tradition," 118–19.

11. Ruíz, *Great Rebellion,* 171.

12. Aguilar Camín, "Relevant Tradition," 119. On Calles, see Enrique Krauze, *Mexico: Biography of Power. A History of Modern Mexico, 1810–1996,* trans. Hank Heifetz (New York: Harper Collins, 1997), 405.

13. Linda B. Hall, *Alvaro Obregón: Power and Revolution in Mexico, 1911 to 1920* (College Station: Texas A & M Press, 1981), 28.

14. Aguilar Camín, "Relevant Tradition," 107–10.

15. Deeds, "José María Maytorena," 24–32.

16. Aguilar Camín, "Relevant Tradition," 110.

17. Alexander Dye, U.S. Consul at Nogales, to Secretary of State, 23 Oct. 1911, National Archives (NA), Washington, D.C., decimal file (dec.) 812.5045/24, micro. M-274, reel 167.

18. Aguilar Camín, "Relevant Tradition," 107–10.

19. Aguilar Camín, *La frontera nómada,* 161–67; Alexander Dye, U.S. Consul at Nogales, to Secretary of State, 23 Oct. 1911, National Archives (NA), Washington, D.C., decimal file (dec.) 812.5045/24, micro. M-274, reel 167.

20. Dye to Secretary of State, 23 Oct. 1911.

21. George Young, Secretary, Cananea Consolidated Copper Company, to Señor Don José M. Maytorena, Constitutional Governor of the State of Sonora, n.d., Arizona Historical Society, Tucson, Cananea Papers (hereafter AHS-CP), MS 1032, box 1. This letter was drafted (but not mailed) at the request of James Douglas, general manager, who provided Maytorena with the information contained in the letter. See Douglas's note at the bottom of the letter cited here. Telegram, Dye to Secretary of State, 18 Oct. 1911, NA, dec. 812.5045/25, M-274, reel 167; Dye to Secretary of State, 19 Oct. 1911, NA, dec. 812.5045/25; *Mexican Mining Journal* 13, no. 5 (Nov. 1911): 36.

22. Dye to Secretary of State, 19 Oct. 1911, NA, dec. 812.5045/25.

23. *Mexican Mining Journal* 15, no. 1 (July 1912): 45; 16, no. 2 (Oct. 1912): 49.

24. George Young, Secretary, Cananea, to Sr. Cirilo Ramírez, Hermosillo, 12 Dec. 1912, AHS-CP, MS 1032, box 1; Young to Ramírez, 13 Dec. 1912, AHS-CP, MS 1032, box 1; Young, Cananea, to L. C. Ricketts, New York City, 23 Dec. 1912, in U.S. Consul to Secretary of State, N.A., dec. 812.5045/49, M-274, reel 167.

25. George Young, Cananea, to L. D. Ricketts, New York City, 23 Dec. 1912, in U.S. Consul to Secretary of State, N.A., dec. 812.5045/49, M-274, reel 167.

26. Aguilar Camín, *La frontera nómada,* 260–61, 280–81.

27. Ibid., 280–87.

28. Ibid., 280–87, 289, 294, 316–32.

29. *Engineering and Mining Journal* 95, no. 17 (26 Apr. 1913): 868; 95, no. 19 (10 May 1913): 976.

30. Aguilar Camín, *La frontera nómada,* 341–61.

31. Ibid., 363–67.

32. Quoted in Knight, *The Mexican Revolution,* 2:112.

33. Aguilar Camín, *La frontera nómada,* 384–407.

34. Knight, *The Mexican Revolution,* 2:35–45; Friedrich Katz, *The Life and Times of Pancho Villa* (Stanford, Calif.: Stanford University Press, 1998), 165–75.

35. William H. Beezley, *Insurgent Governor: Abraham González and the Mexican Revolution in Chihuahua* (Lincoln: University of Nebraska Press, 1973).

36. Katz, *Pancho Villa,* chap. 1 on Villa's origins, and 237 on his revolutionary platform. During colonial times, *gachupin* referred to those Spaniards living in Mexico who had been born in Spain. By the early twentieth century its meaning encompassed all persons of pure Spanish ancestry.

37. Quoted in Katz, *The Secret War,* 137.

38. John Reed, *Insurgent Mexico* (New York: International Publishers, 1914), 22.

39. Katz, *The Secret War,* 138.

40. Reed, *Insurgent Mexico,* 144; Katz, *The Secret War,* 139–47; Knight, *The Mexican Revolution,* 2:36–37.
41. Knight, *The Mexican Revolution,* 2:35–45.
42. Ibid., 35–48.
43. Katz, *Pancho Villa,* 217.
44. Knight, *The Mexican Revolution,* 2:109–11; Katz, *The Secret War,* 146, 152, 184–85; Katz, *Pancho Villa,* 326–30, provides the most detailed account.
45. All quoted in John Womack Jr., *Zapata and the Mexican Revolution* (New York: Vintage Books, 1968), 162–63, 165, 168.
46. Quoted in ibid., 170.
47. Katz, *Pancho Villa,* 345–54.
48. Knight, *The Mexican Revolution,* 2:168–71.

CHAPTER 5

1. Alan Knight, *The Mexican Revolution, 1910–1920,* 2 vols. (Cambridge: Cambridge University Press, 1986), 2:251–54.
2. Ibid., 2:254–57.
3. Ibid., 2:254–58.
4. Linda B. Hall, *Alvaro Obregón: Power and Revolution in Mexico, 1911 to 1920* (College Station: Texas A & M Press, 1981), 78, 81.
5. Knight, *The Mexican Revolution,* 2:257–58; Robert E. Quirk, *The Mexican Revolution, 1914–1915* (New York: W. W. Norton, 1960), 102, 105, 114.
6. Knight, *The Mexican Revolution,* 2:260–61.
7. Ibid., 2:259–60.
8. Quirk, *The Mexican Revolution, 1914–1915,* 109.
9. Knight, *The Mexican Revolution,* 2:257 (quote), 260–61; Quirk, *The Mexican Revolution, 1914–1915,* 109–12.
10. Quirk, *The Mexican Revolution, 1914–1915,* 112; Hall, *Alvaro Obregón,* 94.
11. Quirk, *The Mexican Revolution, 1914–1915,* 119–26.
12. Hall, *Alvaro Obregón,* 92.
13. Quirk, *The Mexican Revolution, 1914–1915,* 125–30; Friedrich Katz, *The Life and Times of Pancho Villa* (Stanford, Calif.: Stanford University Press, 1998), 388.
14. Katz, *Pancho Villa,* 371, 447–48.
15. Knight, *The Mexican Revolution,* 2:303.
16. Leon Canova, quoted in John Womack Jr., *Zapata and the Mexican Revolution* (New York: Vintage Books, 1968), 221.
17. Knight, *The Mexican Revolution,* 2:303–4.
18. Ibid., 306–7; John Robert Lear, "Workers, Vecinos and Citizens: The Revolution in Mexico City, 1909–1917" (unpublished Ph.D. dissertation, University of California, Berkeley, 1993), 323.
19. Knight, *The Mexican Revolution,* 2:311–13.
20. Hall, *Alvaro Obregón,* 103–5.
21. Womack, *Zapata,* 221–23. For information on Maderista support of Villa, see

Knight, *The Mexican Revolution,* 2:288–91.

22. Lear, "Workers, Vecinos, and Citizens," 220–344.

23. Knight, *The Mexican Revolution,* 2:321–28; Katz, *Pancho Villa,* 489–91, discusses Villa's overconfidence before the battle of Celaya.

24. Knight, *The Mexican Revolution,* 2:329–42. Katz, *Pancho Villa,* 518, discusses the loss of upper-class and intellectual support. Katz states that the value of Villista currency fell from 30 cents per peso to 1.5 cents per peso during 1915 (511).

25. Katz, *Pancho Villa,* 523.

26. Héctor Aguilar Camín, *La frontera nómada: Sonora y la Revolución Mexicana* (Mexico City: Siglo Veintiuno, 1977), 419; Susan M. Deeds, "José María Maytorena and the Mexican Revolution in Sonora," *Arizona and the West* 18, part II, no. 1 (spring 1976): 145; C. S. Wiswall, Cananea, to Mrs. R. F. Torrance, Albuquerque, 24 June 1949, Arizona Historical Society, Robert Torrance Papers, MS 1033, box 1, fol. 27. Wiswall married William Greene's widow and ran her huge cattle ranch adjacent to the mines. He was an eyewitness to Villa's invasion into the region. See also Hon. Frederick Simpich, U.S. Consul, Nogales, to Secretary of State, 4 Nov. 1915; Charles L. Montague, U.S. Sub-Consul at Cananea, to Simpich, 22 Nov. 1915, in United States of America on behalf of *Mary Greene Wiswall, et al., v. The United Mexican States,* National Archives, Suitland, Md., General Claims Commission, Record Group (RG), 76, agency 1149; *Engineering and Mining Journal* 100, no. 18 (30 Oct. 1915): 739; George Young, Warren, Arizona, to the Hon. D[elbert] J. Haff, Kansas City, Mo., 16 Nov. 1915, Arizona Historical Society, Cananea Papers, MS 1032, box 2.

27. Compare with discussion in chapter 3, above.

28. Katz, *Pancho Villa,* 537–41.

29. "Weekly Report on Conditions Along the Mexican Border," 13 Mar. 1915, National Archives, dec. 812.00/1469, M-274, reel 44.

30. Knight, *The Mexican Revolution,* 2:344; James A. Sandos, *Rebellion in the Borderlands: Anarchism and the Plan of San Diego, 1904–1923* (Norman: University of Oklahoma Press, 1992).

31. Friedrich Katz, "Pancho Villa and the Attack on Columbus, New Mexico," *American Historical Review* 83, no. 1 (Feb. 1978): 101–30.

32. Katz, *Pancho Villa,* 528–29, 552–60.

33. James A. Sandos, "Comment on Friedrich Katz's 'Pancho Villa and the Attack on Columbus, New Mexico,'" *American Historical Review* 84, no. 1 (Feb. 1979): 305–6.

34. Katz, "Pancho Villa," 101.

35. Katz, *Pancho Villa,* 528–29.

36. Knight, *The Mexican Revolution.*

37. Katz, "Pancho Villa," 101, on size of the expeditionary force; Knight, *The Mexican Revolution,* 2:347–60.

38. Knight, *The Mexican Revolution,* 2:349–52. Knight downplays the importance of these demonstrations, citing relatively small turnouts in some places and the fact that some were incited. However, popular outbursts of anti-Americanism

were taken seriously by Carranza and Villa, and by such persons as the U.S. mine manager cited below.

39. George Young, Warren, Arizona, to Delbert J. Haff, Kansas City, 11 July 1916, Arizona Historical Society, Cananea Papers, MS 1032, box 2.

40. Knight, *The Mexican Revolution*, 2:347–60.

CHAPTER 6

1. John Reed, *Insurgent Mexico* (New York: Penguin Books, 1984), 218.

2. E. V. Niemeyer Jr., *Revolution at Querétaro: The Mexican Constitutional Convention of 1916–1917* (Austin, Texas: Institute of Latin American Studies, 1974), 31; Alan Knight, *The Mexican Revolution, 1910–1920*, 2 vols. (Cambridge: Cambridge University Press, 1986), 2:477.

3. Knight, *The Mexican Revolution*, 2:472–75. Occupational data drawn from Peter H. Smith, "La política dentro de la revolución: el congreso constituyente de 1916–17," *Historia Mexicana* 22 (1972–1973): 383.

4. Niemeyer, *Revolution at Querétaro*, chap. 7. Unless otherwise noted, the following discussion of the convention is based on Niemeyer.

5. John Womack Jr., *Zapata and the Mexican Revolution* (New York: Vintage Books, 1968), 291–93; Samuel Brunk, *Emiliano Zapata! Revolution and Betrayal in Mexico* (Lincoln: University of Nebraska Press, 1995), 212–16. Félix Díaz had landed at Veracruz in February 1916. With cash and political support from exiled Porfirian hacendados, he attempted to form alliances with local caudillos willing to listen.

6. Womack, *Zapata*, 308–13.

7. Brunk, *Emiliano Zapata*, 208–12.

8. Womack, *Zapata*, 326–27; Brunk, *Emiliano Zapata*, 221–22.

9. Gilbert M. Joseph, *Revolution from Without: Yucatán, Mexico, and the United States, 1880–1924* (Cambridge: Cambridge University Press, 1982), chaps. 4–6. For a discussion of Sonoran culture, which influenced Alvarado's policies, see Miguel Tinker Salas, *In the Shadow of the Eagles: Sonora and the Transformation of the Border During the Porfiriato* (Berkeley and Los Angeles: University of California Press, 1997).

10. The following discussion is based on Jonathan C. Brown, *Oil and Revolution in Mexico* (Berkeley and Los Angeles: University of California Press, 1993), chaps. 3–4.

11. Wilson's capture of Veracruz was aimed at undermining Huerta, the favorite of U.S. business interests in Mexico, and the Pershing expedition sought to punish Pancho Villa for raiding Columbus, New Mexico, as opposed to protecting U.S. companies in the North.

12. George M. Young, Cananea, to Louis Ricketts, Warren, Ariz., 8 July 1915, Arizona Historical Society, Cananea Papers, MS 1032, box 2; telegram, Young to D. J. Haff, Naco, Arizona, to Kansas City, 24 Aug. 1915, Arizona Historical Society, Cananea Papers, MS 1032, box 2; General Plutarco Elías Calles, Governor and Military Commander of the State, Decree No. 39, 27 Mar. 1916, Hermosillo, in Simpich, U.S. Consul, Nogales, to Secretary of State,

Washington, D.C., 12 Apr. 1916, National Archives, Center for Research Libraries, Chicago, dec. 812.602/24, M-274, reel 204. In January the Carrancista governor of Aguascalientes, where the Guggenheim's American Smelting and Refining Company owned a major smelter, also issued a decree annulling special concessions granted to companies. Gaston Schmutz, U.S. Consul, to Secretary of State, 26 Jan. 1916, N.A., Center for Research Libraries, Chicago, dec. 812.602/23, M-274, reel 204.

13. Haff, Kansas City, to Young, Warren, Ariz., 5 July 1916, Arizona Historical Society, Cananea Papers, MS 1032, box 2. Americans working in Mexico also expressed their displeasure with U.S. policy. Luella Herr, wife of mining engineer Irving Heer, wrote on 3 May 1914: "But don't ask our opinion of Wilson and Bryan. We are too disgusted to talk! It is too insane and a disgraceful page to U.S. history. The United States has gotten herself into a mess and then asks South American countries to help her get out of it!" Quoted in Robert Woodmansee Herr, in collaboration with Richard Herr, *An American Family in the Mexican Revolution* (Wilmington, Del.: Scholarly Resources, 1999), 55.

14. Haff, Kansas City, to Young, Warren, Ariz., 5 July 1916, Arizona Historical Society, Cananea Papers, MS 1032, box 2.

15. "Conference of the American-Mexican Mining and Smelting Interests," New York City, 25 Sept. 1916, and "The Effect of the Revolution in Mexico on American-Mexican Mining Interests," part 2, Sept. 1916, both Arizona Historical Society, MS 1032, box 5; George Young, Secretary, "Statement of the Cananea Consolidated Copper Company, S.A.," re: "How the Company has been Affected by Mexican Revolutionary Conditions, Taxation, etc.," presented before the "Honorable Members of the Mexican-American International Commission," 28 Sept. 1916, New York City, Cananea Papers, Centro Regional de Sonora, Hermosillo, reel 4.

16. See discussion in chapter 5, above.

17. Provisional Governor Adolfo de la Huerta, printed notice, Hermosillo, 12 Oct. 1916, Cananea Company Archive (CCA), 1916 Documental 0038.

18. Sonora's new labor code also included double pay for overtime, one day off per week, provision of a safe working environment, appointment of government safety inspectors, equal wages for natives and foreigners, hiring preferences for natives over foreigners (when qualifications were equal), foreigners' knowledge of Spanish, cash wages (as opposed to goods or tokens), and provision of medical care by Spanish-speaking physicians and pharmacists. In return, workers were instructed to be punctual, hardworking, respectful, and obedient to company rules. Adolfo de la Huerta, Decree No. 71, 10 Oct. 1916, Occidental College, Los Angeles, Special Collections, Labor Issues, Edward Doheny Research Fund, file I-K. The decree only made brief mention of the agricultural sector, which underscores the regime's concern over the more lucrative, volatile, and controversial mining industry.

19. W. D. King, Douglas, Ariz., to George Young, Cananea, 14 May 1917, AHS-CP, MS 1032, box 2; statement by S. Ramírez Sandi, President of the Labor Commission of the State, to Mariano Urrea, Municipal President of Cananea, 8 June 1917, CCA, 1917 Documental, 0004; Young, Cananea, to C. E. Mills, President of Cananea Consolidated Copper Co., Miami, Ariz., 14 Mar. 1917, CCA, 1917 Documental 0005; Young to Mills, 15 Mar. 1917, ibid.; The

Secretary [Young] to Municipal President, [n.d.] May 1917, ibid.; Acting Gnl. Supt. to Charles H. Bates, [n.p], 3 Dec. 1917, CCA 1918 Documental 0083; Adolfo de la Huerta, Hermosillo, to U.S. Consul at Nogales, 24 June 1917, AHS-CP, MS 1032, box 2; Héctor Aguilar Camín, *La frontera nómada: Sonora y la Revolución Mexicana* (Mexico City: Siglo Veintiuno, 1985), 439–40.

20. Public notice: "Obreros Cananenses," Buenavista, Cananea, 19 Sept. 1919, AHS, Torrance Papers, MS 1033, box 5.

21. Gnl. Supt., Cananea, to Louis B. Ricketts, Warren, Ariz., 17 Sept. 1919, CCA, 1919 Documental 0131; George Young, Cananea, to J. W. Allen, Treasurer, New York City, 23 May 1919, AHS-CP, MS 1032, box 1.

22. Acting Gnl. Supt. to Ricketts, 16 Oct. 1919, Gnl. Supt. to Ricketts, 6 Nov. 1919, Gnl. Supt. to Ricketts, 26 Nov. 1919, all in CCA, 1919 Documental 0131; R. B. Armenta, *El Tiempo* (Cananea), 8 Dec. 1919, clipping included in letter, Gnl. Supt. to Ricketts, New York City, 26 Dec. 1919, CCA, 1919 Documental 0128; *El Tiempo*, 27 Nov. 1919, CCA, 1919 Documental 0044; Adolfo de la Huerta, Hermosillo, to Young, Cananea, 5 Dec. 1919, AHS-CP, MS 1032, box 2; *El Tiempo*, 8 Dec. 1919, CCA, 1919 Documental 0128; Memorandum of meeting, C. L. M. [Charles L. Montague], Cananea to Evans, Cananea, 18 Dec. 1919, CCA, 1919 Documental 0006; Gnl. Supt., Cananea, to Ricketts, New York City, 26 Dec. 1919, CCA, 1919 Documental 0128.

23. Héctor Aguilar Camín and Lorenzo Meyer, *In the Shadow of the Mexican Revolution: Contemporary Mexican History, 1910–1989*, trans. Luis Alberto Fierro (Austin: University of Texas Press, 1989), 68–69. See below for discussions of the Conventions of Aguascalientes and Querétaro.

24. Knight, *The Mexican Revolution*, 2:490–93.

CHAPTER 7

1. Information concerning Obregón's youth can be found in Linda B. Hall, *Alvaro Obregón: Power and Revolution in Mexico, 1911 to 1920* (College Station: Texas A & M Press, 1981), chaps. 1–2; and Enrique Krauze, *Mexico: Biography of Power. A History of Modern Mexico, 1810–1996*, trans. Hank Heifetz (New York: Harper Collins, 1997), 374–78.

2. Colin M. MacLachlan and William H. Beezley, *El Gran Pueblo: A History of Greater Mexico* (Englewood Cliffs, N.J.: Prentice Hall, 1994), 252–55; Jean A. Meyer, "Revolution and Reconstruction in the 1920s," in *Mexico Since Independence*, ed. Leslie Bethell (Cambridge: Cambridge University Press, 1991), 201–5.

3. MacLachlan and Beezley, *El Gran Pueblo*, 260–64. For more information on the agrarian reform in Morelos, see the section below entitled "The Agrarian Impulse." Terrazas is discussed in the section below entitled "Caudillos, Old and New."

4. Héctor Aguilar Camín and Lorenzo Meyer, *In the Shadow of the Mexican Revolution: Contemporary Mexican History, 1910–1989,* trans. Luis Alberto Fierro (Austin: University of Texas Press, 1989), 120–25. Data on real wages are from MacLachlan and Beezley, *El Gran Pueblo*, 260–61. Organized labor during the presidential administrations of Calles and General Lázaro Cárdenas will be discussed in chapters 8 and 9, respectively.

5. Friedrich Katz, *The Life and Times of Pancho Villa* (Stanford, Calif.: Stanford University Press, 1998), 720–26.

6. Ibid., 749–52.

7. Ibid., 752.

8. Ibid., 754.

9. Mark Wasserman, *Persistent Oligarchs: Elites and Politics in Chihuahua, Mexico 1910–1940* (Durham, N.C.: Duke University Press, 1993), 35.

10. Ibid., chaps. 1–3.

11. Ibid., 72.

12. Ibid., chaps. 3, 5.

13. John Tutino, *From Insurrection to Revolution in Mexico: Social Bases of Agrarian Violence, 1750–1940* (Princeton, N.J.: Princeton University Press, 1986), 340.

14. Dudley Ankerson, *Agrarian Warlord: Saturnino Cedillo and the Mexican Revolution in San Luis Potosí* (DeKalb: Northern Illinois University Press, 1984), 90–95.

15. The following discussion of agrarian reform in Morelos is based on Arturo Warman, *"We Come to Object": The Peasants of Morelos and the National State,* trans. Stephen K. Ault (Baltimore, Md.: Johns Hopkins University Press, 1980), 133–45.

16. Ibid., 145.

17. Quoted in Ankerson, *Agrarian Warlord,* 97.

18. Ibid., especially chap. 4. There existed other peasant movements led by regional caudillos who supported Obregón. Examples include Governor Adalberto Tejeda in Veracruz and Governor Emilio Portes Gil in Tamaulipas. On Tejeda's movement, see Heather Fowler Salamini, *Agrarian Radicalism in Veracruz, 1920–38* (Lincoln: University of Nebraska Press, 1971).

19. Paul Friedrich, *Agrarian Revolt in a Mexican Village* (Chicago: University of Chicago Press, 1977).

20. Ibid., 105.

21. The following discussion is based on Linda B. Hall, *Oil, Banks, and Politics: The United States and Post-Revolutionary Mexico, 1917–1924* (Austin: University of Texas Press, 1995).

22. Secretary of State Charles Evans Hughes, at about the same time, offered to recognize the Obregón government if Mexico would sign a treaty guaranteeing U.S. property under terms established before the promulgation of the 1917 Constitution. Obregón refused.

23. Hall, *Oil, Banks, and Politics,* 137.

24. Ibid., chap. 7, quote on 149.

25. Jonathan C. Brown, "Why Foreign Oil Companies Shifted Their Production from Mexico to Venezuela During the 1920s," *American Historical Review* 90 (1985): 362–85.

26. According to Hall, Obregón's doubts first arose when de la Huerta, as interim president, pardoned Pancho Villa and gave him the hacienda Canutillo. This could not have caused a definitive breach, however, because Obregón subsequently appointed de la Huerta treasury minister and entrusted him with the sensitive debt-settlement negotiations. See Hall, *Oil, Banks, and Politics,* 159–60.

27. Ibid., 156–70.

28. Katz, *Pancho Villa,* 755–805.

29. Hall, *Oil, Banks, and Politics,* 156–70.

CHAPTER 8

1. Enrique Krauze, *Mexico: Biography of Power. A History of Modern Mexico, 1810–1996,* trans. Hank Heifetz (New York: Harper Collins, 1997), 405–7.

2. Héctor Aguilar Camín and Lorenzo Meyer, *In the Shadow of the Mexican Revolution: Contemporary Mexican History, 1910–1989,* trans. Luis Alberto Fierro (Austin: University of Texas Press, 1989), 99–107.

3. Clark W. Reynolds, *La economía mexicana: Su estructura y crecimiento en el siglo XX* (Mexico City: Fondo de Cultura Económica, 1973), 51; Centro de Investigaciones Agrarias, *Estructura agraria y desarrollo agrícola de México,* 3 vols. (Mexico City: CDIA, 1970), 1:59.

4. Abraham Hoffman, *Unwanted Mexican Americans in the Great Depression: Repatriation Pressures, 1929–1939* (Tucson: University of Arizona Press, 1974).

5. Arnaldo Córdova, *La ideología de la revolución mexicana: La formación del nuevo regimen* (Mexico City: Editorial Era, 1974), 345.

6. Aguilar Camín and Meyer, *In the Shadow of the Mexican Revolution,* 120.

7. Arturo Warman, *"We Come to Object": The Peasants of Morelos and the National State,* trans. Stephen K. Ault (Baltimore, Md.: Johns Hopkins University Press, 1980), 148.

8. Ibid.

9. Ibid., 148–55.

10. Heather Fowler Salamini, "Revolutionary Caudillos in the 1920s: Francisco Múgica and Adalberto Tejeda," in *Caudillo and Peasant in the Mexican Revolution,* ed. D. A. Brading (Cambridge: Cambridge University Press, 1980), 170–92; Christopher R. Boyer, "Old Loves, New Loyalties: Agrarismo in Michoacán, 1920–1928," *Hispanic American Historical Review* 78, no. 3 (Aug. 1998): 419–55; Warman, *"We Come to Object,"* 156; and Dudley Ankerson, *Agrarian Warlord: Saturnino Cedillo and the Mexican Revolution in San Luis Potosí* (DeKalb: Northern Illinois University Press, 1984). Also see below for a discussion of Cedillo's support of Calles during the Cristero Rebellion.

11. Unless otherwise noted, the discussion of the Cristero Rebellion is based on Jean A. Meyer, *The Cristero Rebellion: The Mexican People Between Church and State,* trans. Richard Southern (Cambridge: Cambridge University Press, 1976).

12. Ankerson, *Agrarian Warlord,* 122.

13. Carlos Martínez Assad, *El Laboratorio de la Revolución: El Tabasco Garridista* (Mexico City: Siglo Veintiuno, 1979), 26, 38, 41–50, 71–76. Graham Greene's powerful novel of personal redemption and religious persecution, *The Power and the Glory,* is set in Garridista Tabasco.

14. Luis González, *San José de Gracia: Mexican Village in Transition,* trans. John Upton (Austin: University of Texas Press, 1994), chap. 5.

15. Ibid., 154–55.

16. Ibid., chap. 5.
17. Ankerson, *Agrarian Warlord*, 122–26.
18. Quoted in González, *San José de Gracia*, 166, emphasis added.
19. Ankerson, *Agrarian Warlord*, 127.
20. González, *San José de Gracia*, 127. Regarding León de Toral, William Beezley and Colin MacLachlan write:

> Interrogators determined he was deranged, a supporter of the Cristero movement and a devotee of the charismatic nun Madre Conchita. The nun was quickly arrested and the trial of the two became a public spectacle that intensified both Catholic and anti-Catholic feelings. The defense tried to justify the actions of the defendants with a plea that they were acting on behalf of their God. The claim of divine inspiration did not bring divine intervention. The court ordered the execution of León Toral and sentenced Madre Conchita to thirty years imprisonment at the Islas Tres Marías federal prison off Mexico's Pacific coast. (El Gran Pueblo, 286)

21. MacLachlan and Beezley, *El Gran Pueblo*, 284, 289–94.
22. Meyer, *The Cristero Rebellion*, 61–65. Church-state conflict in the 1930s will be discussed below in chapter 9.
23. MacLachlan and Beezley, *El Gran Pueblo*, 294–95.

CHAPTER 9

1. Enrique Krauze, *Mexico: Biography of Power. A History of Modern Mexico, 1810–1996,* trans. Hank Heifetz (New York: Harper Collins, 1997), 440–42.
2. Ibid.; Christopher R. Boyer, "Old Loves, New Loyalties: Agrarismo in Michoacán, 1920–1928," *Hispanic American Historical Review* 78, no. 3 (Aug. 1998): 419–55.
3. Krauze, *Mexico: Biography of Power,* 440–44; Adolfo Gilly, *El cardenismo, una utopía mexicana* (Mexico City: Cal y Arena, 1994), 415.
4. Krauze, *Mexico: Biography of Power,* 441–44.
5. Ibid., 445–48.
6. Ibid., 448–52; Adrian A. Bantjes, "Idolatry and Iconoclasm in Revolutionary Mexico: The Dechristianization Campaigns, 1929–1940," *Mexican Studies/Estudios Mexicanos* 13, no. 1 (winter 1997): 87–121. Public education and de-Christianization campaigns during the Cárdenas presidency are discussed below.
7. See chapter 7, above, for a definition and discussion of the ejido.
8. Krauze, *Mexico: Biography of Power,* 451. Agrarian reform during the Cárdenas presidency is discussed below.
9. Gilly, *El cardenismo,* 185–86.
10. Krauze, *Mexico: Biography of Power,* 452–54, who quotes Anguiano.
11. Ibid., 454–56.
12. Ibid., 456.
13. Ibid., 456–57.
14. Quoted in ibid, 454.

15. Bassols made the observation in a 1993 interview with Mexican publisher Julio Scherer. Quoted in Gilly, *El cardenismo,* 284–85, n. 28.

16. Gilly, *El cardenismo;* Alan Knight, "Cárdenas, Caciquismo, and the Tezcatlipoca Tendency" (paper presented at the XXI Congress of the Latin American Studies Association, Chicago, Sept. 1998); Alan Knight, "Cardenismo: Juggernaut or Jalopy?" *Journal of Latin American Studies* 26, no. 1 (Feb. 1994): 73–109; Alan Knight, "The Rise and Fall of Cardenismo, c. 1930–c. 1946," in *Mexico Since Independence,* ed. Leslie Bethell (Cambridge: Cambridge University Press, 1991), 241–320; and Adrian A. Bantjes, "Cardenismo: Regional Perspective and Revisionism" (paper presented at the XXI Congress of the Latin American Studies Association, Chicago, Sept. 1998).

17. Enrique Krauze unfairly criticizes Cárdenas for laying the foundation for the emergence of the all-powerful, corrupt, antireform Partido Revolucionario Institucional. Alan Knight and Adrian Bantjes offer the provocative counterargument that Cárdenas's dependency on volatile regional caudillos undermined his presidential authority and that the power of Mexican presidents has been, in general, exaggerated. See Krauze, *Mexico: Biography of Power,* chap. 16; Bantjes, "Cardenismo"; and Knight, "Cárdenas." Also instructive is Jeffrey W. Rubin's observation that regional variations in politics, culture, and geography helped shape the contours of state building since the 1930s. In Rubin's words:

> The Mexican state and regime should be seen as parts of a complex and changing center that consists with, and is indeed constituted through and embedded in, the diversity of regional and cultural constructions that have evolved throughout Mexico since the 1930s. . . . State formation in the 1930s involved particular, localized, and changing forms of resistance and accommodation concerning not only land reform, labor legislation, and party affiliation, but such matters as religious practices and Indian identity as well.
>
> From his *Decentering the Regime: Ethnicity, Radicalism, and Democracy in Juchitán, Mexico* (Durham, N.C.: Duke University Press, 1997), 12–13.

18. Krauze, *Mexico: Biography of Power,* 457.

19. Knight, "Rise and Fall of Cardenismo," 273. For Calles's views toward Sonora's miners during the revolution, see Gonzales, "U.S. Copper Companies, the Mine Workers' Movement, and the Mexican Revolution, 1910–1920," *Hispanic American Historical Review* 76, no. 3 (Aug. 1996): 503–34.

20. Knight, "Rise and Fall of Cardenismo," 274–75.

21. Ibid., 253–55.

22. Krauze, *Mexico: Biography of Power,* 458–60.

23. Arturo Warman, *"We Come to Object": The Peasants of Morelos and the National State,* trans. Stephen K. Ault (Baltimore, Md.: Johns Hopkins University Press, 1980), 108.

24. Paul Friedrich, *Agrarian Revolt in a Mexican Village* (Chicago: University of Chicago Press, 1977).

25. Jennie Purnell, *Popular Movements and State Formation in Revolutionary Mexico: The Agraristas and Cristeros of Michoacán* (Durham, N.C.: Duke University Press, 1999).

26. Luis González, *San José de Gracia: Mexican Village in Transition,* trans. John Upton (Austin: University of Texas Press, 1994).

27. Ibid., 186.

28. Ibid., 188.

29. Ibid., 189.

30. Ibid., 195–214, quote on 214.

31. John Gledhill, *Casi Nada: A Study of Agrarian Reform in the Homeland of Cardenismo* (Albany, N.Y.: Institute of Mesoamerican Studies, 1991).

32. Warman, *"We Come to Object,"* 159–91.

33. Barry Carr, *Marxism and Communism in Twentieth-Century Mexico* (Lincoln: University of Nebraska Press, 1992), 80–104.

34. Bantjes, "Cardenismo"; and Mark Wasserman, *Persistent Oligarchs: Elites and Politics in Chihuahua, Mexico 1910–1940* (Durham, N.C.: Duke University Press, 1993).

35. Censo de 1940, quoted in James W. Wilkie, *The Mexican Revolution: Federal Expenditure and Social Change Since 1910*, 2d ed. (Berkeley and Los Angeles: University of California Press, 1970), table 9–8, 230; Table 9–5, 223.

36. Warman, *"We Come to Object,"* 108.

37. Wilkie, *The Mexican Revolution*, table 10–8, 264; Table 10–6, 260; and Stephen H. Haber, *Industry and Underdevelopment: The Industrialization of Mexico, 1890–1940* (Stanford, Calif.: Stanford University Press, 1989), 170–74.

38. Bantjes, "Idolatry and Iconoclasm," 87–121.

39. Quoted in ibid., 97.

40. Quoted in ibid., 98.

41. Bantjes, "Idolatry and Iconoclasm"; Marjorie Becker, *Setting the Virgin on Fire: Lázaro Cárdenas, Michoacán Peasants, and the Redemption of the Mexican Revolution* (Berkeley and Los Angeles: University of California Press, 1995), esp. chap. 6.

42. Mary Kay Vaughan, *Cultural Politics in Revolution: Teachers, Peasants, and Schools in Mexico, 1930–1940* (Tucson: University of Arizona Press, 1997), 36.

43. Ibid., 58.

44. Ibid.

45. Ibid.; and Becker, *Setting the Virgin on Fire*. The latter presents a detailed reconstruction of iconoclasm at the village level, which she links to questions of patriarchy and agrarianism.

46. Bantjes, "Idolatry and Iconoclasm."

47. Vaughn, *Cultural Politics in Revolution*, esp. chaps. 6–7.

48. Ibid., chap. 5.

49. Becker, *Setting the Virgin on Fire*, 126–27.

50. Vaughn, *Cultural Politics in Revolution*, 122.

51. Becker, *Setting the Virgin on Fire*, 125.

52. Quoted in Bantjes, "Idolatry and Iconoclasm," 116.

53. Peter Lester Reich, "Mexico's Hidden Revolution: The Catholic Church in Politics Since 1929" (Ph.D. dissertation, University of California, Berkeley, 1991). Published with comparatively minor revisions as *Mexico's Hidden Revolution: The Catholic Church in Law and Politics Since 1929* (Notre Dame, Ill.: University of Notre Dame Press, 1995).

54. Quoted in Bantjes, "Idolatry and Iconoclasm," 119.

55. Ibid.

56. Vaughan, *Cultural Politics in Revolution,* 25.

57. Jonathan C. Brown, "Acting of Themselves: Workers and the Mexican Oil Nationalization," in *Workers' Control in Latin America, 1930–1979,* ed. Jonathan C. Brown (Austin: University of Texas Press, 1997), 45–49.

58. Ibid.

59. Lorenzo Meyer, *Mexico and the United States in the Oil Controversy, 1917–1942,* trans. Muriel Vasconcelos (Austin: University of Texas Press, 1972), 154.

60. Ibid., 152–54.

61. Brown, "Acting of Themselves," 58–60.

62. Josephus Daniels, *Shirt-Sleeve Diplomat* (Chapel Hill: University of North Carolina Press, 1947), 221.

63. Ibid., 213–30.

64. Ibid., 223–25.

65. Meyer, *Mexico and the United States,* 154–65.

66. Quoted in Gilly, *El cardenismo,* 43, my translation.

67. Quoted in Meyer, *Mexico and the United States,* 167–68.

68. Quoted in Friedrich E. Schuler, *Mexico Between Hitler and Roosevelt: Mexican Foreign Relations in the Age of Lázaro Cárdenas* (Albuquerque: University of New Mexico Press, 1998), 46. Schuler argues that Mexico's increasingly professional diplomatic corps and federal bureaucracy gave Cárdenas valuable analysis and advice.

69. Meyer, *Mexico and the United States,* 169–74. Cárdenas agreed to compensate the oil companies for the value of their surface property, such as oil rigs, drilling equipment, storage tanks, and so forth. The companies, however, also insisted on compensation for the value of untapped petroleum reserves. The difference was unbridgeable.

70. Ibid., 174–226. Ankerson argues that Cedillo had been badly treated by Cárdenas. After appointing the agrarian leader minister of agriculture, Cárdenas and Múgica isolated him within the cabinet and party circles. Cedillo also grew critical of the *ejido*-based agrarian reform (Dudley Ankerson, *Agrarian Warlord: Saturnino Cedillo and the Mexican Revolution in San Luis Potosí* [DeKalb: Northern Illinois University Press, 1984], chap. 6). Although we do not know if the petroleum companies bankrolled Cedillo, Cárdenas told U.S. historian Frank Tannenbaum that El Aguila would pay Cedillo $500,000 to start a revolt. See Gilly, *El cardenismo,* 416.

71. Daniels, *Shirt-Sleeve Diplomat,* 246–48, quote on 247.

72. Gilly, *El cardenismo,* 255.

73. Meyer, *Mexico and the United States,* 220–26. On the anti-Cardenista politics of the Monterrey industrial elite, see Alex M. Saragoza, *The Monterrey Elite and the Mexican State, 1880–1940* (Austin: University of New Texas Pressm 1988), chap. 8.

74. Meyer, *Mexico and the United States,* 220–226.

75. Lorenzo Meyer, *Su Majestad Británica contra la Revolución Mexicana, 1900–1950: El fin de un imperio informal* (Mexico City: El Colegio de Mexico,

1991), 496–521.

76. Meyer, *Mexico and the United States,* 227–29. On the oil companies' shift in interest from Mexico to Venezuela, which began in earnest in the 1920s, see Jonathan C. Brown, "Why Foreign Oil Companies Shifted Their Production from Mexico to Venezuela during the 1920s," *American Historical Review* 90 (1985): 362–85.

77. Beezley and MacLachlan, *El Gran Pueblo,* 325–26; Warman, *"We Come to Object,"* 189–90.

78. Ibid.; Roderic Ai Camp, *Generals in the Palacio: The Military in Modern Mexico* (Oxford: Oxford University Press, 1992), 22, 78–79.

79. Camp, *Generals in the Palacio,* 78.

80. Quoted in ibid., 78.

81. Ibid., 79.

82. Warman, *"We Come to Object,"* 189–90.

83. Knight, "Cárdenas"; Bantjes, "Cardenismo."

84. Gilly, *El Cardenismo,* 415.

85. Ibid., 260.

86. Quoted in González, *San José de Gracia,* 204.

assassinations, 98–99, 104–5, 161, 167, 180, 200–201, 215–16

Association of Petroleum Producers in Mexico, 249

atheist clubs, 213

Avila Camacho, Manuel, 223, 256–57; as a presidential candidate, 253–55

Baca Calderón, Estebán, 66, 83, 118–19

Baja California, 46

Banco de Mexico, 205

banking industry, 9, 55, 205; laws governing, 24

Barrazas, Salas, 200

Bassols, Narciso, 229, 241

Becker, Marjorie, 244

Benton, William, 129–30

Blanquet, Aureliano (General), 97–99, 98, 104

Bonilla, Manuel, 82

Bonillas, Ignacio, 178

border region conflicts, 153–55

Bracamonte, Pedro, 121

Bracero Program, 238

bribes (mordidas), 14, 208

Brittingham, John, 57

brokers fronterizos, 122

Brown, Jonathan C., 173

Bryan, William Jennings, 103–4

Bucareli Accords, 198–99, 206

Bulnes, Francisco, 70

Cabral, Juan, 83, 118

Cabrera, Luis, 108, 135

Calles, Juan Bautista, 203

Calles, Plutarco Elías, 117–18, 176; El Maximato, 215–20; power struggle with Cárdenas, 230–31; presidency, 116, 117, 199, 203–8; revolutionary activities, 145, 151, 174

camarillas (regional political networks), 13

Camp, Roderic, 256

Campa, Emilio, 88

Cananea, Sonora: attacked by Villa, 151; copper mines, 24, 48, 50–52, 119–20; strikes by miners, 67, 83, 116, 122, 176

Cananea Consolidated Copper Company, 174

Canutillo hacienda, 187

capital in the Mexican economy, North American, 69. See also foreign corporations

capital vs. labor, 119

Carden, Sir Lionel, 106, 110, 130

Cárdenas, Francisco, 98–99

Cárdenas, Lázaro, 221–23, 222, 259–60; expropriation of foreign assets, 245–55; as Governor of Michoacán, 225–27; land reforms, 232–39; political alliances, 193, 256–59; power struggle with Calles, 230–31, 257; presidency and governing coalition, 2–3, 228–32; promoting secular education, 239–45; revolutionary activities, 223–25

Cárdenas, Miguel, 42, 114

Carnegie, Andrew, 5

Carrancistas vs. Villistas, 157, 159

Carranza, Emilio, 113

Carranza, Jesús, 113

Carranza, Venustiano, 153, 179; assassination, 180; Constitutionalist movement, 113–15, 122–24, 126; and copper companies, 174–77; opposing U.S. policies, 109–10, 130; and petroleum companies, 171–74; political compromises, 131, 133–38; political platform, 139–43, 147; presidency, 81, 160–80; revolutionary activities, 80, 82, 107

Carrasco, Florencio, 51

Carrasco, Juan, 122

Carreón, Juan, 84

Carrillo Puerto, Felipe, 171

Carrizal, Chihuahua, 157

Casa del Obrero Mundial, 146–47, 186

Casa España, 253

casta divina, 33

INDEX

Continental Rubber Company, 41
contract laborers, 169
Contreras, Calixto, 75
Convention of Aguascalientes, 134–38,
    145, 162
Coolidge, Calvin, 200, 248
copper, 275n. 85; map of economic
    activity, 58
copper companies, 48; and Carranza
    presidency, 174–77
Copper Handbook, 48
copper mines, 24, 46–48, 50–52,
    119–20; strikes, 83, 116, 122, 176
corn patches (milpas), 28
corn prices, 31, 38
Corral, Ramón, 40, 78, 115; as a vice
    presidential candidate, 70–72
El Correo de Chihuahua, 78
Cosmes, Francisco, 70
cotton, 31
cotton agro-industrial complex, 40–41,
    236
counterrevolution, 92–99, 111; Huerta
    in power, 99–102; U.S. military
    intervention, 103–10
cowboys, 43–44, 126
Creel, Enrique, 45, 56, 68, 189
Creelman, James, ("Creelman
    Interview"), 38, 71
Cristero Rebellion, 204, 208–15,
    218–19
CROM (Confederación Regional de
    Obreros Mexicanos), 186, 204, 210,
    230
crops, 31; failures, 45
Cruz Gálvez trade school, 241
CTM (Confederación de Trabajadores
    Mexicanos), 230–31, 235, 245,
    256–57
cultural revolution, 269–70

dam construction, 205
Daniels, Josephus, 248–52
debt peonage, 32–33, 35, 51, 165;
    abolishing, 169
Decena Trágica, 94, 95

Dehesa, Teodoro, 63
de la Huerta, Adolfo, 116, 174–77; as
    interim president, 184; negotiations
    with Lamont, 197; negotiations with
    Villa, 187; revolt against Obregón,
    199–201
de la Rocha, Heraclio, 75
Díaz, Félix, 92–94, 96–97, 98, 104;
    exile, 106
Díaz, Porfirio, dictatorship, 1–2, 5, 6,
    70, 82; commercial agriculture,
    28–46; economic development,
    20–28; industrial development,
    55–59; mining, 46–52; petroleum
    industry, 52–55; as a politician, 8,
    10–20, 78; strike settlements, 63–64
Díaz, Porfirio, Jr., 56
Díaz Soto y Gama, Antonio, 66, 137,
    191
Diéguez, Manuel, 83, 118–19, 121,
    145, 150–51
Dios Bojórquez, Juan de, 231
Doheny, Edward, 52, 107, 172, 196,
    198, 200
Domínguez, Belisario, 104–5
donations to compensate the oil
    companies, 252
Douglas, Walter, 68
Dresden (German battle cruiser), 132
Dublán, Manuel, 20
Dublán Convention, 20
Durango, 40
dynamite, 56

economic crises, 45, 62–70
economic development, 5, 20–28,
    205–7; social consequences of, 26–28
economic inequities, 164
economic nationalism, 266–67
economic reforms, 116, 124, 168–70
economic status quo, 120
education, public, 169–70, 218,
    225–26, 239–45, 263
egalitarian society, 126
ejidatarios (communal landowners),
    190–91, 236–37